Industrial Approaches to Media

Matthew Freeman

Industrial Approaches to Media

A Methodological Gateway to Industry Studies

Matthew Freeman
Bath Spa University
Bath, UK

ISBN 978-1-137-55175-7   ISBN 978-1-137-55176-4   (eBook)
DOI 10.1057/978-1-137-55176-4

Library of Congress Control Number: 2016948429

Printed on acid-free paper

This Palgrave Macmillan imprint is published by Springer Nature
The registered company is Macmillan Publishers Ltd. London
The registered company address is: The Campus, 4 Crinan Street, London, N1 9XW, United Kingdom

FOREWORD: MEDIA INDUSTRY STUDIES IN PRACTICE

Media industry studies certainly has come a long way. Roughly a decade ago, when we began drafting the introduction to our edited collection, *Media Industries: History, Theory, and Method,* Jennifer Holt and I observed that there remained 'a dearth of formal gatherings and conferences for those researching the media industries, as well as an absence of journals or anthologies devoted specifically to the study of media industries as a coherent discipline' (2009: 1). Oh, how things have changed. As of this writing in early 2016, the Society of Cinema and Media Studies (SCMS) has a Media Industries Scholarly Interest Group as does the International Communication Association (ICA).[1] There is a now an open-access, peer-reviewed journal, *Media Industries,* and several universities, including University of California, Santa Barbara (UCSB) (with its Media Industries Project) and the University of Nottingham (with its Institute for Screen Industries Research), have initiatives dedicated to critical, qualitative industry-focused research.[2] A range of scholars have published articles and books in which they explicitly position their projects within media industry studies.[3] In addition, courses on media industry studies are now offered at both the undergraduate and graduate level at a variety of institutions.[4] Given its survey and synthesis of industry studies scholarship to date, its timely engagement with issues ranging from social media to transmedia, and its personalised, interdisciplinary case studies, it is easy to see this book quickly becoming a required text in many such courses.

Clearly, media industry studies has become one of the most dynamic subfields of media studies. The ongoing transformations taking place in the media industries themselves, along with the evolution of scholarship about these industries, make it an exciting time to undertake such work. It is within this context that *Industrial Approaches to Media* arrives and moves media industry studies forward in crucial ways. Perhaps most significantly, this book's focus on how, where, and why we undertake media industry studies encourages continued self-reflexivity. As Matthew Freeman and his contributors note, it is imperative that we come to terms with our own politics, ethics, and goals for conducting industry-related research. Choosing to focus on the industry as an object of study—and choosing to work *with* or *for* industry practitioners—is often a complicated, fraught process both in terms of the specific mechanics of building and sustaining such relationships and in terms of the broader social, political, and cultural ramifications of such work. Freeman does not shy away from such issues but rather forces us to assess our own investments in conducting media industries research. As he and the book's contributors make clear, there are stakes involved in every choice we make. From formulating research questions to deciding which people, sites, and objects we wish to analyse, from determining our audience(s) to choosing the appropriate publication formats and venues for our research, we are part of the process of shaping the protocols and practices of a still-emergent field.

Certainly there is no shortage of books focused on media and communication methods.[5] And several articles or book chapters discussing media industry studies methodologies have been published in the past.[6] In our collection, Holt and I made an effort to address some of the methods and approaches employed by media industry studies scholars. However, as Freeman notes, *Industrial Approaches to Media* represents the first attempt to look explicitly at the practical, theoretical, and ethical principles of conducting media industry studies—crossing the humanities and social sciences, culture and economics. In so doing, this book can benefit both emerging and established industry scholars in distinct ways. For those relatively new to the study of the media industries, what is offered here is a valuable guidebook—a book that simultaneously engages with macro-level political and epistemological issues and with the pragmatic, micro-level 'how to' concerns so essential to developing scholars. On offer are valuable first-hand examples, reflections, and advice from some of the most prominent media industry researchers in the US and UK. These researchers cover wide-ranging historical and contemporary examples across a range of media forms and industry sectors including radio, film, television, journalism, sports, music, and social media. Their voices, placed in conversation with Freeman's own prose, illustrate the benefits—as well as the complexities and complications—of speaking about, with, or for 'industry'. Those new to the subfield of media industry studies are provided with a road map for how—and why—one might undertake such research. Meanwhile, what more experienced industry scholars and researchers will find here is a vital and logical next step in the evolution of the rapidly developing field of media industry studies. Back in 2005, Holt and I began soliciting contributors for our edited collection. At the time, we were motivated to assemble that collection for a number of reasons. First, we recognised the dramatic transformations taking place in the structures, practices, and products of the media industries as a result of 'convergence, technological growth, and global exchange' (2009: 2). Such developments, we felt, merited greater scholarly consideration. As noted in the introduction to our collection, we recognised that there was already a great deal of critical, qualitative work being undertaken about the media industries. The problem was that such work lacked a home. While scholars based in sociology, anthropology, media economics, communication, media studies, film and television studies, journalism (and more) had been undertaking research on the media industries for decades, they often operated on parallel tracks, failing to engage in conversation with each other.

Thus came our second major motivation in assembling the collection—and in deploying the phrase 'media industry studies'.[7] Namely, *Media Industries* sought, through the form of a collection featuring twenty scholars at various career stages, to further facilitate a dialogue, to provide a name to then-dispersed work focused on the media industries. In addition, we incorporated the perspective of a media professional, executive Jordan Levin, in the interest of initiating greater cross-fertilisation between the industry and the academy. With *Industrial Approaches to Media*, Matthew Freeman picks up where we (and many others) left off, assessing both the larger stakes of industry–academy engagement as well as the pragmatics involved in undertaking such relationships.[8]

By constructing a collection that included scholars and practitioners from diverse disciplinary backgrounds, we believed that we could enable greater coherence and conversation.[9] Although their theories, methods, and politics were diverse—and they frequently disagreed about how or why one should 'do' media industry studies—the participation of these twenty-one individuals in our collection signified their recognition of the value and necessity of placing such work under a singular, umbrella label. This label, in turn, enabled us to move beyond the long-standing,

well-worn, and, from our perspective, by-then paralysing 'political economy *versus* cultural studies' debate.

It is no longer necessary to make the case for media industry studies.
Hundreds of us are now talking about industry-related scholarship to each
other at conferences, online, in classrooms, and beyond. The next step
involves figuring out how best to conduct such research. We now have so
much to work with—so many social media posts from creatives, historical
artefacts in archives, interviews and podcasts with executives waiting to
be downloaded or streamed. And yet, paradoxically, we often have *so little*
to work with—internal communications that stay forever hidden (if not
deleted), promising contacts who refuse to return our requests for interviews, passes that remain unavailable for visits to sets or studio lots. Within
this context, it is more important than ever for us to have ongoing conversations—with each other and with industry practitioners—about the value
of this work. There may be disagreement regarding the conditions under
which researchers should work with industry, or if they should do so at all.
But there is no longer any disagreement that media industry studies has
arrived. For its provocations regarding the scope and goals of this subfield,
as well as its attentiveness to methods, practices, and politics, this book
represents an important advance in media industry studies.

NOTES

1. See http://www.cmstudies.org/default.asp?page=groups_media_indust and
   http://community.icahdq.org/ohana/groups/details.cfm?id=174.
   Accessed 31 January 2016.
2. *Media Industries* was launched by a collective of institutions including
   UCSB, The University of Texas at Austin, Georgia State University,
   Queensland University of Technology, The University of Nottingham, and
   The Chinese University of Hong Kong. http://www.mediaindustriesjour-
   nal.org/index.php/mij/about. For information about UCSB's Media
   Industries Project, see http://www.carseywolf.ucsb.edu/mip. For informa-
   tion about Nottingham's Institute for Screen Industries Research, see
   http://www.nottingham.ac.uk/research/groups/isir/index.aspx.
   Accessed 31 January 2016.
3. For a few examples, see: Brooke Erin Duffy, *Remake, Remodel: Women's
   Magazines in the Digital Age*. Champaign, IL: University of Illinois Press,
   2013; Daniel Herbert, *Videoland: Movie Culture at the American Video
   Store*. Oakland, CA: University of California Press, 2014; Eric Hoyt,
   Hollywood Vault: Film Libraries Before Home Video. Oakland, CA: University

of California Press, 2014; Eva Northrup Redvall, *Writing and Producing Television Drama in Denmark: From* The Kingdom *to* The Killing. New York: Palgrave McMillan, 2013.

4. Among the institutions offering courses on media industry studies include Northeastern University, University of Liverpool, the University of Michigan, Arizona State, University of Copenhagen, UCLA, and Northwestern University.

5. Among the books I recommend to students, depending on their research interests and background, are Jane Stokes, *How to Do Media and Cultural Studies* (2nd ed.). Thousand Oaks: SAGE, 2013; David Deacon, Graham Murdock, Michael Pickering, and Peter Golding, *Researching Communications: A Practical Guide to Methods in Media and Cultural Analysis* (2nd ed.). London: Bloomsbury, 2007; Thomas R. Lindlof and Bryan C. Taylor, *Qualitative Communication Research Methods* (3rd ed.). Thousand Oaks: SAGE, 2011; and most recently, Richard Rogers, *Digital Methods*. Cambridge, MA: MIT Press, 2015.

6. I have contributed my own take to this body of literature recently with "The Trick of the Trades: Media Industry Studies and the American Comic Book Industry," in Miranda J. Banks, Vicki Mayer, and Bridget Conor (eds.) *Production Studies: The Sequel! Cultural Studies of Global Media Industries*. New York: Routledge, 2016, pp. 227–237. Also see John Thornton Caldwell, "Cultural Studies of Media Production: Critical Industrial Practices," in Mimi White and James Schoch (eds.) *Questions of Method in Cultural Studies*. Malden, MA: Blackwell, 2006, pp. 109–153.

7. In trying to find a name for what we were doing, I recall running searches on both Google and various library databases for the phrase 'media industry studies'. Beyond finding a couple of syllabi from business and management programs, only Jennifer Holt's work and my own came up in the search results.

8. Our own inspiration for industry–academy dialogue came from a number of sources, including Horace Newcomb and Robert Alley with *The Producer's Medium: Conversations with Creators of American TV*. Oxford: Oxford University Press, 1983 and Richard Ohmann (ed.), *Making and Selling Culture*. Hanover, NH: University Press of New England, 1996. A more recent example of such industry–academy dialogue can be found Derek Johnson, Derek Kompare, and Avi Santo (eds.) *Making Media Work: Cultures of Management in the Entertainment Industries*. New York: New York University Press, 2014.

9. Significantly, we were not alone in our impulses. Published within months of our collection were both the first edition of Vicki Mayer, Miranda J. Banks, and John Thornton Caldwell (eds.) *Production Studies: Cultural Studies of the Media Industries*. New York: Routledge, 2009 and Timothy

Havens, Amanda Lotz, and Serra Tinic, "Critical Media Industry Studies: A Research Approach," *Communication, Culture & Critique* 2:2 (June 2009): 234–253. While each of these publications conceptualises media industry studies in slightly different ways, they are all driven by similar goals of providing and encouraging dialogue and debate among previously disparate voices located across diverse disciplines.

Alisa Perren

Acknowledgements

The ideas and perspectives in this book derive in part from a research methods training event held at the University of Nottingham in June 2014. I would like to thank everybody who contributed to that event, as well as to its accompanying website, especially Paul Grainge, Catherine Johnson, Elizabeth Evans, Roberta Pearson, Paul McDonald, Steve Benford, and Steve Presence, who all acted as workshop speakers, interview participants or advisers, and Sam Ward and Leora Hadas, who co-organised the event and ensured its smooth running. My thanks also go to the Department of Culture, Film and Media at the University of Nottingham for lending the financial support necessary to hold this event in the first place.

Beyond the training event that set the *Industrial Approaches to Media* project in motion, getting this book completed has been a journey of data, perspective, and insight gathering, talking to and interviewing as many of the subfield's most esteemed academic voices as it has been possible to find, as well as engaging with a whole wealth of media industry practitioners so as to compare and theorise the discussions. The perspectives in this book come from an extensive data pool of interviews and case study contributions, comprising Henry Jenkins, Michele Hilmes, Amanda Lotz, Derek Johnson, Alisa Perren, Paul Grainge, Catherine Johnson, Steve Presence, Paul McDonald, Elizabeth Evans, Daniel Ashton, John Mateer, Eva Novrup Redvall, Jon Hickman, Hanne Bruun, Sam Ward, Leora Hadas, and Elinor Groom, amongst others. My sincere thanks to all of these people, not only for taking the time and effort to think carefully and critically about why they actually do the sorts of things that they do, but also for producing streams of answers, observations, insights, and methodological tips for how one can best go about studying today's media industries. It goes without saying that my contributors' insights are the very foundation, bedrock, and heartbeat of this book, and without their involvement, suggestions, and general sense of support, this project could never have existed.

And, as always, my eternal thanks go to Carley, my wonderful wife, partly for her constant support in my academic endeavours, but more so just for being her.

CONTENTS

LIST OF CASE STUDIES

NOTES ON CONTRIBUTORS

Emily Caston is a Senior Lecturer at London College of Communication. She is a board member of Film London, the public agency for strategic development of the capital's screen industries, a member of BAFTA and a member of D&AD. She was Visiting Professor in Communications at Al Akhawayn University in Morocco for several years, and education advisor to the MOBO Foundation (Music of Black Origin Foundation). For fifteen years she was a leading executive producer of music videos at Ridley Scott Associates in London and Los Angeles and at Propaganda Films Europe, where she produced over 100 award-winning videos for artists such as Madonna and Oasis and directors such as Chris Cunningham and Spike Jonze.

Elizabeth Evans is Assistant Professor in Film and Television Studies at the University of Nottingham. She is primarily interested in the relationship between technology and the experience of narrative, and her research focuses on film and television audiences, in particular in relation to the development of cross-platform narrative forms. She is also concerned with issues such as interactivity, agency, and immersion, and her first book, *Transmedia Television*, explores the attitudes, opinions, and values of audiences towards the development of the Internet as forms of extension of and alternatives to the television set.

Dave Harte is a Senior Lecturer in Media and Communication and award leader for the MA in Social Media at Birmingham City University. He researches the emerging trend of local community 'hyperlocal' news websites and has published widely on the subject. He has a track record of working with local media companies to support the growth of the creative economy. For many years he has worked closely with Birmingham's vibrant digital media sector, acting as a link between the public sector and the business community. Dave has published on the role of social media in media education and has also managed funded research projects for the

Communities and Culture Network, part of the UK Digital Economy research strand.

Michele Hilmes is Professor of Media and Cultural Studies in the Department of Communication Arts at the University of Wisconsin-Madison. Her work focuses on media history and historiography, particularly in the areas of transnational media and sound studies. She is the author or editor of several books in this field, including *Radio Voices: American Broadcasting 1922–1952* (1997), *Network Nations: A Transnational History of British and American Broadcasting* (2011), *Only Connect: A Cultural History of Broadcasting in the United States* (2013), and *Radio's New Wave: Global Sound in the Digital Era*, co-edited with Jason Loviglio (2013). She was a 2013–14 Fulbright Research Scholar at the University of Nottingham, UK and is currently researching the history of British/American television co-production.

Petros Iosifidis is Professor of Media and Communication Policy at City University London. He is a media policy academic, working on the social, political, and economic aspects of the media industry. He currently heads the Centre for International Communications & Society in the Department of Sociology. As part of this group he has developed extensive expertise in the areas of broadcasting, telecommunications, and digital media policies, global media market structures, regulatory frameworks, and the public interest. His most recent books include *Global Media and National Policies: The Return of the State* (2016), *Global Media and Communication Policy* (2013), and *The Political Economy of Television Sports Rights* (2013), with Tom Evans and Paul Smith. Professor Iosifidis serves on the Peer Review College of the Economic and Social Research Council and he is Books Editor of the *International Journal of Digital Television*.

Henry Jenkins is Provost Professor of Communication, Journalism, Cinematic Arts and Education at the University of Southern California. As one of the first media scholars to chart the changing role of the audience in an environment of increasingly pervasive digital content, Jenkins has been at the forefront of understanding the effects of participatory media on society, politics, and culture. His research gives key insights to the success of social-networking websites, networked computer games, online fan communities and other advocacy organizations, and emerging news media outlets. Jenkins has played a central role in demonstrating the importance of new media technologies in educational settings. His most recent book, *Convergence Culture: Where Old and New Media Collide* (2006) is recognised as a hallmark of recent research on the subject of transmedia storytelling. His other published works reflect the wide range of his research interests, touching on democracy and new media, the 'wow factor' of popular culture, science-fiction fan communities, and the early history of film comedy.

Paul Kerr is Senior Lecturer and programme leader in Television Production at Middlesex University. He is the author and editor of a number of books and articles on television and film. He started his career at the British Film Institute but for twenty years was an award-winning television producer, making dozens of programmes for the BBC and Channel Four as well as a number of international co-productions. He began his TV career by specialising in major series about the media, first as researcher on *Open The Box* (C4 1986), then as producer on *The Media Show* (C4 1987–90), and subsequently as Series Editor of the award-winning cinema series *Moving Pictures* (BBC2 1990–96), and then developed into working on a range of documentaries about the arts and history. His research interests include drama documentary, documentary, 'quality' television, Hollywood, the independent production sector in film and television, and international art cinema. He was Co-Investigator on an AHRC research project on British television documentary television and independent production between 2010 and 2012.

Paul McDonald is Professor of Culture, Media and Creative Industries at King's College London. Paul has played a leading role in developing the field of critical media industry studies. His current research is focused in the areas of screen media industries, political economy and history of media piracy, digital distribution of film and television, symbolic commerce of Hollywood film stardom, and interactions between Hollywood and the law. His most recent books include *Hollywood and the Law* (2015, edited with Emily Carman, Eric Hoyt, and Philip Drake), *Hollywood Stardom* (2013), and *The Contemporary Hollywood Film Industry* (2008, edited with Janet Wasko). Before entering academia, Paul trained as a professional actor at the Royal Academy of Dramatic Art and worked in various areas of the media industries, including animated film production, studio photography, and film exhibition.

Alisa Perren is Associate Professor in the Department of Radio-Television-Film at the University of Texas at Austin. Her research interests include television studies, media industry studies, US film and television history, and media convergence. She is co-editor of *Media Industries: History, Theory, and Method* (2009, with Jennifer Holt) and author of *Indie, Inc.: Miramax and the Transformation of Hollywood in the 1990s* (2012). Her work has appeared in a range of publications, including *Film Quarterly, Journal of Film and Video, Journal of Popular Film & Television, Cinema Journal, Managing Media Work*, and *Moving Data*. Her current book project examines the growing interrelationship between the American comic book industry and Hollywood in the 2000s. From 2010 to 2013, she served as Coordinating Editor for *In Media Res*, an online project experimenting with collaborative, multi-modal forms of scholarship. Presently, she is a co-founder and co-managing editor for *Media Industries*, an online, peer-reviewed, open-access journal.

Sarah Ralph   is Lecturer in Media and Cultural Studies at Northumbria University. Prior to this she was Research Associate in the Department of Film, Television and Media Studies at the University of East Anglia working on the AHRC-funded research project *Make Me Laugh: Creativity in British Television Comedy* (2012–2015) and also a Part-Time Lecturer in both the Film, Television and Media Department and in UEA's Interdisciplinary Institute for the Humanities. She has published in the journals *Celebrity Studies*, *Participations*, and *Critical Studies in Television*, and recently co-authored *Alien Audiences: Remembering and Evaluating a Classic Movie* (2015, with Martin Barker, Kate Egan, and Tom Phillips).

CHAPTER 1

Introduction: Media Industry Studies—What and Why?

Matthew Freeman

In November 2014, news broke of what became known in the press as the Sony Pictures Entertainment hack, an infamous release to the public of confidential email data belonging to the media company and its staff. The hack led to a wide range of private information concerning Sony's employees, executive salaries, and previously unreleased Sony films becoming public knowledge. Allegedly, Angelina Jolie was branded 'a minimally talented spoiled brat', and insensitive jokes concerning President Obama's favourite African American film became public news stories. Moreover, the leak suddenly provided statistical evidence regarding long-suspected salary discrepancies between Hollywood's male and female stars. Assumptions about work practices and the burden of promotional campaigns on actors and publicists—all important components and considerations in today's film industry—were suddenly revealed for public consideration in a way rarely seen in the traditionally secretive media industries. Sony's co-chairman quickly departed the company, such was the level of controversy surrounding the openness of the hack and the release of private email correspondence.

Perhaps above all else, the widespread public fascination with the Sony hack highlights just how interested we all are in the people in charge of

M. Freeman (✉)
Bath Spa University, Bath, UK

© The Editor(s) (if applicable) and The Author(s) 2016   1
M. Freeman, *Industrial Approaches to Media*,
DOI 10.1057/978-1-137-55176-4_1

making the so-called dream factory of Hollywood film. And it is hard to argue against the contention that at least some of the information released during the hack adds new depths of understanding about the workings of a giant media conglomerate like Sony to those of us on the outside looking in. As Emily Carman (2015) notes, 'while the hack is clearly an invasion of privacy, it is also a vital resource for scholars because contemporary Hollywood reveals so little about its internal operations and business practices.' The inner workings of the media industries are indeed often associated with veils of mystery, rather like fiction's the Great Wizard of Oz, whose face and work were so famously hidden from the world behind a curtain. Much like the Wizard from the L. Frank Baum fairy tale and MGM iconic musical, the media industries may connote magic and mysticism; the creative, escapist lure of the films and television programmes media industries produce can evoke within audiences a sense of awe and wonder. People are drawn to stories, to characters, to worlds. Without emotions of awe, wonder, intrigue, and relish, many of these same film and television programmes would surely cease to capture the public's imagination in ways necessary for these forms of entertainment to succeed. And so it is little wonder then that the media industries at large attempt to operate on a behind-the-scenes basis, upholding a strictly wizard-behind-the-curtain approach.

Yet the understandable secrecy of many media industry operations also causes a major problem for those wishing to research and study them. In a sense, the Sony hack crystallises not only how many people are now interested in learning about the workings of media industries, but even more so the importance of learning how to learn about the workings of media industries: how does one go about researching the media industries strategically and ethically?

John Mateer (2015) directly links the closed-door facade of the media industries and their tendency to often withhold information for commercial advantage to an increased difficulty of gaining access and forging mutually beneficial relationships between academia and industry. For Mateer (2015), 'this has made meaningful research into certain aspects of media industries much more difficult and required academics to be more creative in ways to procuring relevant data.' And yet understanding the inner workings behind the proverbial curtain of the media industries is crucial to anyone interested in studying, working in, or perhaps even shaping the future of the media industries. As Huw Jones (2014) rightly notes, 'knowledge of the media industries is essential to understanding the media's wider social, cultural, political and economic significance. Yet few graduate or postgraduate degrees offer the necessary skills and training to research this area.'

It may actually be true, as Michele Hilmes (2014) argues, that 'all of us who have been doing media studies have, from the very beginning, been doing media industry studies—since the first films were instituted and the first television programmes were studied.' Nevertheless, the specified turn to focusing critically on the industrial structures, processes, and practices of the media's workings—or media industry studies—has emerged explicitly only recently within the last ten years or so, which for Hilmes (2014) has 'to do with a lot of changes in the industry itself.' In the UK, as of 2014, the creative industries are now worth £71.4 billion per year to its economy, a growth of almost 10 % since 2012 (Gov.uk 2014). As such, the wider creative industries have emerged as one of the most celebrated sectors of the UK economy, framed and endorsed as part of a new knowledge economy for a global digital society. As such, as Daniel Ashton and Caitriona Noonan (2013: 1) assert, 'the media industries, or more accurately their partial political successor, the creative industries, are associated with ideals of flexibility, enterprise, competition and modernity [...] [I]n the UK the sector is often framed as a panacea to numerous financial and social ills, including economic development, urban regeneration and social inequalities.'

There has been sizable academic interest in the media industries, too—something that Ashton and Noonan tie, at least in part, to 'the various government-led programmes which have attempted to provide a strategic plan for the industry in the UK' (2013: 2).[1] In the academy, moreover, it is surely no coincidence that media industry studies has been quite similarly framed as a panacea to any perceived limits to studying media—with 'industry' here becoming a shorthand for collaboration and utopic partnerships across borders. As Catherine Johnson (2013) discusses, in 'the current research funding environment in the UK, a key factor in contemporary higher education policy ... is the emphasis placed on the impact of research conducted within universities and funded through public money.' Linked to this, Johnson continues, 'government policy on higher education research has also placed increased emphasis on knowledge exchange and knowledge transfer.'

With media industry studies certainly emerging as a priority at several major UK and US universities, finding ways to enhance the relationships between universities and businesses are becoming increasingly important to emerging researchers, and this, of course, is impacting the type of research that best affords such priorities. Producing work that is not only about the business of the media but also seeks, as part of its in-built research agenda, to actually shape or perhaps reshape the future business strategies of the media industries themselves is thus now becoming increasingly crucial to supporting this broader shift in the focus of UK policy towards the development of a thriving media-based knowledge economy.

And yet it is fair to suggest that the relative lack of clear and fully developed methodologies for conducting research about the media industries often impedes the formation of lasting collaborations between academia and the media industries that may well benefit both parties. Many emerging scholars often lack the resources necessary to approach and engage with media companies, studios, and organisations. Perhaps this is because the best media industry research draws from such a diverse range of disciplines. But in practice, this multi-disciplinarity means that novice researchers can sometimes find the methodological landscape of media industry studies difficult to navigate. While some scholars have attempted to outline approaches to studying media industries in the past, much of this work is quite conceptually broad and lacks clear direction. Jane Stokes (2003: 107–108), for instance, asserts that in researching the media industries, 'there are two kinds of evidence: *documentary* evidence (such as written sources) and *people* (such as interviews and participant observation.' Stokes is right in her assessment, but what exactly is the value of documentary evidence for our understanding of media industries? For what types of studies is documentary evidence most appropriate? Similarly, how does the evidence gained from people differ from that gained from written sources? And how does one go about finding relevant people?

THE AIMS OF THE BOOK

So, despite the prominence of industry engagement, theoretical understandings of the actual methodological processes for studying media industries remain vague. This lack is not particularly surprising given the relative infancy of media industry studies as a focus of scholarly research. In 2009, Jennifer Holt and Alisa Perren published *Media Industries*, a hugely important publication that aimed to define the critical study of media industries as a coherent discipline. Holt and Perren acknowledged that 'the media industries themselves have been experiencing a period of unprecedented influence, prosperity, cultural debate, and transformation'

(2009: 1). The growth in the importance of the media industries has been matched in academic circles with the founding of new research groups and academic journals based on the study of the media industries, such as the Media Industries Scholarly Interest Group of the Society for Cinema and Media Studies and the *Media Industries* journal, which both exemplify the surge of interest in these industries. But if the focus of our scholarly research is as vast and often as intangible as an entire media industry or set of media industries, then how exactly do we research this vastness? How precisely do we get close to this intangibility? What is the industry as a 'text' or what are these industries as an object of study? What are the appropriate methods for examining specific aspects of the media industries—and how does one navigate those methods in light of complex industrial deterrents such as copyright law or policy regulations, not to mention the aforementioned difficulty of gaining access to the innards of media industries outside of unethical public hacks?

Indeed, while the above scholars, groups, and journals have all been pivotal in developing media industry studies into a coherent discipline, there remains a notable lack of understanding about how to actually *do* research in this particular discipline. For as Paul McDonald (2013) observes, 'labelling a field of inquiry […] suggests there is a distinct and coherent body of purposes, principles or perspectives at work, although any survey of scholarship on media industries is immediately confronted by the enormous diversity of approaches and critical preoccupations.' In fact, as Holt and Perren (2009: 1) also note, 'to explore the media industries in the twenty-first century is to engage with an extraordinary range of texts, markets, economics, artistic traditions, business models, cultural policies, technologies, regulations, and creative expression.' And yet, while such a vast array of critical emphases have been crucial to the definition and topicality of media industry studies as a field of enquiry, thus far there has been little sustained effort to unify the broad approaches of this work under a more coherent methodological framework.

Responding to this need, *Industrial Approaches to Media* aims to offer a guidebook for those interested in undertaking study of the media industries. Its goal is twofold: one, to conceptualise the objectives and critical orientations of media industry research, as well as to conceptualise media industries as an object of study; and two, to provide guidance, most pointedly to postgraduate students and early career researchers, in developing a methodology for researching the media industries. In particular, this book looks to provide such guidance in ways that might be best suited to

more effective, collaborative, and valuable dialogue between media industry scholars and the media industry professionals that those scholars may
interact with in the course of their research.

The book therefore extends the work done by Jennifer Holt and Alisa
Perren, amongst many others, by attempting to offer a set of practical,
theoretical, and ethical principles for researchers new to the area of media
industry studies. I build on the likes of Holt and Perren (2009), Havens
et al. (2009), and Wasko and Meehan (2013), who have all called for a
more unified methodological approach in media industry studies. Given
that scholars based in the US have done a large proportion of the ground-
work of media industry studies, moreover, this book will primarily offer
a UK perspective on what it means to conceptualise the media industries
as an object of study—an approach that seems especially important given
that at least some of the forces bringing industry and academics into collaboration may be unique to the UK, as noted previously. Many of the
book's contributors have a strong knowledge of the UK media landscape,
offering insight into particular production and academic cultures that lend
greater nuance to media industry studies approaches. That being said, I do
not intend this book to be entirely specific to the UK setting; on the contrary, media industry studies requires an increasingly globalised approach
to research given the global ecology of today's media industries. While
not attempting to generalise what are certainly different worlds of research
and industry between the UK, the US, and other national contexts, the
book will make use of insights and case studies from scholars based outside
the UK so to realise the aim of establishing a more unified methodological
understanding of media industry studies.

It is certainly not my intention, in other words, to profess some kind of
complete radicalisation of media industry studies methodology, but rather
to pull together the numerous, if occasionally contradictory, insights about
ways of researching the subfield of media industry studies into a single,
coherent resource that provides more depth and with more elaboration
than has been outlined previously. Specifically, this book aims to demonstrate, in a rather nuts-and-bolts sense, and via contemporary examples and points of guidance, how the differing yet highly complementary
methodologies of trade paper and social media analysis, interviewing and
ethnography, political economy, cultural studies, and social theory can
all be used in media industry studies as what Havens et al. (2009) have
called an overarching *Critical Media Industries Studies* approach. A critical
media industries approach is a multi-method, multiperspectival approach

to studying media industries, bringing together a variety of different methods as part of a holistic analysis, paying equal consideration to economic, corporate, and discursive contexts.

The first objective of this book, therefore, is to theorise, methodologically, how emerging researchers can go about conceptualising the media industries as a coherent object of study, and in turn to research those industries. The second and somewhat intertwined aim of this book is to conceptualise, in a similarly nuts-and-bolts fashion, the notion of media studies as genuinely and productively engaging with industry. McDonald (2013: 146), in his work on mapping and characterising media industry studies as a field of enquiry, observed the field's dual purpose of serving both academia and industry in equal measure as one of its opportunities and its potential limits: 'Preserving a distance from the object of inquiry is frequently considered a necessary condition for the scholarly production of critical knowledge about industry. But if that knowledge is to achieve any influence beyond the academy, it is important to consider—How can studies of media industries engage in productive dialogue with the very industries they study?' Jennifer Holt (2013), too, notes that such a notion of productive dialogue with industry brings opportunities for academics but also additional considerations, most notably she asks, 'How can we frame our scholarly research in ways that render our lines of inquiry productive for such exchanges? Is this "translation" a necessary component of research design moving forward if we strive to create new partnerships? What is gained—or lost—in collaborating with the industry we study?'

In many respects, McDonald's and Holt's remarks are themselves the underlying critical questions of this book, and so I will endeavour to not only explore the methodological approaches to doing academic research *about* the media industries, but also to theorise the implications—practical, theoretical, and ethical—of producing academic research that is potentially equally *for* the media industries. In what ways then might one go about 'translating' academic media research to a media industry audience and for a more open media industry context?

Indeed, how precisely can academics go about providing answers to the media's search for knowledge, what exactly is that knowledge, and how might the media industries in turn help shape academia in terms of how it shapes those questions? John Mateer (2015), whose own research aims to interrogate academia–industry collaborations more broadly and explores perceptions of media practitioners working in higher education today, initially suggests that

[i]t is arguable that those who have worked in industry are best placed to be involved in research concerning the media industries, yet the bulk of the research into the area has been conducted by those who have never directly engaged in it. This is a significant shortcoming and one that has potentially led to a skewed understanding of industry but also has meant that certain aspects of industry may have been missed or misrepresented.

It might stand to reason then that any first-hand experience of working in the media industries would help in the process of teaching the workings of the media industries. But this book does not argue that those interested in researching the media industries need experience working in industry. On the contrary, I will explore how the sort of industry-engaged media studies suggested above emerges, first, from multiperspectival research methodologies and, second, from collaboration and partnership—making use of the insights and exchanges across the different fields of academia and industry. Derek Johnson (2014), in fact, argues that it is important for media industry studies as a subfield to 'figure out that it does not need full access to start making significant interventions into how we all understand industry and how that industry might be imagined to work.' Says Johnson (2014),

> I think it is important that we try to address the voices of industry pro-fessionals in our work—but I don't know that we need to celebrate the scholar's ability to get inside [industry]. The industry is already talking to us—via Twitter, in trade articles, and more—and so acting like we have to get inside ourselves to understand how practitioners are trying to negotiate and make sense of their work seems a little unnecessary.

Though Johnson (2014) does acknowledge that getting inside the industry and looking for access can yield terrific insights, he believes that the role of the scholar is to 'try to understand media industries from all pos-sible perspectives'—and that means conceptualising the methodology of media industry studies as being about much more than mere access to industry itself. In fact, Johnson goes so far as to indicate that relying on industry access for research about the media industries might be as 'limit-ing as it is enabling' (2014). As we will see through the pages of this book, knowledge about the media industries can come from a whole range of places and spaces—and only by fully embracing the cultural circuits and the ephemerality of the media industries (i.e., the discourses that circulate around them, the bits and pieces of text that surround their core products, the social context in which media industries work, etc.) can a methodology of media industry studies be fully understood.

Still, it is true, as Mateer (2015) elaborates, that 'researchers need to have a rich understanding of a domain in order to ask pertinent questions that can uncover more nuanced elements of the subject.' In other words, before beginning to understand a methodology of media industry studies, or before exploring ways of engaging with media industries, let us first go about defining media industry studies.

DEFINING MEDIA INDUSTRY STUDIES

'Media industry studies is really more of a practical approach to theory by the means of theory.'[2] This seemingly throwaway remark, uttered by an undergraduate student tasked with writing a critical blog about the idea of researching the media industries, is actually a far more insightful and useful observation than meets the eye. For this remark in fact goes straight to the heart of what makes media industry studies at once so important and yet so difficult to navigate as an emerging academic researcher.

The comment indicates a bridging between notions of theory and practice, between the creation of ideas and the pragmatics of media making. This idea of bridging will be examined in more depth later on, particularly in Part III of this book, but for now the principle question remains: what exactly *is* media industry studies?

As Paul McDonald (2014) notes that while 'there are a number of ways to respond to a question such as "what is media industry studies?"', it can be defined, in the simplest and more directive terms, as,

> [m]edia industry studies is the umbrella label that we give to the whole body of research and of teaching that is principally concerned with wanting to critically examine the histories, processes, procedures, structures, policies, mechanisms, and professional ideologies that relate to the workings of the media industries.

Acting as a forum in which to study and in turn shape media and cultural production then, media industry studies encompasses those industries involved in the production and circulation of media texts, such as television, radio, film, music, and newspapers. As Paul McDonald (2013: 145) insists, 'media industry studies is not a "discipline"; rather, media industry studies revels in disciplinary heterogeneity.' McDonald, indeed, declares media industry studies 'a subfield with defined limits', arguing that it 'operates in the "*über*-fields" of the humanities and social sciences.' In fact, media industry studies is a specific subfield of culture, media, and film studies that additionally draws from and crosses over into a whole range of other disciplinary areas, including film studies, mass communications studies, cultural studies, sociology, and business and management studies—adopting a cross- and inter-disciplinary stance on the study of the media so as to provide a greater and more richly contextualised understanding about its specific objects of study. While McDonald (2014) notes that 'there are arguments that have been voiced to say that media industry research is a particular methodological approach to media industries', he himself prefers to see the label as 'a collective title for a whole bunch of different perspectives.' Says McDonald (2014), '[t]here is a whole range of different subject areas that have been concerned with the media industries.' Thus, while some scholars may address industrial questions from a film and media studies perspective, there is other work from the disciplines of 'economics, sociology, business and management studies, and elements of economic geography as well.'

There is a broad spectrum of interests that make up the fabric of media industry studies then, and this broadness comes from its history. Holt and Perren (2009: 2) argue that 'many of the foundational ideas about the media industries emerged in critical/scholarly writing from the 1920s through the 1950s.' They point here to the significance of, first, the Frankfurt School scholars of the twentieth century and their coining of the term 'culture industry' to critique the influence of mass production, commerce, and consumerism on the reshaping of cultural forms, and second, the rise of mass communication theories that sprang up in the wake of Theodor Adorno and Max Horkheimer as well as other Marxist theorists. One can trace the influence of these Marxist perspectives on conceptualisations of media industries, with the former's critique of the mass commodification of media and culture arguably informing David Hesmondhalgh's *The Cultural Industries* (2007), where Hesmondhalgh identifies the business of media industries as a complex, intertwined, if problematic, relationship between 'art' and 'commerce'.

Philip Schlesinger (2015) meanwhile suggests that the rise of media industry studies was built up during three distinct phases over the past fifty years or so, and that we are now in the third of these phases. For Schlesinger, phase one of media industry studies was the research taking place in the US in the 1950s and 1960s. At this time, much media research focused on the idea of gatekeeping, which led to researchers typically going into news organisations, for example, in order to learn about what stories are broadcast or published and which are not. This era of media industry research was indeed rooted in the study of media organisations, seeing the newsroom or the production studio as a transparent system to be deciphered and mapped.

Schlesinger suggests that this organisational phase was then followed by a second phase of media industry studies in the 1970s and 1980s; this second phase would see a turn towards a more ethnographic approach, which has since seen a renaissance more recently. Says Schlesinger (2015), '[t]his second phase was about thinking of industry "relationally", which means you step outside of the company and think about the relationships between what is going on culturally (outside) and within the industry (inside)'. This approach is well adapted to the networked nature of today's media culture, allowing for the creation of a study with a kind of centre that then works to map connections to outside factors or influences. As such, ethnographic research is now very important to the methodology of media industry studies.

Lastly, Schlesinger argues that a third phase of media industry studies has emerged in the last ten years or so, and this phase involves conducting both of the former approaches *together*—that is, attempting to do the sorts of in-depth organisational analysis that we saw in the past whilst combining this with more culturally minded ethnographic analysis. This more contextualised, nuanced approach to media industry studies can be detected in the publication of John Thornton Caldwell's hugely influential *Production Culture: Industrial Reflexivity and Critical Practice in Film and Television* (2008) together with *Production Studies: Cultural Studies of Media Industries*, edited by Caldwell with Vicki Mayer and Miranda Banks (2009). In contrast to many organisational studies of the past century, which indeed tended to focus on large-scale work structures, patterns of ownership, and the dominant control exercised by large corporations, Caldwell et al. reconceived the notion of media industry studies as more of a *cultural practice* involving levels of 'ordinary' workers, professionals, organisations, and more informal, less highly regulated networks—thus thinking of industry as a cultural rather than an exclusively economic phenomenon. And in emphasising cultures of production with their own codes, meanings, and rituals, media industry studies soon shifted from its earlier Marxist or sociological orientation to a more combined anthropological and ethnographic approach. In doing so, and as Andrew Spicer (2015) articulates, media industry studies 'retained an attention to the wider forces of international capitalism [while] attempting to embrace the often competing claims of political economy studies and cultural studies, and therefore to be equally attentive to economic, technological and political forces, to ownership, regulation and the marketplace, as well as to the activities of media workers and the production of specific media texts.'

Attempting to map all of these different and notably vast forces of industry is precisely the challenge for researchers; media industry studies' apparent refusal to tie down its prescribed focus of study to any particular approach—while itself crucial to the objectives of this subfield—simultaneously exemplifies the methodological challenge of doing this kind of research. But as we will see, what is meant by media industry studies today is principally *contextualisation*—it aims to trace connections between the micro and the macro, between production and culture, so as to better understand *how* and *why* the media industries ultimately work the way that they do. All media industries essentially operate as a complex blend of creativity and enterprise, translating culture into economy. Contextualisation affords a valuable insight into the processes and practices of this translation, be they big or small.

Given this emphasis on crossing subjects and disciplinary boundaries, however, it is crucial to narrow down our definition of what studying the media industries might actually mean. McDonald (2013: 145–146) argues that 'even within the academic fields to which it belongs, media industry studies is limited in its disciplinary borrowings: Economics is clearly important to any study of media industries, but the impetus toward social and cultural criticism motivating much scholarship in media industry studies has seen the influence of political economy exerted'. As will be explored throughout this book, within this umbrella of media industry studies we can identify a series of defined yet crucially overlapping critical frameworks. These frameworks include the political economy of communications, the production of culture, media, and cultural economics, the sociology of media occupations, and some elements of film historiography, such as film funding history.

All of these aforementioned frameworks have something in common: they are all principally concerned with understanding the relationship between discourse and economics, between art and commerce, between storytelling and production. And so it is important to begin to conceptualise media industry studies in such terms. As will be outlined in Chap. 5, Michele Hilmes (2014) defines media industry studies very specifically as 'the study of authorship'—by which she means understanding modes of corporate and discursive production across multiple sites of creation and industrial development, not to mention wider cultural terrains. And it is in that sense that we can say that media industry studies is about contextualisation. For Hilmes (2014), doing this kind of contextualised media research 'brings us into examining structures, workings and policies'—things that go beyond the actual text and place media within a wider, vital context of numerous overlapping principles of study.

Let's call the first of these three principles the *societal context*, where the operations of the media industries emerge as the outcome of deep structures in society. The second of these can be called the *corporate context*, which concerns the working practices that make up production cultures within the media industries. And the third of these principles can be called the *discursive context*, which concerns not actual practice but the discourses communicated by media industry practitioners, and thus the ways in which media practitioners narrativise the transformation of deep social structures into clear sets of meanings and understandings about the media industries.

Each of these three contexts of media industry study will be explored and elaborated on further throughout the book, but what is important to emphasise at this stage is the idea of studying a sprawl, a sense of looking across borders—be it vast economic borders, narrower corporate borders, or discursive cultural borders. As we shall see, thinking of media industries not just as industrial places—i.e., sectors, organisations, producers—but also in terms of circuits around industries, as socio-political-cultural enterprises, is crucial to the process of conceptualising media industry studies, and this book is partly about exploring how best to navigate those conceptual borders.

APPROACHING MEDIA INDUSTRY STUDIES

Conceptually, indeed, a fundamental methodological perspective of media industry studies would be that products of the media (i.e., everything from films, television programmes, radio podcasts, video games, and so on) are at once both *symbolic* and *economic* entities. That is to say, they are at once texts of creativity designed to articulate layers of cultural meaning and substance and enjoyment to audiences as stories, and equally commodities intended to generate profits.

In other words, for the doing of media industry studies we need to adopt perspectives that afford an understanding of both media's artistry and of media's business. It is, as John Caldwell (2013: 157–159) encourages, about better understanding the multifaceted nature of media industry workings and their embedded nature within industrial networks, routines, and cultures. As Caldwell (2013: 158) elaborates, 'one trap would be to construe *the* industry … as a clean, self-evident sphere or as a bounded site for research that does not simultaneously involve the vagaries of human subjects and culture's thick complexities.' And if an overriding aim of media industry studies is to somehow 'account for these messy aspects of industrial, corporate activity' through research, the ensuing chapters of this book will attempt to identify a set of clearer methodologies for how to account for the media industry's pluralised, multifaceted vagaries and thick complexities, mapping specific methodological approaches and strategies to particular research interests and objectives.

So, exactly what are the overriding research questions, interests, and objectives that media industry studies can address? As McDonald (2013: 146) explains, an array of questions are suggested by the subfield, each of which will be considered in this book:

How have media industries been organized and structured at different times? What are the functions and processes at work in making, selling, and circulating the outputs of the media industries? How does a company or the media industry at large respond to disruptive technological change? What struggles have confronted organized labor? How do patterns of ownership and control define economic and ideological power? What relationships exist between the media economy and the wider economy? How do media industries construct "audiences" and "consumers"? Why, how, and with what consequences do governments regulate the conduct of media industries? What impact do transnational firms, forms, and flows have on the operations of media industries? In what ways are digitization and convergence challenging traditional business models? How do spatial concentrations of media companies and institutions in clusters or cities shape geographies of media business? What systems of belief and value are produced and circulated among media practitioners? How can media industries support or impede democratic communication? What impact do technological obsolescence and the electronic waste produced by the disposal of media hardware have on the environment? Finally, there is the metacritical question: what frameworks can we construct for making sense of the preceding questions?

McDonald's detailed and thorough outline of media industry studies' possible research questions provides us with a useful place to begin conceptualising research in this area. And McDonald's acknowledgement of a need to find clear frameworks for answering any or all of the above research questions also goes some way to justifying the intentions of this book. That few clear methodological frameworks exist for either actually studying media industry studies or the processes involved in formulating, constructing, and articulating studies that speak mutually to academia and to the media industries at large is surely the greatest barrier currently impeding the future development of media industry studies as a subfield of academic enquiry.

THE STRUCTURE OF THE BOOK

Having outlined the aims of the book, we now turn to a breakdown of the structure of the book and an explanation of my methodology. As the first book to provide readers with the methodological tools they need to start doing media industry studies, *Industrial Approaches to Media* aims to bring researchers to a point of methodological coherence in this area of study—providing a more definitive full-scale exploration of the topic rather than merely pointing towards it. And providing a more definitive full-scale exploration of media industry studies methodology means drawing on perspectives and insights from the subfield's most established and esteemed academic voices as well as from industry practitioners. The perspectives in this book come from an extensive data pool of interviews and workshops conducted with both media industry professionals and international media studies academics.[3] This data pool includes many of the most esteemed academics now working in media industry studies—from the UK and beyond. From the UK this includes Paul McDonald, John Mateer, Elizabeth Evans, Daniel Ashton, Jon Hickman, Paul Grainge, Catherine Johnson, and Steve Presence, with Henry Jenkins, Michele Hilmes, Amanda Lotz, Derek Johnson, Eva Novrup Redvall, and Hanne Bruun lending global perspectives.

Using the perspectives and experiences of these scholars as a starting point, this book will then focus on thinking about ways to better bridge academia and industry via the methodologies of doing media industry studies—defining what those methodologies are along the way. To do this, the book is divided into three parts, each designed to build on the last. Part I, titled 'The Ideologies & Ethics of Media Industry Studies', works to justify the importance and examine the politics of engaging with the media industries for academic purposes, looking at the ways in which the current professional ideologies of academia and the media industries (at least in the UK) do in fact overlap, before going on to discuss the political and ethical dimensions and implications of doing media industry research in this UK setting. The politics of producing academic research that can be 'translated' to a media industry audience and for a media industry context will also be examined in depth throughout this part.

This first part is split into three chapters. Chapter 2, 'The Professional Ideologies of Academia and Industry', aims to interrogate the diverse and overlapping ways in which UK academia and media industries perceive their own roles and objectives, looking to see where the through lines might be for the advancement of greater academia–industry collaboration. This chapter also features a contribution from Paul Kerr, who explores this question of comparing the professional working ideologies in academia to those in the media industries by reflecting on his past experiences in television. Chapter 3, 'The Politics and Ethics of Media Industry Studies', moves on to explore the political and ethical principles and complexities of developing collaborations between academia and media industries, interrogating the political principles of producing media industry studies for multiple parties before outlining a number of best practice approaches for the researcher. These approaches will be supported and demonstrated via Elizabeth Evans and Paul McDonald's case study contribution, reflecting on the process of partnering with commercial media.

In Part II, titled 'The Theory & Practice of Media Industry Studies', the book then moves on to identifying specific methodological approaches for studying media industries, exploring which methods might be best suited to various objects of study and theoretical interests—be it the societal context, the corporate context, or the discursive context. Nevertheless, it is important to stress at this stage that while I structure this book around separate methodological approaches, I will show how each of these methodological contexts also complement one another—revealing different facets of different media industry workings—as strands of what Havens et al. (2011) defined as an overarching *Critical Media Industries Studies* approach.

This second part is divided into four chapters. Chapter 4, 'Socialised Authorship: Conceptualising Media Industry Studies', begins by theorising the very idea of studying media industries in the light of twenty-first century transformations in technology, ownership, structures, and working conditions. Here I return to the idea that media industry studies methodology is about tracing connections between political economic, corporate, and discursive contexts, as suggested above, and I highlight the importance of authorship as a concept for thinking of media industries, at least in the broadest conceptual sense. I also explore the importance of particular social theories on understanding how one might approach the study of media industries. In other words, Chap. 4 is where I set out an overarching conceptual framework for conceiving of the media industries as an object of study, with the ensuing three chapters in this part demonstrating the different components of this framework in reference to specific methodological approaches and techniques. For this chapter, Michele Hilmes provides a case study about ways of conceptualising media industry studies as a study of authorship across borders of personnel, subdivisions, and subsidiary corporations, using radio studies as an example.

Chapter 5, 'Media Industries as Structure: Objectivism and the Societal Context', begins our exploration of the key methodological approaches for doing media industry studies, with this chapter looking at the approach of deep social structure and the modes of studying the impact of political economic contexts on the workings of media industries. In so doing, I also consider the idea of what is known as 'objectivism' in business and management studies, linking this ontological notion to political economy in media industry studies. Petros Iosifidis ends the chapter with a case study detailing how he himself employed political economy in his research to reveal crucial insights into television sports rights and the larger sports industry.

In Chap. 6, 'Media Industries as Interaction: Constructivism and the Corporate Context', I look at the study of media industries from a more localised, people-orientated perspective, thinking about researching media industries through the lens of the corporate context. To do so, I consider the relationship between the notion of 'constructivism' and what interviewing and ethnography—two long-standing and traditional research methods—mean in the more collaborative media industry studies mould outlined in earlier stages of the book. This chapter is filled with reflections, insights, and suggestions for how to approach media industry practitioners in the hope of obtaining interviews, how to make best use of those interviews, and how the researcher might wish to conceptualise the role of the media industry practitioner in this case. Sarah Ralph, too, contributes a short section about her own experiences of doing interviews with members of the UK television industry.

Lastly, in Chap. 7, 'Media Industries as Modality: Culturalism and the Discursive Context', I end this second part of the book by considering the sorts of media industry studies that can be tackled by analysing the peripheral documentation that surrounds the media industries; the sorts of extra materials like trade papers and social media webpages that are produced by the media—and sometimes for the media—but which are not necessarily the promoted commodities we as media scholars tend to call texts. I draw on the study of culturalism to best understand this approach, showing that since media industries are essentially communication tools, the likes of trade papers are crucial to understanding media industries as cultural sprawls of information. In particular, I argue that taking a cultural studies approach to gauging the discursive context of the media industries can work to bridge the gulf separating the macro-economic considerations of media industries and the individual scale of creative decision making, positioning everyday ephemeral documentation as the productive middle ground between questions of political economy and agency. Dave Hart then demonstrates how this approach might work in practice, ending the chapter with a case study about researching the workings of journalism via social media.

In Part III, 'The Reciprocity & Publishing of Media Industry Studies', I move on to examine the means by which academic research might be best 'translated' to a media industry audience. Chapter 8, 'Approaching Knowledge Exchange', offers some pointed reflections about the importance of seeing media industry partners as precisely that—as long-standing, ethically regarded partners who require equal benefits from scholarly research as the academic partners developing the project. As well as examining precisely what knowledge exchange might actually mean in the context of media industry studies, the chapter ends with a piece by Henry Jenkins, who offers invaluable insights into how future generations of researchers might go about conceiving of research projects built on this notion of reciprocity, with Jenkins ultimately pinpointing the need for what he calls 'multiperspectival' work. Finally, Chap. 9, 'Publishing Media Industry Research', ends by exploring the implications of producing academic research that is both *about* and *for* industry on academic publishing, and specifically the tensions involved in satisfying academic publishing demands and desires to reach more public industry expectations. To demonstrate this shift towards looser, more publically accessible publishing potentials—itself a core implication of producing collaborative media industry research— Emily Caston offers a final case study contribution that reflects on her own approaches to 'publishing' research via her collaborations with members of the British music video industry.

As has been hinted above, and as will be explored clearly throughout the pages of this book, media industry studies is so much more than a subfield of various disciplinary concerns. Rather, it is an approach of study that taps into the utopic possibilities of what academic research could—or maybe even *should*—be, for it sees theory and practice as mutually beneficial, as arenas of applied thought and process that may be bound together via clearer and more productive avenues. And that is precisely why more work that aims exclusively to identify further methods for actually doing this kind of collaborative, multidisciplinary, and contextualised research across multiple borders and fields is so important—because it is difficult.

NOTES

1. The work of Galloway and Dunlop (2007) and Hesmondhalgh (2008) also charts the etymology of the terms 'creative industries' or 'cultural industries' in the UK, showing how the ambitions for the UK's cultural industries in the 1980s were eventually subsumed by the conformist and largely market-driven agenda of the New Labour political party which came to power in 1997.

2. This same student usefully went on to conceptualise a methodology of media industry studies thusly: 'Media industries are flourishing at an unprecedented speed and they are arguably the most loyal mirror of what we are as a society, and so making sense of the media artefacts we produce and consume daily is vital for the industry practitioners, scholarly researchers and for the general public. The various ways in which media industries can be studied are therefore ample and diverse and most of them do not start from books, only end in them.' Saud [said? This?] student is right: there are indeed few books about how to study media industries—until now.

3. Indeed, the findings and specific focus of the book is expanded from work conducted at the University of Nottingham, where the project began as a funded research methods training initiative. The project gathered practical information on the methodological issues and techniques involved in doing media industry research, acting as a starting point for thinking about a how-to for ways of embarking on future collaborations between academia and media industry professionals. The project worked to bring together both media industry professionals and a host of international media studies academics, together exploring a range of untapped dialogues between industry and academia. The project website can be found here: www.nottingham.ac.uk/research/groups/isir/projects/industrial-approaches-to-media/index.aspx.

BIBLIOGRAPHY

Ashton, D., & Noonan, C. (Eds.). (2013). *Cultural Work and Higher Education*. Basingstoke: Palgrave Macmillan.

Caldwell, J. T. (2008). *Production Culture: Industrial Reflexivity and Critical Practice in Film and Television*. Durham and London: Duke University Press.

Caldwell, J. T. (2013). Para-Industry: Researching Hollywood's Blackwaters. *Cinema Journal, 52*(3), 157–165.

Carmen, E. (2015). Illicit Archive: Sony Hack as Access for Media Industry Studies. *In Media Res* (March 10). Available at: http://mediacommons.futureofthebook.org/imr/2015/03/10/illicit-achive-sony-hack-access-media-industry-studies.

Creative Industries worth £8 million an hour to UK economy. (2014, January 14). Gov.uk. Available at: https://www.gov.uk/government/news/creative-industries-worth-8million-an-hour-to-uk-economy

Galloeway, S., & Dunlop, S. (2007). A critique of definitions of the cultural and creative industries in public policy. *International Journal of Cultural Policy, 13*(1), 17–31.

Havens, T., & Lotz, A. D. (2011). *Understanding Media Industries*. Oxford: Oxford University Press.

Havens, T., Lotz, A. D., & Tinic, S. (2009). Critical Media Industries Studies: A Research Approach. *Communication, Culture & Critique* 2:2(June): 234–253.

Hesmondhalgh, D. (2007). *The Cultural Industries* (2nd ed.). London: SAGE.

Hesmondhalgh, D. (2008). *The cultural industries* (2nd ed.). London: SAGE.

Hilmes, M. (2014). An Interview with Professor Michele Hilmes. *Industrial Approaches to Media – The University of Nottingham*. Available at: http://www.nottingham.ac.uk/research/groups/isir/projects/industrial-approaches-to-media/index.aspx.

Holt, J. (2013). Two-Way Mirrors: Looking at the Future of Academic-Industry Engagement. *Cinema Journal, 52*(3), 183–188.

Holt, J., & Perren, A. (Eds.) (2009). *Media Industries: History, Theory, and Method*. Malden: Wiley-Blackwell.

Horkheimer, M., & Adorno, T. (1944). The Culture Industry: Enlightenment as Mass Deception, in Cumming, J. (ed. and translated) *The Dialectic of Enlightenment*. New York: Continuum, 120–149.

Johnson, C. (2013). The Mutual Benefits of Engaging with Industry. *CST Online*. Accessed December 3, 2015, from http://cstonline.tv/mutual-benefits

Johnson, D. (2014). Understanding Media Industries From All Perspectives. *Industrial Approaches to Media – The University of Nottingham*. Available at: http://www.nottingham.ac.uk/research/groups/isir/projects/industrial-approaches-to-media/derek-johnson.aspx

Jones, H. (2014). Industrial Approaches to Media Conference. *MeCETES* (June 6). Available at: http://mecetes.co.uk/industrial-approaches-media-conference/

Mateer, J. (2015). Author Interview: *Industrial Approaches to Media*. 15 June.
Mayer, V., Banks, M. J., & Caldwell, J. T. (2009). *Production Studies: Cultural Studies of Media Industries*. New York: Routledge.
McDonald, P. (2013). Introduction: In Focus – Media Industries Studies. *Cinema Journal, 52*(3), 145–149.
McDonald, P. (2014). An Interview with Professor Paul McDonald. *Industrial Approaches to Media – The University of Nottingham*. Available at: http://www. nottingham.ac.uk/research/groups/isir/projects/industrial-approaches-to-media/index.aspx
Schlesinger, P. (2015). PhD Workshop on Researching Media at a Time of Transition, presentation at the University of Glasgow (Glasgow, June 10).
Spicer, A. (2015). 'Production Studies', introductory address at the conference of *New Directions in Film and Television Production Studies* (Bristol, April 14–15).
Stokes, J. (2003). *How to Do Media & Cultural Studies*. London: SAGE.
Wasko, J., & Meehan, E. I. (2013). Critical Crossroads or Parallel Routes? Political Economy and New Approaches to Studying Media Industries and Cultural Products. *Cinema Journal, 52*(3), 150–156.

PART I

The Ideologies and Ethics of Media Industry Studies

It would be easy to cut to the chase and explore the nature of methods in media industry studies and provide the reader with advice on how best to choose between and implement them. After all, many people might expect a book with the title of the present volume to be concerned with the ways in which different methods in the media industry researcher's arsenal can be employed. And indeed it is. Yet the practice of media industry studies does not exist in a bubble hermetically sealed off from the social sciences and the many intellectual allegiances that their practices hold.

So, if Part II of this book will offer a practical theorisation and exploration of the best methodical approaches and conceptualisation necessary to conducting effective and collaborative media industry research, and Part III will later offer a theorisation of ways to go about translating academic research to a media industry audience, then Part I must first contextualise these later claims and approaches by focusing on the political and ethical dimensions of why we might do both of the former in the first place. In fact, the politics and ethics of when—or if—emerging academics might conceive of their research projects as somehow being *about* or especially *for* media industries is crucial to laying out the overall goals of this book.

Across two chapters then, this first part aims to explore the different priorities and working assumptions that characterise academia—at least in the UK—compared to those in the UK media industries. Chapter 2 reflects on the professional ideologies that mark out academia from industry—by which I mean specifically media studies compared to media industry—while aiming to explore the potential through lines between these two sectors in the hope of identifying a clear set of overlaps between the needs, wants, priorities, and agendas of both academia and the media industries. Here, Paul Kerr—an academic with vast experience of working in the UK television industry—also reflects on these questions with a valuable case study. Then, having laid out a number of interesting points of overlap between the professional ideologies of both academia and industry in this first chapter, Chap. 3 goes on to detail and examine the political and ethical dimensions of thinking across academia and industry by doing collaborative, impactful media industry research, highlighting issues of intellectualism and knowledge across the academia/industry border. Centred on the UK landscape, this chapter goes on to offer useful points of practical advice concerning the ethical dimensions of doing media industry studies, highlighting the complex and multifaceted ethical responsibilities of doing this kind of research. To support these points, Elizabeth Evans and Paul McDonald offer their reflections about the ethics of collaborating with corporations in the media industries.

CHAPTER 2

The Professional Ideologies of Academia and Industry

Matthew Freeman

This chapter will identify the changing ideologies that have come to characterise the world of academia compared to that of the contemporary UK media industries. This chapter explores the potentials for bridging these divergent professional ideologies, asking how the academic researcher can retain critical distance from the market or commercial agendas of the media industries. Drawing on insights from both academics and from media industry practitioners, this chapter makes use of multiple voices and perspectives, framed around a case study contribution by Paul Kerr.

So, just what are the differences in terms of how media is constructed and enforced in media studies as an academic discipline compared to how media is constructed, perceived, enforced, and sold as a business in the media industries? What exactly is different in terms of the professional ideologies that make up those working in academia compared to those working in industry? Are these sectors really that different—and if not, what are the overlaps and through lines between the perceived roles of media in academia and those in industry? Where precisely are the shared interests and overlapping priorities across these two sectors? These are all fundamental and crucial questions to begin with, for in order to understand

M. Freeman (✉)
Bath Spa University, Bath, UK
e-mail: m.freeman@bathspa.ac.uk

M. Freeman, *Industrial Approaches to Media*,
DOI 10.1057/978-1-137-55176-4_2

25

the best methodological approaches to producing scholarly research that is not only *about* but also potentially *for* the media industries—as was identified as the crux of media industry studies in the introduction—it is first necessary to understand the potential overlaps (as well as the continuing barriers) between the professional ideological standpoints of the academy compared to those in the media industries. In one sense, overcoming any deep, historic ideological divide between the notion of media as a field academic study and the notion of media as industrial professional practice—and the gulfs between these two worlds—underpins the entire rationale of this book.

Contextual Relationships

Despite any subtle differences that may continue to stand between the worlds of academia and industry in the UK, the past few decades have seen a rapid evolution in the relationship between academia—and, by extension, universities—and the media industries. In the UK at least, the global growth of the wider cultural and creative industry sectors, occurring in parallel to the dramatic changes in the role and funding of higher education, has seen the relationship between academia and industry become more formal, more directed, and more calculating. From the perspective of many universities in the UK, more explicit connections to industry have increased the employability potentials of prospective students. As Kate Oakley (2013: 26) puts it, 'the argument is that the best way to prepare students for work in the media industries is to provide them with a mix of knowledge, skill and judgment, together with the network of contacts.'

Much of the thinking in the UK which advocates more collaborative arrangements between universities and industry derives from government policy papers produced over the last couple of decades. Discussing relationships between universities and the cultural economy, the likes of the Lambert Review, the Leitch Review of Skills, and the Browne Review (Department of Business, Innovation and Skills 2010) all made, as Stefan Collini has noted, a 'contribution to economic growth the overriding goal of a whole swathe of social, cultural and intellectual activities.' The Wilson Review later crystallised these ideas more clearly, positioning universities in the UK as 'an integral part of the supply chain to business.'

With UK universities and the cultural and creative industries thus positioned as integrally beneficial to one another, it is hardly surprising that media industry studies—a subfield that places collaboration across academic and industrial borders at its heart—has risen in prominence in recent years. Still, as I indicated at the start of this chapter, academia and industry are not the same thing—and there remains a number of profound ideological and practical barriers between these two sectors that continue to keep the work of academics and media practitioners separate.

A Gulf Between Two Worlds

Indeed, even at a time when media industry studies is ascendant within the academy, particularly in the US and the UK, it is hard not to observe the apparent sense of divide that still stands between academia and industry. Many challenges, pitfalls, and obstacles remain for those researchers seeking to both study and work with the media industries in the name of research. And many of these obstacles come from the value—or perhaps the lack thereof—that academia is seen to be able to offer industry, and to a far lesser extent vice versa. This is all in spite of the fact that studying and developing understandings of industrial practices is crucial to media studies. Media industry operation always provides a vital backdrop to understanding media texts and media audiences. For Amanda Lotz (2014), in fact, when beginning to think about what the media industries can contribute to scholarly media studies today, and indeed vice versa, 'I cannot really divorce media industries from media studies—it is a constitutive component.' Yet, at the same time, Lotz (2014) remarks, 'I am not sure that industry workers recognise that academics have insights that can be of value. It is challenging to write simultaneously for both audiences, and so it is not surprising that those in the industry who have encountered academic conversations are uncertain of our relevance.' Such views are in contrast, Lotz argues (2014), to the 'calls for greater collaboration between academics and industries. [...] It is difficult to find the time for broad thinking and paradigm reimagining in industry when there are always more immediate crises requiring attention.'

In terms of the more specific perceptions of media academics and media industry practitioners, John Mateer (2015) indicates that, at least based on his own surveys and interviews on this subject, there appears to be demonstrable differences between academics and industry personnel in the ways that they each view their own domains as well as each other's: 'Many in industry whom I have spoken with often feel that traditional media studies analysis of what they do is either off-base or ill-considered, which has made them distrustful (and perhaps reinforced negative stereotypes surrounding media studies) [...] feeding perceptions of a disconnect between "studies" and "the real world".' Says Mateer (2015),

[m]any in industry have are rather romantic notion of academia but tend to feel that academics cannot truly understand industry. Likewise, academics often consider those in industry to somehow lack insight or understanding into their own domain in terms of formally analysing it yet often marvel at the interesting work that industry can produce (coincidentally practitioners working in academia are often perceived to be "lesser" by both groups). As the two groups become closer out of both commercial and academic necessity, these preconceptions are beginning to lessen somewhat.

Mateer (2015) argues that the gradual shifts in perception between academia and industry is also partly a result of the increasing number of media personnel moving from industry to academia—a factor that Paul Kerr will also extensively elaborate on in his case study later in this chapter. Indeed, because of the previously discussed changes in universities, UK academics now find themselves in closer contact with media practitioners than ever before. And yet, in contrast, 'whether we like it or not,' Paul McDonald (2014) insists, 'there is still a kind of gulf between the academic field and the industry field, and that gap I think materialises in several different ways, most principally in terms of issues of *access*—how one can gain contact to talk to people within industry.' But for McDonald (2014), this so-called gulf between academia and media industries happens for a number of reasons, one of which can be as simple as the matter of commercial confidentiality—that is, the fact that people within industry are not readily going to disclose information because they are in a field of commercial competition where they do not want to share knowledge and insights with people who wish to disclose it to the eyes of potential competitors.

This issue of confidentiality will be discussed in further depth in Chap. 3, but on a broad level McDonald also highlights a possible distrust between academia and industry, one that speaks about wider issues in terms of the relationship between the academic and industry communities. The reason for such distrust might stem from the simple fact that in media industry studies, the industrial workings (and thus their people) are the object of study, rather than the voices of support lending credence to a particular argument that may be used to provide evidence in more text-focused media studies. As McDonald (2014) explains more clearly,

[t]here is a very strong critical imperative whereby there is a focus on not simply accepting an industry point of view or an industry account of things, but to find ways of challenging such views as a way of offering fresh insights or insights that might reveal points of view that are otherwise ignored or intentionally pressed towards the margins. Thus that critical imperative is very important, and one thing that has happened in media studies generally but particularly in media industry studies is a tendency to hold industry at a distance as this almost very separate critical object.

McDonald (2014) goes on to say, 'I think that sense of distance comes with a certain number of problems, most notably the potential to misinterpret the field of media industry research as a lofty or arrogant group of researchers who see industry and industry professionals purely as objects that are there to be investigated.' Moreover, such a sense of critical distance can be seen to entirely oppose the more utopic possibilities of media industry studies— possibilities that derive from potentials for new understandings, new critical insights, new partnerships and collaborations. And so for such 'utopic' possi- bilities to emerge, the gulf between academia and industry must be fully bro- ken down—and that means, at the very least it seems, a better understanding of the points of overlap between these two sectors is needed.

As a way into beginning to understand these points of possible overlap and shared interest between the academy and the media industries, Paul Kerr will now share his experiences of working in both the media indus- tries and in the academy, discussing his own insights into the areas of pos- sible overlap between these two sectors.

CASE STUDY: THE APPRENTICE'S SORCERER: TELEVISION IN/AND THE ACADEMY

Paul Kerr
School of Media & Performing Arts, Department of Media
Middlesex University London

For television, academia is essentially a one-stop shop for presentable faces and expert interviewees in front of the camera, and a reliable relay of un(der)paid runners behind it. For universities, television is a subject of study for specialist staff and an aspirational career for students, whilst remaining little more than an embarrassment for the rest of higher edu- cation—somewhere on the spectrum between a default teaching aid and a digital distraction. But in today's austere economic climate, while the television industry remains a sought-after employer for graduates, it is also a putative partner in research projects and powerful evidence of public impact. For me, an eye-opening early experience in academia was the submission of four of 'my' final television documentary productions for the 2008 RAE, and their being awarded four-star-status as 'world-leading research'. Since I was the titular researcher on none of the four productions and had long been a published critic of auteurism, the implicit academic myopia about media production proved surprising to say the least.

I abandoned television—or, more accurately perhaps, television abandoned me—in 2007. I had been working in television for almost 25 years, making arts and history programmes for the BBC and Channel 4, starting out as an archive researcher and working my way up to series and executive producer. My accidental entrée into production had been facilitated by an assumed expertise about film and television as subjects, at a time when the media were seen, albeit briefly, as legitimate arts topics for primetime programming. And so I was initially hired to work on media programmes—beginning in 1984 with a one-off documentary spin-off from a book I co-edited about MTM Enterprises, the makers of *Hill Street Blues*. That in turn led to jobs on *Open the Box* and *The Media Show*, and then being offered the chance to set up and launch 'my own' cinema series for BBC2, *Moving Pictures*. In this sense, my television career began as media studies by other means—and I still believe television remains potentially the best medium for understanding how film and television actually work, textually and technically. Several colleagues with media and cultural studies backgrounds also moved into film and television production about the same time—an influx about which I have written elsewhere (Kerr 1991).

This phenomenon, which could be called a kind of academic entryism into television, was facilitated by the advent of Channel 4, the rapid explosion of the independent sector that fed it, and a heady moment of expansion and relative experimentalism in British television. In 2008, I wrote a belated sequel, tracing the pessimistic inverse of this story, featuring a comparable and more or less enforced exodus from television, not just of ex-academics and cultural workers like myself, but also of independent filmmakers, and many of those with radical or even traditional public service ambitions for the medium (Kerr 2008).

The two programme categories, arts and history, in which I worked as a programme-maker both fall, institutionally, into what is often referred to by broadcasters nowadays as specialist factual, though both history and music and arts were their own relatively independent commissioning departments when I started working in television. The reduction of public service obligations on terrestrial broadcasters began to impact on arts and history television well over a decade before public funding was completely removed from teaching humanities courses in the universities. But as a broadcaster I rarely gave any thought to the predicament of higher education. Working in—and worrying about—public service broadcasting proved to be a full-time occupation, though as a freelancer at the end of my television career, a full-time occupation was precisely what I lacked.

Since 2007, therefore, I have been working full-time in higher education. My first post-television job was teaching on a media studies degree, but since 2013 I have taught a bachelor of arts in television production. This academic transition provides an apt metaphor, or reprise, for my wider career—from media studies to media production, from teaching critical thinking about the media to providing professional and vocational training for them. I had begun my working life as a freelance film and television critic for the broadsheets and magazines, and had then started teaching extra-mural evening classes in both film and television studies. These freelance jobs led to a series of short-term contracts at the British Film Institute and eventually a staff position there in the National Film Archive, which in turn gave me the time and space to contribute to a number of academic publications, one of which, as mentioned above, led, entirely accidentally, to a career in television.

Having feet in both camps—sometime academic, sometime practitioner—has led to those with similarly schizophrenic CVs being described as amphibians, able to survive on academic land and in televisual waters with equal 'success'. However, as the above sketch of my extended television 'sabbatical' reveals, that survival was temporary and how long I will be able to earn a living as an academic remains to be seen. Certainly the habitats of both the public service broadcaster and the academic media scholar have recently undergone and continue to undergo dramatic change in the UK. Of course there have been many other émigrés from television into academia—among them Rod Stoneman, who was a commissioning editor in UK television. Stoneman recently co-wrote with Duncan Petrie *Educating Filmmakers: Past, Present and Future* (2014), which whilst primarily about film schools does have some things to say about television production courses and their relationship with the television industry.

Petrie and Stoneman (2014: 3) note the coincidence of the development of the first post-war European film schools and the national art cinemas that began to flourish in those years. What they do not point out, equally tellingly, however, is that this development also coincided with a decline in mass cinema attendance and the replacement of film as the most popular art by television. And this, in part, explains why many film courses endorse the filmmaker as artist, whilst many television production courses endorse both multi-skilling and a more market and industry-facing curriculum.

Having written about the perils of the market for public service media in various publications over the years, I was probably unforgivably naïve about the impact of precisely the same neoliberal forces on higher education. My relief on getting a full-time, pensioned, salaried job in higher education after the insecurities of a precarious freelance existence for the last eight years of my television career was perhaps understandable. I thought I was saying goodbye to a world of short-term contracts, outsourcing, deregulation, cost counting, marketing and monetising, franchising and formats, and an abiding obsession with ratings and audiences. Little did I know that the world of the university was already and increasingly in thrall to its own market-led revolution, with a dizzying metrics all its own—recruitment, retention, progression figures, quality assurances, and all of the other paraphernalia of a monetised public service. The open plan offices and hot-desking I have encountered in academia have felt familiar from those I came across when I worked in television.

Of course both television and the university sectors in the UK were once seen as public services where questions of profitability were, if not entirely absent, certainly not the final determinants of what filled the schedules of screens, seminar rooms, and lecture theatres. But while public service broadcasting in the shape of the BBC has had to become increasingly reliant on income other than that secured by the license fee, under first the coalition and now the new Conservative government (and Channel 4 long ago lost its funding formula with ITV), so too the universities have increasingly relied on student fees which have replaced government grants, making consumers the prime funders of higher education as they are, through advertising, of British television beyond the BBC.

Massimo De Angelis and David Harvie (2015) have written about the intrusion into academia of neoliberal metrics and methods—learning outcomes, programme specification forms, benchmarks, progression and retention rates, league tables, employment figures, widening access, international rankings, deregulation, outsourcing, franchising, the influx of private providers, the emphasis on outputs (analytics and hits paralleling the ratings and overnights in television). And if established academics suffer such discomforts, the next generation is threatened with a future of precarity and a zero hours culture. This eerily echoes the situation in television, in which graduates of courses like the one I teach are expected to work as unpaid runners for work experience or in internships, which function to privilege those living off the bank of their parents. No diversity campaign in broadcasting, however well intentioned, is likely to change the demographics of production until and unless the existence of unpaid internships is brought to an end. Much the same, of course, could be said about the tripling—and more—of university fees.

At its best, television studies 'openly subscribes to a multi-disciplinary approach that recognizes the industry, the texts and the consumption in equal measure' (Weissmann 2014). But this three-headed hydra is not always in balance. Indeed, in my own experience students of television studies and television production courses often learn quite a lot about texts and/or techniques respectively but sometimes considerably less about the institutional and economic contexts that determine both those programme forms and the techniques which help shape them. *CST Online (Critical Studies in Television)* is one very useful source for discussions about how to teach television and indeed what to teach when we teach television. In television studies the holy trinity seems to be text, industry, and audience, with the central role being taken by textual analysis. In television production courses, on the other hand, the stress tends to be on multi-skilling and technical and editorial training. In television studies the second priority tends to be the audience, just as in television production courses it is, or ought to be, the industry itself.

Much of my own academic output, before I began working in television, whether about film or television, took this industrial turn, if only to restore the equilibrium, including a *BFI Reader* about Hollywood as industry (1986), which anthologised an article of mine about the industrial determinants of film noir (Kerr 1980). The first funded research I undertook once I became a full-time academic was as Co-Investigator on a major AHRC project, led by Dr James Bennett, on the impact of independent television and digital production companies on public service broadcasting,[1] which involved, among other things, one hundred interviews with factual television and digital professionals. More recently, I have published on the industrial determinants of both specific television forms and cinematic network narratives.[2] Furthermore, my experience in the industry—and in teaching film and television and media studies—only reinforced my belief that an understanding of how the media industries are organised is crucial both to academic analysis and practitioner employability, and should be included in all studies of audio-visual media. However, if one of the rhetorical tropes of neoliberalism is that the customer is always right, then in both higher education and in British television the student and the viewer are now assumed to be right also. Follow the money, as the saying goes. Teaching a media audiences module at my previous employer I came across Tamar Liebes' 'Viewing and Reviewing the Audience: Fashions in Communications Research' in *Mass Media and Society* (2005), edited by James Curran and Michael Gurevitch. Liebes offers a provocative analysis of why certain kinds of audience research have predominated at certain times. He bases his essay on John Ellis' *Seeing Things: Television in the Age of Uncertainty* (2000), which conceptualised the history of television into three eras—scarcity, availability, and plenty.

The dominant research paradigms in these three periods are, according to Liebes, initially a tradition assuming powerful effects (and a passive audience), secondly a period characterised by concepts like encoding/decoding and uses and gratifications (and an active audience), and finally an era marked by postmodern ethnography, with its stress on specific demographic fractions (and interactive audiences). If Liebes is right, then it is striking that the age of broadcast plenty—in an age of economic austerity—has seen a deluge of publications about and familiarity with notions of the viewer and what seems to be, to this ex-programme-maker, a worrying lack of focus on—or analysis of—the television industry itself. The disproportionate attention to the viewer over the industry in much television studies of the past is worrying enough, but perhaps it is even more worrying that many of the graduates of television production courses I have met—while still in television—share the same misconceptions about UK broadcasting as their media studies peers.

I wrote recently about the impact of the shift from BBC in-house to independent production on the weekly cinema series, *Moving Pictures*, which I produced for BBC2 in the 1990s (Kerr 2013). Arts magazine programmes like *Moving Pictures* are scarcer on British television now than they were in the heady days of the 1980s and 1990s, but television documentary, about which I have also written, is still with us.[3] I currently co-teach a module about documentary, but of course documentary, too, is under siege from reality television, itself one of the symptoms of our neoliberal culture. Couldry and Littler (2011) have written usefully about reality television in relation to programmes like *The Apprentice*. Their article discusses the relationship between *The Apprentice* and the working cultures of neoliberalism in the UK, arguing that the programme re-enacts, through ritualised play, some of the skills required by the UK's 'flexible' work economy: emotional commitment, entrepreneurial adaptability, and a curious combination of team conformity and personal ambition. But while this may help to explain what—and why—audiences recognise and enjoy such programmes, its analysis is perhaps too much at the macro level to satisfactorily account for how they come to be produced in the first place. To do that we would need to know rather more about the precise production cultures in which such series are generated. That is one of the functions of teaching students about television as an industry, regardless whether they want to work in television or to study it.

But beyond questions of curriculum, do such courses have any real impact on that industry? Certainly organisations like Creative Skillset, the industry skills body for the creative industries in the UK, think they do, and courses like the one I teach are recipients of their coveted accreditation. However, Mark McGurl's recently published book, *The Program Era: Postwar Fiction and the Rise of Creative Writing* (2011), poses this question in a much more provocative manner, as it makes a case for the extent to which creative writing courses have helped shape the post-war American novel. Is there a comparable question to be asked about the extent to which film and television production courses in British universities have contributed to shaping contemporary British television and cinema?

McGurl (2011) argues that the creative writing programme has exercised the single most determining influence on post-war American literary production, and that such courses have led to a premium being put on writers finding their individual voices (read: virtuoso technique) and writing about what they know (dirty realism, regionalism, the campus novel, ethnic and émigré fiction). The parallel with some film production courses could not be clearer with their built-in auteurism and reflex antagonism toward the film industry. Indeed, at the joint final year screening of our film and television degree graduation films—this year held at the BFI Southbank—there was a marked contrast between the individual, auteurish art-house nature of several of the film projects and the generic characteristics of many of the television projects. Petrie and Stoneman point to what they describe as the 'valorization of the creative vision of the individual filmmaker and a progressive engagement with contemporary society' as characteristic of film schools, which seems to uncannily echo McGurl's diagnosis of creative writing schools and courses (Petrie and Stoneman 2014: 6).

However, the authors point out that such creativity is increasingly being curtailed in film schools just as it has been in the teaching of television. They note that there has been 'a shift away from an emphasis on cinema as a potent form of auteur-driven, socially relevant cultural expression, and towards a new focus on the moving image as a market-oriented, global entertainment business' (Petrie and Stoneman 2014: 6). They describe three phases in the development of filmmaking in the academy—and while there is an elision between film and television courses in their book, there are also parallels between the teachings of the two media. For Petrie and Stoneman (2014), the initial formative phase of development is marked by a spirit of exploration and the strong integration of both industrial and cultural factors and of theory and practice. For the authors, the second phase is one of freedom of expression and the third involves 'a new emphasis on an industrial imperative and with it a reaffirmation of the importance of the training of craft specialists and a greater appreciation and understanding of the marketplace' (Petrie and Stoneman 2014: 42). This seems to me to echo the way in which craft skills and industrial and economic logics increasingly enter the curriculum of television, even whilst acknowledging that they were, perhaps, present in the founding of the discipline in ways not evident—or considerably less centrally—in the teaching of filmmaking. Television, inherently, refers to an industry and to broadcasting institutions, albeit with more and less mainstream aspects to its production. Film, on the other hand, is a medium that implies nothing about whether the focus is a commercial and industrial or art cinema or indeed independent/avant garde practice.

Television production courses are different, more pragmatic perhaps, and less experimental—which is not necessarily a good thing. What television production curricula underline is less the 'authorised' director or screenwriter than the multi-skilled technician and the editorially adept Jill-and-Jack-of-all-trades. But what else do we teach our students? Among the, perhaps anachronistic, watchwords I learned in television were to ensure that all of my projects had a Unique Selling Point and that any pitch included an answer to the following question: Why now? What else do I try to convince my students to do—watch television, not least in order to learn the modes and mannerisms of contemporary broadcasting? If 'creative' writing and, by extension, filmmaking is about finding your own voice, often (too often?) television is about repressing that voice and learning to become a ventriloquist.[4]

British television's appetite is to tell stories that we do not know—or to retell those we do know, but in surprising new ways. It is to find and tell stories that are counter-intuitive. One progressive alternative for television practitioners, unable to use their own voices, is to find ways of amplifying the voices of others, those too often unheard in our media. This is, perhaps, one way of enabling us to avoid the charge of preparing our students for what might be called the Television Programme Era.

For if today's television production course is not the online begetter of our current television culture, it is certainly a magical helper, a source—if not the sorcerer—conjuring a reality in today's television that makes unpaid apprentices of our graduates. These realities about British public service television reinforce my argument about the relative importance of a political economy of television alongside technical training and textual analysis in television studies. Of course it is important to understand how programmes make sense and communicate meanings and to learn how they are made—and how to make them. But if, as someone once said, the point is to change it, then perhaps first we have to ensure that we do not lose the public service broadcast economy and ecology we have got—before we try to reform it. And to do that we have to understand how—and why—it still works, for all its undeniable problems. As I write, public service broadcasting in Britain is in danger of being stolen from us, with the threatened privatisation of Channel 4 and the diminution if not outright destruction of the BBC, both on the political agenda.

In a blog on *CST Online* titled 'True Detective and Practical Criticism', Jason Jacobs (2014) has written eloquently of his own study of television as 'a species of practical criticism, with close reading as the method.' Jacobs (2014) is adamant:

> For me, industrial studies of television can only be interesting if they include the special fact that an aesthetic object is its primary outcome—something expressive and intended by human agents, rather than constructed by, or somehow emanating from, discursive forces. I am interested in television that is able to transcend its time and conditions of making; in television that is something we typically call art.

This is a powerful argument and one with which I have some sympathy—as one of those human agents who worked in television and attempted to produce programmes that would stand the test not just of primetime but of time itself. But we live in a culture in which there are other contenders for 'primary outcome' including increasing obligations of profitability and residual commitments to public service, neither of which are necessarily conducive to quality. However, while some television programmes can and do 'transcend' their own time, they are always produced and transmitted within it—and it is those conditions of existence that help determine the possibilities of such work. If, like Jacobs, I want to experience expressive aesthetic objects on television—unlike him I want to insist that the structures and strategies of television in this country, the policies and political economy that sustain such programming are protected. Without them Jacobs will have nothing to admire or analyse so passionately and productively. When he characterises his interest in television as 'articulating the value of the experience particular television shows provide', I want to argue that, in Britain as elsewhere, it is particular structures and policies, specific funding mechanisms and production modes which ensure that particular shows are provided. Taking one's eye off the industry assumes that the shows one admires are somehow autonomous objects produced only by human agents. But whilst human agency is crucial, so too is the specific form the industry takes—which employs (and hopefully pays) those human agents. Television professionals and television academics alike should at least agree about that.

WHEN WORLDS COLLIDE: EMPLOYABILITY

Building on and looking beyond Kerr's more personalised affirmation of the apparent similarities between academia and the media industries in terms of work conditions, how does the world of the media industries overlap with the world of scholarly media studies in the UK—and how might these overlaps help forge productive connections and shared research interests? For Daniel Ashton (2015), whose research explores the connections between higher education and the media industries in the UK, 'the link between the media industries and media studies is often around *employability*.' Notably, the importance of employability was also noted by Kerr in his discussion of university verses industry skill sets— defined by Kerr as what he called 'entrepreneurial adaptability'. Ashton (2015) elaborates:

> The contribution of a media studies degree course, although this course title can cause consternation in some quarters, is increasingly aligned with the employability agenda of higher education and the need for graduate "talent". Even where we distinguish different types of "media" degrees (e.g., "production" degree courses compared to 'studies' degree course), the link to working in industry is ever present.

In researching the UK video games industry, Ashton has been able to explore some of the broad policy priorities, for example the 'talent pathways' set out in the DCMS *Creative Britain* report (see Ashton 2011), and some of the higher education priorities, for example as set out in the Department of Culture, Media and Sport (2008) *Creative Britain* report. 'Through an interview with a representative from Creative Skillset,' Ashton (2015) explains, 'the UK sector skills council, and through attending events, such as the *Game Careers Fair*, I was able to gain an understanding of industry priorities for recruitment and training. A picture emerged here of "pipelines" in which higher education would supply "industry-ready" graduates.' Though part of this pipeline perspective would involve concerns over what Ashton calls 'skills shortages' and the relevance of higher education degree courses, Ashton argues that 'many recent publications such as Nesta's *Creative Economy Manifesto* (Bakhshi, Hargreaves and Mateos-Garcia 2013) continue to voice concerns about a disconnect between what businesses need from graduates and what universities are teaching' (2015). This is stark contrast to established UK governmental policies about the role of UK universities. As Kate Oakley (2013: 25) discusses, 'government expectations of what universities should deliver still includes contributing to economic prosperity, nurturing skills development and offering professional training.'

The so-called disconnect between what UK universities are teaching and what UK media industries need goes back to what McDonald described as the gulf between academia and industry, and partly explains Lotz's aforementioned assumption that the media industries sometimes struggle to see the relevance of academic approaches to the theoretical study of media. And yet the theme of *employability* does indeed emerge from Ashton's, Kerr's, and Oakley's work at least, as a key foundation on which both sectors depend. The nature of work too is not radically dissimilar across academia and industry, at least in the way that both academics and media practitioners aim to work for larger institutions while simultaneously doing their own personally developed work, i.e., individual research projects or personal films, respectively.

As was also noted by Kerr above, moreover, today's UK television industry is increasingly dependent on people with multiple skills and areas of expertise—those who understand media not from a single perspective, such as filmmaking only, but from various cross- and multi-medial perspectives. There is the strong sense that multi-skilling is significant in an industry still adapting to the multiplicities of digital transformations across convergent media platforms. In an academic context as well, those who understand this multiplicity, i.e., those who study media from the more contextualised, holistic, and theoretically practiced perspectives that media industry studies affords, are arguably more adaptable to the multi-skilled employability demands of the twenty-first century UK media industries at large.

WHEN WORLDS COLLIDE: KNOWLEDGE ECONOMY

Beyond the shared interest in employability, however, what else do academia and the media industries have in common? Broadly, and as will be highlighted throughout much of this book, the very notion of engaging in media industry studies, for Catherine Johnson (2013), means generating 'shared research'—meaning that the overlaps in agendas and interests between academia and media industries should be mutual. Yet even the differences in what the word 'research' actually means in an academic context compared to in an industrial one can pose challenges when attempting to formulate a shared project. Says Johnson (2013),

> '[w]e were operating with very different understandings of the term "research"; for [industry practitioners], research referred specifically to audience research—questionnaires and focus groups used to develop and test new and on-going projects. As an established part of a media business, they have little need for external academics to undertake such work.'
> But in Johnson's experience, having 'explained that we were interested in their company specifically and their work as an object of research, they were surprised that they themselves might be a valuable subject of academic enquiry.'

So, what is the primary value of collaboration with academics? What are the shared professional interests and ideologies? Johnson (2013) suggests that when she posed this same question to one of her own industry collaborators, interestingly 'the answer was *not* the intellectual insights that we might offer or the alternative perspectives that we might bring to their work' (though this is not to underestimate the value of these aspects of the collaboration). Instead, for Johnson, the shared professional interests between herself as an academic and her media industry partners as corporate businesses was conceptualised as the shared and mutual interest in *critical knowledge* of the wider media landscape. More than just taking an interest, indeed, many media organisations depend on such critical insight on what is going on in the wider media and cultural landscape in order to stay one step ahead of the competition in what has of course become a highly competitive and fragmented digital media culture. And in that sense, explains Johnson (2013), 'It has been interesting to note that the more industry practitioners that we speak to, the more it becomes apparent that we are asking essentially the *same questions*, and that the insights from academia offer unique and impartial perspectives not driven by commercial imperatives.'

The focus on gaining new and impactful critical insights is thus another overlapping professional ideology of both academia and industry. Perhaps more than anything else, it is the concept of *knowledge economy* that unites the academy with the media industries: Both the media academic and the media practitioner thrive on new ideas and skilled insights into how best to use those ideas. But let us not forget that both sectors are also highly collaborative in nature, and are open to dialogues with external partners in the hope of establishing a more globalised operation and presence. As Johnson (2013) puts it, the media industries often can be drawn to 'the prestige of collaborating with a major UK university.' Johnson elaborates further:

> Industry's recognition of the value of the informal exchanges that are taking place through the process of our collaboration suggests that the real benefits of such research lie less in the giving of academic knowledge to businesses or vice versa, but in the collision of different perspectives that might arise from the interactions between academic researchers and industry professionals.

Thus for Johnson (2013), 'the divergence between the needs of academic research and the needs of media business in this case emerges less in the shared research questions than in the nature of the answers that are generated to these questions, how those answers are communicated, and the applicability of those answers within a commercial business setting.' This is an important point that echoes Kerr's aforementioned discussion of working in the UK television industry. Just as Kerr noted that many television projects in the UK are chosen based on the pitcher's clear articulation of a unique selling point and a clear answer to the question of 'why now?', so too are many instances of collaborative media industry research right now. Media industry partners need to be able to see the uniqueness, the relevance, and indeed the point of a potential research project with a university, just as they need to understand—clearly and explicitly—the whys and the future benefits of embarking on such a project. Make no mistake: Both academia and the media industries, at least in the UK, are thinking explicitly about the *future*—and the subfield of media industry studies, in its most utopic, collaborative sense, can help to understand that future.

CONCEPTUALISING RELEVANCE

Precisely how such a relationship might work, in the broadest and most conceptual of ways, means thinking about what academia and industry do not have but need. Ashton suggests that 'the contribution of media industries to media studies is "industry insight", and the contribution of media studies to media industries is "critical space".' This idea is about the ways that media industries—constantly under day-to-day pressures and putting out immediate fires, as Lotz put it earlier—often lack the space to conceptualise or to re-think their established industry practices and processes for the better. For Ashton (2015), 'the use of the word "space" is important, because "space" suggests that proximity and involvement do not necessarily limit the development of different perspectives and the emergence of critical questions. Rather, for those working in industry on a day-to-day basis, space can present the possibilities for considering assumptions and unchallenged thoughts and practices.'

There may well be shared questions across academia and industry, but academia promises to offer space in which to understand these assumptions and unchallenged thoughts about industry (Ashton 2013b). And in its reciprocal fashion, Ashton characterises the benefit of industry to academia as 'industry insight'—that is, the real-world, day-to-day knowledge of industry workings that lend weight and context to any theoretical understanding, thus deepening and strengthening that theoretical understanding. As Derek Johnson (2014) articulates, however, 'this is not necessarily to suggest that we take the lead of industry uncritically, but to recognise that media practitioners have an on-the-ground perspective that we lack as scholars and might benefit from hearing, helping us to hone our insights, critiques and suggestions.'

Moving towards the potential for collaborative arrangements between academia and media industries then, there may well remain a gulf, as McDonald called it, between the worlds of these two sectors. But this is a gulf that is now breaking down, not least of all because of the shared interests of media studies and the media industries. Both sectors, as Kerr noted, are preoccupied with a need to better understand and conceptualise media *audiences*. But both sectors are equally required to develop clear strategies around the theme of employability of skillsets; scholarly research that aims to capture new and innovative understandings of creative work will be of value to industry, as will research that succeeds in mapping the changes in industry in ways that can provide new insights into its potential futures.

However, and perhaps most importantly, both media academics and media industry practitioners are characterised equally by the professional ideology of knowledge economy or 'thought leadership'—that is, by their needs, commercial or otherwise, to carve new knowledge about the media landscape and in turn to apply that knowledge strategically. And to re-cite Johnson (2013), the carving of such new knowledge comes from 'the collision of different perspectives that might arise from the interactions between academic researchers and industry professionals.' Just as multidisciplinarity is now encouraged in academia on account of its potential to add insights, so too can the multiperspectival insights of the media industries.

Of course, there are political dimensions and challenges to overcome when approaching academia-industry collaborations, as I will explore in the next chapter.

NOTES

1. Full details of this research project are: James Bennett, Paul Kerr, Niki Strange, Andrea Medrado, (2012) *Multiplatforming Public Service Broadcasting: The Economic and Cultural Role of UK Digital and TV Independents*. AHRC/Royal Holloway/University of Sussex/London Metropolitan University.
2. For the latter, see Paul Kerr, (2010) 'Babel's Network Narrative: Packaging a Globalized Art Cinema', *Transnational Cinemas* 1:1 (February): 37–51.
3. See, for instance, Paul Kerr, (2009) 'The Last Slave (2007): The Genealogy of a British Television History Programme', *Historical Journal of Film, Radio and Television* 29:3 (September): 381–397.
4. See Bill Nichols, (2005) 'The Voice of Documentary' in Rosenthal, A and Corner, J. (eds.) *New Challenges for Documentary*. Manchester: Manchester University Press.

BIBLIOGRAPHY

Ashton, D. (2011). Pathways to Creativity: Self-learning and Customising in/for the Creative Economy. *Journal of Cultural Economy, 4*(2), 189–203.

Ashton, D. (2013a). Creative Contexts: Student Voices and Reflection on Work Placements in the Creative Industries. *Journal of Further and Higher Education, 39*(1), 127–146.

Ashton, D. (2013b). Industry Professionals in Higher Education: Values, Identities and Cultural Work. In D. Ashton & C. Noonan (Eds.), *Cultural Work and Higher Education* (pp. 172–192). Palgrave Macmillan: Basingstoke.

Ashton, D. (2013c). Cultural Workers in-the-Making. *European Journal of Cultural Studies, 16*(4), 468–488.

Ashton, D. (2014). Creative Contexts: Work Placement Subjectivities for the Creative Industries. *British Journal of Sociology of Education.* doi: 10.1080/01425692.2014.916602.

Ashton, D. (2015). Author Interview: *Industrial Approaches to Media.* 17 June.

Couldry, N., & Littler, J. (2011). Work, Power and Performance: Analysing the 'Reality' Game of The Apprentice. *Cultural Sociology, 5*(2), 263–279.

De Angelis, M., & Harvie, D. (2015). 'Cognitive Capitalism and the Rat-Race: How Capital Measures Immaterial Labour in British Universities. *Historical Materialism, 17*(3), 3–30.

Department of Culture, Media and Sport. (2008). *Creative Britain*, Department of Culture, Media and Sport, London.

Ellis, J. (2000). *Seeing Things: Television in the Age of Uncertainty.* London: I.B. Tauris.

Jacobs, J. (2014). True Detective and Practical Criticism. *CST Online.* Available at: http://cstonline.tv/true-detective-and-practical-criticism

Johnson, C. (2013). The Mutual Benefits of Engaging with Industry. *CST Online.* Accessed December 3, 2015, from http://cstonline.tv/mutual-benefits

Johnson, D. (2014). Understanding Media Industries From All Perspectives. *Industrial Approaches to Media – The University of Nottingham.* Available at: http://www.nottingham.ac.uk/research/groups/isir/projects/industrial-approaches-to-media/derek-johnson.aspx

Kerr, P. (1979). Out of What Past? Notes on the B Film Noir. *Screen Education, 32*(3), 45–65.

Kerr, P. (Ed.) (1986). *The Hollywood Film Industry.* London: Routledge.

Kerr, P. (1991). Opportunity Knocks. *Screen* 32:4(Winter 1991): 357–363.

Kerr, P. (2008). Thinking Outside the Box. *Screen, 49*(3), 316–323.

Kerr, P. (2009). The Last Slave (2007) The Genealogy of a British Television History Programme. *Historical Journal of Film, Radio and Television* 29:3 (September): 381–397.

Kerr, P. (2013). Making Film Programmes for the BBC and Channel 4: The Shift from In-House 'producer unit' to Independent 'Package Unit' Production. *Historical Journal of Film radio and Television* 33:3 (October): 434–453.

Liebes, T. (2005). Viewing and Reviewing the Audience: Fashions in Communications Research. In J. Curran & M. Gurevitch (Eds.), *Mass Media and Society.* London: Hodder Education.

Lotz, A. D. (2014). Media Industry Studies: Challenges, Pitfalls, Obstacles. *Industrial Approaches to Media – The University of Nottingham.* Available at:

http://www.nottingham.ac.uk/research/groups/isir/projects/industrial-approaches-to-media/amanda-lotz.aspx
Mateer, J. (2015). Author Interview: *Industrial Approaches to Media*. 15 June.
McDonald, P. (2014). An Interview with Professor Paul McDonald. *Industrial Approaches to Media – The University of Nottingham*. Available at: http://www.nottingham.ac.uk/research/groups/isir/projects/industrial-approaches-to-media/index.aspx.
McGurl, M. (2011). *The Program Era: Postwar Fiction and the Rise of Creative Writing*. Massachusetts: Harvard University Press.
Nesta's *Creative Economy Manifesto*. (2013). Bakhshi, Hargreaves and Mateos-Garcia.
Oaklley, K. (2013). Making workers: Higher education and the Cultural Industries Work Force. In D. Ashton & C. Noonan (Eds.), *Cultural Work and Higher Education* (pp. 25–44). Basingstoke: Palgrave Macmillan.
Stoneman, R., & Petrie, D. (2014). *Educating Filmmakers: Past, Present and Future*. Bristol: Intellect.
Weissmann, E. (2014). Teaching Television: Where Do I Start? *CST Online* (April 7). Available at: http://cstonline.tv/teaching-television-where-do-i-start

CHAPTER 3

The Politics and Ethics of Media Industry Studies

Matthew Freeman

This third chapter aims to consider and theorise the politics and ethics of doing media industry studies—by which I mean the political expectations that underpin research in this subfield, and in turn the ethical responsibilities of doing this kind of research. First, I will explore important political issues of ownership and confidentiality that may arise when crossing between academia and the media industries; as has been identified in Chap. 2, both of these sectors encompass quite different legal and political rights over their work. This chapter will therefore provide clear examples of how a research agenda can change the application of research findings, and I specifically look at how the workings of commercial media organisations can impact academic research directions (via embargos, release dates, and so on). Second, I then turn to the ways in which the academic media researcher can go about balancing different obligations and responsibilities when working with commercial media partners, while also discussing the potential legal challenges.

This chapter then builds on the discussions of the previous chapter by considering the question of whether—at least when conceived through the lens of the politics of media industry studies—the academic study

M. Freeman (✉)
Bath Spa University, Bath, UK
e-mail: m.freeman@bathspa.ac.uk

© The Editor(s) (if applicable) and The Author(s) 2016   47
M. Freeman, *Industrial Approaches to Media*,
DOI 10.1057/978-1-137-55176-4_3

of media is (or even should be) understood and applied as some sort of *extension* of the media industries, thus exploring the possible ethical implications of such a status. Lastly, I discuss the more immediate ethical concerns for researchers seeking to collaborate with the media industries for the purposes of scholarship, offering a set of best practice principles based on the ideas and experiences of those currently doing this kind of research. To demonstrate these ideas, Elizabeth Evans and Paul McDonald provide a case study which discusses the difficulties faced when working with commercial media partners.

THE POLITICS OF COLLABORATION

Beyond the perceived difficulty of gaining access to the media industries, perhaps the single greatest challenge for emerging academic researchers when engaging with media industry partners lies in the politics of negotiating such a partnership. Who exactly is in charge of the research? Is the industry the subject or the audience—or both? Steve Presence (2014) highlights the role that power dynamics can play in any researcher's attempts to engage with the media industries: That power might assert itself on account of what Presence characterises as 'the unspoken sense of irrelevance that marks academia through the eyes of industry'—again, the so-called gulf between these sectors rearing its head—or alternatively via the 'intellectual hierarchies' that might unwittingly distinguish the academic researcher from the media industry practitioner.

Elizabeth Evans (2014) breaks down and categorises the unwritten politics of working with media industry practitioners into two main dimensions, which she calls (1) *commercial sensitivity* and (2) *ownership.* With regards to the former, Evans (2014) argues that it is about 'being aware of who your industry partners are, when they work, what they are working on, etc.' For example, an example of such an instance of commercial sensitivity might be the use of embargos, where media scholars may be prohibited from publically releasing documentations or publications of findings related to a particular research project, usually until a specified date has passed.

In terms of the issue of ownership, secondly, Evans (2014) indicates that this becomes especially prevalent when doing research *with* the media industries as opposed to research *on* the media industries. She notes: 'Sometimes there is a question about whose project it actually is.' If, for instance, it is a media organisation that is funding the research project, then to some extent it is industry that is driving the direction of the research question and, in particular, the objects or areas of study. As such, Evans highlights the degree of compromise that is needed when doing academic research with media organisations, and again the question of ownership over the project emerges as a key ethical consideration to be considered in advance.

Exactly where then are lines of ownership between the work of the academic and the work of the media organisation? 'In terms of the argument itself,' Evans (2014) insists, 'that is yours—that is your ownership. The transcript—the words—that is theirs; how I interpret those words, that is mine.' Says Evans (2014), '[y]ou can write up an argument that remains incredibly respectful even as you are being incredibly critical. [...] It is about respecting both your industry partners and your own integrity as a researcher.' Perhaps the greatest political danger of embarking on collaborations with the media industries in this way, therefore, is the danger that media industries essentially choose and approve your research questions. And yet the way forward, perhaps, if indeed industry and academia are indeed asking much the same questions, is to identify shared goals and produce outputs of mutual benefit.

THE ETHICS OF COLLABORATION

It is certainly fair to suggest that the issue of ownership identified by Evans raises not only political but also ethical questions about the role and function of scholarly research in the context of media industry studies. But just how does one go about respecting both your media industry partners and your own integrity and aims as a researcher? As will be explored in the later sections of this book, the very idea of producing scholarship that is both *about* and potentially *for* media industries suggests that we need to identify and develop research questions that the media industries need answers to. In turn, however, this raises a number of complex issues—in the narrowest sense, to do with the perceived necessity to get access to media industries, but in a much broader, more ethical sense, to do with the implication that academia merely becomes a response to industry wants, serving as an outsourcing regime for the media industries to make more money and to improve their commercial standing.

On this subject, Steve Presence (2014) suggests that, in the worse case scenario, any academic–industry engagement risks the outcome of manipulation and, worse still, coercion. More pressing, Presence (2014) adds, is the potentially 'real danger that we can present our scholarly work as something that is fairly cheap', here noting that the tendency of the researcher may well be to pitch one's engagement with industry as a kind of 'free business analysis'. Moreover, Presence (2014) notes that there is the very real ethical question of at what point a piece of scholarly research—one which began as an academic, critical enquiry—ultimately morphs into something that simply no longer serves the imperatives and critical agendas of scholarship.

It is true then that prospects of collaboration between academia and the media industries raises more and more ethical issues, for both sides of the equation. Collaboration between academics and the media industries may mean dealing with the legal or political tangles noted above—including those to do with government, funding bodies, investors, public and cultural policy, research politics, audience agendas, economic imperatives, institutional goals, and so on. But it is important to continually discuss such implications and how best to remain ethical throughout.

So, what are the key ethical challenges of media industry studies? For Emily Caston (2015) the aforementioned issue denouncing media academics as potential outsourcing regimes of the media industry's commerce boils down mostly to *trust*—that is to say, it is closely tied to the so-called gulf standing between academia and the media industries, and which impacts how one sees and uses the other. For Caston (2015), at least, strategies of overcoming this potential ethical problem include approaching media industry studies in its most utopic of imaginings—that is, as a process whereby academics work closely with media industries to set goals and make progressive change, thus occupying a collaborative space where 'we can use our skills as academics to make a difference to industry.'

Caston's emphasis on 'progressive goals' that are also 'shared industry–academic goals' immediately implies a sense of ethical rigour in so far as all parties involved are established as equal beneficiaries of the research, rather than as 'objects' or 'subjects' within another person's research project. Caston (2015) demonstrates how such a set-up can work by pointing to her experiences collaborating with the BFI National Archive and the British Library, where Caston asked members of the music video industry to conceptualise a canon of music videos that would be entered into the National Archives as artistically and culturally significant (see Chap. 8). Ethically, all partners had an equal role to play in the research, and gained equally from it too:

What is the value of this research? The value is to enrich and enhance perspectives and understanding—media industry studies allows us to illuminate intentionality by considering different perspectives; it is by its very nature expansive and allows us to contextualise. For example, by having music producers sitting in a room, they can identify intertextual practices; they don't call it this but that insight and perspective is crucial that expands scholarly and industry understandings of that concept (Caston 2015).

Both ethically and practically then 'a good tip is to pitch and situate one's media industry partners as "co-researchers"' (Caston 2015). For as Caston (2015) elaborates, 'These practitioners don't need you to tell them how to do their job. But they often don't get the room or the time to reflect on their everyday working processes.' Working together—as equal partners or co-researchers with equal access to the overarching aims of the research project—can provide this critical space and time to develop new strategies, methods, and outputs relevant to both academia and to the media industries. Thus whilst the danger is that the media industries ultimately choose the research questions, Caston maintains that the way forward is to identify shared goals that tap into the sorts of questions that cross the academia/industry divide—i.e., the sorts of topics and interests identified by McDonald and in Chap. 2—with media industry practitioners understanding the value and meaning of this research.

Importantly, Caston (2015) further reminds us that 'industry practitioners may be economically minded, but that is not to say that these people aren't critical and analytical. If anything, it is that critical edge that has got them where they are in the industry.' After all, let's remember that the contextualisation at the heart of media industry studies affords researchers a chance to understand media (films, television programmes, radio podcasts, video games, etc.) as equally *symbolic* and *economic* entities—both as creative and as business enterprises. In other words, as researchers we must not lose sight of the fact that media industry practitioners are also required to be just as analytical as any academic would be. And this means that the role of media academics is not to theoretically re-imagine the workings of the media industries, but rather to create new and holistic understandings together via the sharing of alternate perspectives and approaches. As Caston (2015) eloquently concludes, 'honestly, industry sees the value of academia as being able to contextualise their work.'

Balancing Obligations and Responsibilities

Still, even in the face of such utopic ideas of maintaining ethical principles via the process of collaboration and partnership with media industries, there are of course many additional ethical difficulties and challenges that the media industry researcher must overcome. Presence (2014) characterises the practice of engaging with media industries and indeed maintaining professional relationships with those industries throughout the process of research as 'a fine balancing act between obligations and responsibilities to different sets of interest groups within both academia and industry.' Presence (2014) highlights the obligation to ourselves and to our peers, but also our obligation as researchers to make our research accessible to an array of readerships.

In the most basic sense, Evans (2014) insists, 'ethics in research is about good practice, being professional, maintaining integrity; it is about being honest and open.' And in the context of media industry studies, Evans (2014) argues that ethics refers to *'relationships*, and specifically managing those relationships.' Says Evans (2014), '[r]emember, the industry is your audience, and you may wish to go back to them.'

In that sense too Evans (2014) points out that one should not necessarily approach the practice of media industry research and media audience research as diametrically different or opposed, arguing instead that 'there is actually a lot of overlap between media industry and media audience research—and specifically a lot of ways that the two approaches can speak to each other.' Yet Evans (2014) highlights a further methodological distinction that is important here: 'Rather than talking about research *on* the industry, I prefer to talk about research *with* the industry, or *for* the industry'—an important three-way distinction that will be further unpacked shortly.

At this stage, doing research that is about, with, or for the media industries brings yet another party into this relationship: the research participants. As the researcher, you are responsible for managing not only your relationship with both the media industry partners and the research participants, but also their relationship to each other. As Caston (2015) explains, 'always ask yourself as a researcher: Who is your audience?' Evans (2014) insists that two of the biggest ethical priorities for researchers engaging with media audiences in the context of media industry research—which can then take on an added dimension when dealing with commercial media organisations—is, first, the need to maintain honesty, and, second, attempts to combat issues around privacy. Says Evans (2014), '[w]hen you are doing audience research for a commercial media partner, those audiences need to know that the research is for that commercial media partner, and sometimes that may make people want to answer your questionnaire, simply because of the idea that their responses might somehow get back to the sorts of people who can take the audiences' perspectives on board.'

The involvement of commercial media partners can also work to legitimise academic research in the eyes of audiences—branding scholarship with familiar corporate media logos, for instance. Evans (2014), however, also suggests that the involvement of commercial media partners in academic research can be problematic: 'If you are doing research around online viewing habits, for example, which naturally raises issues around privacy, if your audience participants then think, "hang on, you are researching me and you are then going to talk to Warner Bros. about all the illegal Warner Bros. films that I have downloaded," then those participants may not wish to be involved, for obvious reasons.' Thinking then about the potential impact of your audience participants' own honesty is a key consideration, as are the circumstances of your research project. An investigation into fandom, for example, may benefit from the involvement of commercial media partners because there is the promise of feeding the views of fans back to media producers—a promise of a relationship that fans may well find attractive—while an investigation into illegal, taboo, or more personal audience activity may likely suffer from any legitimate corporate industry branding.

In terms of how such a relationship actually works and how the researcher should begin, Evans (2014) notes that such an investigation breaks down into the following steps: '(1) What are you planning to do with the data? (2) How are you collecting it? (3) Who will you show that data to, i.e., commercial partners? And (4) How will those commercial partners use it?' Ensuring that all participants are fully briefed about each of these four questions is crucial before any research takes place. Getting written consent for the views of audiences to be shared with industry partners should also take place before the start of any study. And as for *after* the research has taken place, issues of privacy should also continue to be upheld; this is likely to include keeping personal details and contact addresses private from the commercial media industry partners, with only the necessary reports or findings made viewable.

Presence (2014) accordingly emphasises the importance of *strategy* when engaging with the media industries: 'Being clear about one's objectives and approach is a must for any researcher,' while 'approaching media companies and saying, "you should work with me because I have got a lot to teach you" is *not* the best strategy for beginning a healthy working relationship with media industries.' Instead, Presence (2014) concludes, 'we would all do well to bear in mind that academics are *skilled learners* and that we have a lot to learn from industry as well as lots to offer it.'

Ethics as Critical Distance

Such talk of both teaching and learning from the media industries may raise smaller—though no less critical—ethical considerations, especially for the emergent media industry researcher. 'More justifiably', Presence (2014) adds, 'we need critical distance from all of our objects of study'— for without it, or at least without the establishment of clear, shared goals, to use Caston's earlier expression, the danger of much media industry studies is that researchers become unethical to themselves.

For Evans (2014), 'acting ethically means everything that being an academic means: It is being objective, it is maintaining critical distance, and it is making it politely clear that you are not a conduit between the industry and audiences; instead, you are separate from both of these parties, but you are nevertheless managing that relationship between them.' In other words, a key ethical principle for media industry researchers is to be aware of the aforementioned issues that arise from such research, identifying which issues apply to your study, and putting in place steps for how you can overcome any or all of these issues. Be relatively upfront about your research questions, but do not imply the answers, and certainly do not overlook your own role.

Accordingly, and perhaps above all else, it is a key ethical responsibility not to forget and always to recognise the true *value* of academic media studies research. Says Presence (2014), 'I would argue that bringing critical, historical, and theoretical perspectives on the media industries is essential to a healthy society; we need to identify and understand media industries as huge phenomena that come from society but also shape it in really serious and significant ways.'

Now, to demonstrate how all of the aforementioned ideas, issues, concerns, and considerations might manifest in the context of actual media industry research, consider the following case study by Elizabeth Evans and Paul McDonald. Here, Evans and McDonald reflect on some of the ethical and political dimensions of their own media industry research, pointing out further considerations along the way, while also categorising differences between research that is on, with, or for media industries.

CASE STUDY: ON, WITH, OR FOR: PERSPECTIVES
ON ACADEMIC/INDUSTRY COLLABORATIONS

Elizabeth Evans
Department of Culture, Film and Media
University of Nottingham

Paul McDonald
Department of Culture, Media and Creative Industries
King's College London

Combining conceptual perspectives and practical methodologies from a range of research traditions, academic studies of media industries now represent a diverse and eclectic subfield in academic media research (Herbert 2014; Holt and Perren 2009; McDonald 2013). While there is no singular line or direction to work that might be identified as belonging to this subfield, nevertheless there is some commonality or shared ground to how these studies proceed, for in one way or another, the necessary descriptive work of explaining how these industries work meets a critical imperative to interrogate and evaluate the conduct of those industries. To generalise, this critical imperative involves looking beyond the showbiz gloss to make known how the media industries function as actors in, and arenas for, enacting economic, political, social, and cultural power. Media industries research poses alternative, oppositional, or radical challenges to the ways in which the media industries work, purposefully saying things that otherwise might be left unsaid about those industries.

This results in a certain abstract spatiality, for critical integrity seemingly necessitates a conscious and principled separation between the academic researcher and the media industries. 'Industry' is held at an analytic distance as an object of enquiry, positioned as a thing to be studied and interrogated. Even if the work of research involves going native by meeting and mixing with media professionals, subject/object relations still keep industry at a distance. Consequently, in one way or another, the academic is placed in the position of producing research *on* the industry. At the same time of course, the media industries themselves are systematic producers of research. Consumer research is regularly commissioned to better know behavioural characteristics in markets for cultural goods and services. To persuade policymakers to act in their interests, media industries must have the data resources at hand to present a convincing evidence base. If there is any questioning in this work over how the media industries operate, it is concerned with how businesses might operate more efficiently to meet their commercial objectives. Work from this direction might therefore be described as research *of* the media industries, knowledge produced by industry for industry.

So what happens when the academic/industry divide is crossed in media scholarship? This question might be applied from various quarters in media research but is obviously pertinent for a subfield where industry is itself the very object of study. Engagements between academic researchers and the media industries can take many different forms, and it might be useful to think of these as inexact points on a continuum. At one end, research *on* industry represents a kind of sub-continuum in its own terms. It covers differing degrees of engagement that range from desk research involving very little or no actual contact with industry actors, where industry is engaged with but at a discreet distance, to investigations that depend on empirical mixings with media professionals and firms. At the other end is what can be called research *for* industry, where the academic researcher is commissioned to fulfil a brief as specified by the industry client. Here, industry is catalytic, for the research only takes place because of industry interests and the academic researcher has the status of hired hand. Between these poles sits the potential for research *with* industry, where both academic and industry partners take mutual gains from a shared process of investigation. This is not to say both parties take the same things away from the research but rather that each reaps respective benefits from the findings.

The divisions outlined so far raise many questions about the practicalities, ethics, and politics of media industries research: what are the gains and losses potentially at play in exchanges between academic media industries research and its object of enquiry; should, and if so can, that research speak to the media industries in meaningful ways; do such engagements compromise or boost criticality; and what can this relationship tell us about the status and value of academic knowledge?

Thinking of the benefits of engagement, several come to mind. Whether through formal interviews or informal conversations, encounters with media professionals provide access to specialist first-hand knowledge and insights otherwise unavailable from other sources. Talking with professionals not only serves information gathering purposes but also illuminates understanding of the operational thinking and belief systems that produce and are produced by industry practice. In these various ways, engagement extends the range and volume of available data feeding the research. Secondly, the insights of industry practitioners may actually open up new avenues of enquiry that productively inflect and redirect a programme of research. Those inside the industry may generate fresh perspectives, ideas, and questions not immediately evident to those from outside. Third, engagement with industry offers opportunities to test theoretically constructed arguments against industry realities; what might have seemed a rock solid argument may just not hold water when exposed to empirical actualities. Fourth, the input of media professionals has the potential to correct the presumptions, misunderstandings, or errors that might underpin an entire project. Fifth, if talking to and learning from media professionals can result in research of greater relevance to industry, then industry engagements may extend the audience for academic research beyond the academy. After all, does media industries research only want to talk to the academic community? If so, what is its purpose? And on that note, finally, considering the critical imperative behind media industries studies, only by engaging with practitioners can media industries studies hold any hope of bringing about change in the conduct or polices of industry. Criticality depends on viewing media industries with at least some degree of scepticism, but blankly erecting barriers against industry arguably remains counterproductive if that means 'writing them off from the outset and then, in a self-fulfilling prophecy, criticizing them again when they seem to affirm one's direst functionalist predictions' (Bennett 1992: 32). None of the benefits of industry engagement outlined above presents a logical or inevitable obstacle to preserving criticality. Rather, if engagement can help the researcher to better understand the complex contradictoriness of what is studied, and thereby strengthen argument, it can only enhance criticality.

On the other hand, encounters with industry are loaded with frictions and frustrations. Academic scepticism towards the industry may frequently be reciprocated, with the whole research endeavour placed in doubt by the dismissive question 'what's the point of all this?' While eliciting industry knowledge from practitioners can enrich the data collected, necessary and respectful observance of ethical protocols can present obstacles if this results in requests from participants to excise statements or information given in the course of interviews or let slip when 'off the record'. The impact of this is particularly evident when it is considered that maybe the very reason such requests are made is precisely because the statements or information concerned are the most revelatory. Similar obstructions arise if industry-produced data is known to exist but access is denied to the researcher. These are just some of the ways in which industry encounters cease to positively shape the research and tip over into negatively defining the research by casting questions over the independence and freedoms of academic enquiry. Bringing the findings of critical research to non-academic communities can certainly extend the audiences for and uses of that work. At the same time, these exchanges always face the possibility that because academic researchers are not of the industry community, there is a credibility or legitimacy gap, for they just 'don't know what they are talking about' and so the work is simply regarded as 'irrelevant'. Critical research seems particularly vulnerable to such reaction, for the point is to produce *un* common knowledge of industry by thinking outside of, or actively challenging, the forms of understanding and belief most familiarly operating within industry. In such situations, it is reasonable to speculate whether such dismissive responses are actually defences against the arguments presented in critical research.

Given this mix of potential advantages and disadvantages, rather than cast any blanket *a priori* judgment—either categorically for or against industry engagement, regardless of circumstances—it would seem wise to consider tensions between the benefits and weaknesses as dynamics that are constantly at work in critical media industries research, whose effects are always context specific and can only ever be judged and negotiated on a case-by-case basis. To do so, we shall turn to our own experience of working on collaborative media industry projects. We have both worked on a number of projects, with a range of different partners, that can be classified as *on* or *with* industry partners or practitioners. Our case study here, however, represents a project we conducted in conjunction with a major Hollywood studio. The project received a small amount of funding from the studio and evolved through conversations between the studio's representative and ourselves both before and during the research process. Rather than researching the industry itself in order to reflect critical insights on its operations and structures back to those working within them, this project consisted of conducting research *for* our studio partners into audience behaviour and attitudes.

Audience research can be seen as offering a highly useful and productive space for collaborative academic–industry projects. At a basic level, attracting audiences is the primary purpose of the entertainment industries, but audiences remain the most unknowable element of their business, heightening the value of any available insights. Beyond this, there is a natural alignment between academic and industry interests in audiences. Both academia and the industry seek to understand roughly the same phenomenon (the reception and consumption of screen texts), and both have long traditions of audience research, often with shared methodologies.

Audience-oriented projects equally lack the potential difficulties of the research partner also being the research subject, of feeding back critical or negative insights to those who have contributed to the research process.

However, our experience of conducting audience research within the US studio system highlighted core differences in approach and method, and in particular the tensions inherent with conducting research *for* an industry partner, rather than *on* or *with* them. The project involved running questionnaires and interviews exploring how audiences were responding to changes in the film and television viewing landscape. The result was a short written report and a presentation to a group of studio executives, some of whom worked in directly related areas and some who did not. We also naturally had more academic forms of dissemination in mind. At various stages of the research process our industry partner asked us to make changes. These ranged from significant re-orientations of the research subjects to the inclusion of specific questions in the primary research that we otherwise would not have asked. As academics, we were keen to explore the messiness of screen consumption, to ask questions that explored the complexities of taste and value through a smaller sample that could interrogate the nuance of screen experiences. Our partners, however, became increasingly concerned with what could be described as more 'functional' questions that directly related to relatively small strategic decisions and were far more specific. These were then tied to the value of larger datasets that could offer generalisations, rather than the potentially contradictory detail that can emerge from smaller scale qualitative work. Rather than generalising, our method sought to interrogate and map a complex set of factors and behaviours that are difficult to articulate through multiple choice survey questions. Such surveys, however, generate datasets that can be argued as 'representative' and therefore supportive of major, multi-million dollar investments. A tension therefore emerged between our aims as a research team and what our partners perceived the project's value to be.

Much of this tension emerged from the fact that the project was funded by the studio, a situation that raised questions over who maintained ownership over the project. To what extent could we exert our own control over the project's direction, and to what extent should we prioritise meeting the requirements of our funders? This is an issue that equally encompasses publically funded research, with projects often having to meet the agenda of funding bodies such as those of the UK's major government-funded research councils. These funders regularly offer strategic directives that encourage certain kinds of research questions and methods over others. However, our industry funders operated with less flexibility than academic funders and were less open to the project's potential evolution along more academically focused lines. When having conversations with our partner studio as the project developed, there was a clear sense of having to ensure it encompassed their interests first, with any alignment with our own interests acting as a bonus.

These tensions ultimately led to some doubt over the effectiveness of the research as a collaborative project and a sense that it had to serve two very different purposes. One was the more academic concerns of critical interrogation, whilst the other was the more administrative concerns of a multi-billion dollar, multi-national entertainment enterprise. Although the same methodology, even the same questionnaire, could be used to answer both concerns, they required not only different interpretations but also different specific questions. The end result was a project that had to serve two aims simultaneously, with two very different interpretation and dissemination processes. For us, the process did ultimately result in both an interesting dataset and the chance to explore that dataset through research outputs. Any potential satisfaction that our studio partners may have found in the process is harder to determine. Initial feedback seemed less than positive, and they do not seem to have followed through with the strategies they were contemplating when the research took place. We've had so sense from them, however, on the direct impact our research findings may or may not have had on these decisions.

Although this specific project resulted in our questioning of its value to our industry partner, it should only be seen as a way to highlight the potential pitfalls of academic–industry research, not as a warning against such research. We have both had far more positive experiences of working for and with industry partners, and it is necessary to recognise the importance of the *kind* of partnership involved. The fact that our partner was a major Hollywood studio should not be underestimated. Large media organisations are fundamentally bound up in the pressures and requirements that emerge from making multi-million (or billion) dollar decisions, often on relatively short notice. The nature of the media industries as businesses means that these decisions require easily digestible findings. The minutiae and nuance of critical media industries research do not always fit neatly into this environment. We equally found significant differences between the individual attitudes of the various studio personnel that we worked with. Whilst some were open to exploring the potential of differing approaches to their audiences, others were less so. A different sector of the industry, or even different personnel, could lead to a very different collaborative experience. Catherine Johnson, for instance, has discussed research she and Paul Grainge conducted with Red Bee Media, a leading UK digital agency. She describes the experience as benefiting both sides of the collaboration. For herself and Grainge, the project allowed them to 'apply and evaluate our existing research from inside the largest company working in this sector in the UK and to analyse the strategies that they were using to manage the fast-changing media environment that is a focal interest for our own research' (Johnson 2013). Such a process was reliant on the access that only a collaborative project could allow for. For Red Bee, the project offered not only the promotionally valuable 'prestige' of working with a university but also the potential for 'opportunities for industrial self-reflexivity' that could 'enhance Red Bee's corporate image as 'thought leaders' in a period of rapid change and thus increase their economic competitiveness' (Johnson 2013).

The growth of media industry studies has reached a point at which critical reflection on both the scope and potential of such work, and on the relationships formed between scholars and industry practitioners is helpful and necessary. Contemplating the state of screen industry studies, Jennifer Holt has advised that 'Going forward, our job will be to strike the right balance between being critical and being engaged with our object of study as we cultivate more terrain for collaboration' (2013: 183). The ability to distinguish, and move, between research on, for, and with industry offers a way for achieving such balance and to understand the subtle but crucial differences in the kinds of relationships screen studies academics can form with the media industries. A greater critical reflexivity on the scope, process, and potential of such research can only help the field not only develop its critical frameworks but also meet the increasingly prevalent agendas calling us to produce work of value to those outside of the academy. Collaboration with industry offers genuine insight into the workings of the screen industries, insights that are simply not available via other means. Understanding, and preparing for, potential tensions between industrial and academic priorities provides us the chance to take advantage of such insights with our eyes firmly open.

Bibliography

Bennett, T. (1992). Putting Policy into Cultural Studies. In L. Grossberg, C. Nelson, & P. A. Treichler (Eds.), *Cultural Studies* (pp. 23–37). London: Routledge.

Caston, E. (2015). Author Interview: *Industrial Approaches to Media*. 20 June.

Evans, E. (2014). Ethics in Industry and Audience Research. *Industrial Approaches to Media – The University of Nottingham*. Available at: http://www.nottingham.ac.uk/research/groups/isir/projects/industrial-approaches-to-media/industrial-approaches-to-media-inaugural-event.aspx

Herbert, D. (2014). Putting the "Me" in "Method": Perspective, Positionality and Embodied Knowledge in Media Industry Research. *Creative Industries Journal, 7*(1), 45–49.

Holt, J. (2013). Two-Way Mirrors: Looking at the Future of Academic-Industry Engagement. *Cinema Journal, 52*(3), 183–188.

Holt, J., & Perren, A. (2009). Introduction: Does the World Really Need One More Field of Study? In J. Holt & A. Perren (Eds.), *Media Industries: History, Theory, and Method* (pp. 1–16). Malden, MA: Wiley-Blackwell.

Johnson, C. (2012). The Mutual Benefits of Engaging with Industry. *CST Online*. Accessed December 3, 2015, from http://cstonline.tv/mutual-benefits

McDonald, P. (2013). Introduction: In Focus – Media Industries Studies. *Cinema Journal, 52*(3), 145–149.

Presence, S. (2014). The Ethics and Politics of Media Engagement. *Industrial Approaches to Media – The University of Nottingham*. Available at: http://www.nottingham.ac.uk/research/groups/isir/projects/industrial-approaches-to-media/industrial-approaches-to-media-inaugural-event.aspx

The Theory and Practice of Media Industry Studies

Now that I have explored some of the key political reasons for why collaboration with the media industries is important, as well as offering some important ethical considerations for this kind of research, Part II of this book will move on to broadly explore the actual doing of media industry studies. I posit that a methodology of media industry studies is most principally a process of contextualising media amidst wider contexts, influences, and impacts, and of course a process of understanding those contexts. As identified in the introduction, I categorise these wider contexts thusly:

Creativity Context—Production Context—Cultural Context

Still, how exactly can these increasingly widening contexts of investigation be harmonised—or as Paul McDonald (2013: 146) asks, 'How can different levels of analysis be effectively integrated in studies of industry?' In addressing this particular question, across the next four chapters I shall examine the strategies and practicalities for how to best utilise specific methodological approaches in particular areas of media industry studies enquiry—be it for understanding the creativity context, the production context, or the cultural context. I will also outline the affordances of specific methodological approaches as well as their potential applications to a range of studies so as to identify how certain methodologies might best suit particular scholarly interests. Each of the ensuing four chapters also comes complete with case study contributions. Michele Hilmes, Dave Harte, Sarah Ralph, and Petros Iosifidis each offer reflective case studies about how best to adopt approaches comprising trade paper and social media analysis, interviews and ethnographic analysis, and political-cultural economy, respectively, to the study of the media industries, with these case studies highlighting the kinds of claims and conclusions that can be drawn from the use of particular methodologies.

BIBLIOGRAPHY

McDonald, P. (2013). Introduction: In focus—media industries studies. *Cinema Journal, 52*(3), 145–149.

CHAPTER 4

Socialised Authorship: Conceptualising Media Industry Studies

Matthew Freeman

Before I get to outlining and exploring the specific methodological tactics and strategies that can be employed in media industry studies, it is first crucial to conceptualise what such a methodology might actually look like. For as I noted in the introduction to this book, my aim is partly to conceptualise the goals and critical orientations of media industry research, as well as to conceptualise media industries as an object of study. Indeed, as was also questioned in the introduction, if the focus of our scholarly research is as vast and often as intangible as an entire media industry or even a whole set of media industries, then how should one approach this research? What is the industry as a 'text', or rather the industrial object of study?

This chapter aims to answer these questions by theorising the very idea of studying media industries in light of twenty-first century transformations in technology, ownership, structures, working conditions, and so on. Here I return to my central notion of media industry studies methodology as essentially processes of tracing connections between political economic, corporate, and discursive contexts, and more specifically as processes of identifying and understanding media industry operations as modes of authorship across multiple sites of macro and micro processes.

M. Freeman (✉)
Bath Spa University, Bath, UK
e-mail: m.freeman@bathspa.ac.uk

© The Editor(s) (if applicable) and The Author(s) 2016
M. Freeman, *Industrial Approaches to Media*,
DOI 10.1057/978-1-137-55176-4_4

To demonstrate this methodological perspective, Michele Hilmes provides a case study looking at ways of conceptualising media industry studies as indeed a study of authorship across borders of multiple creative personnel, subdivisions, and subsidiary corporations, using her past studies of the US broadcasting industries as an example.

More broadly, however, conceptualising media industry studies as studies of authorship means understanding the larger social structures in which media industries operate, and indeed the importance of researching those industries as part of larger webs. In essence, all media industries operate as a complex blend of creativity and enterprise, translating culture into economy. In other words, media industries do not exist in a vacuum; instead, their everyday practices tap into social, political, economic, and cultural phenomena, and must therefore cross what academia would often deem opposing disciplinary perspectives. As Ashton and Noonan (2013: 1) assert, 'the sector is often framed in relation to economic development, urban regeneration and remedying social inequalities.' This comment—pointing to the relationships between media industries themselves and far larger developments in the economy, politics, culture, and society—is especially important to the aims of this book. For it signals the importance of thinking of the study of media industries not just in terms of industries themselves—sectors, organisations, producers, writers, etc.—but also in terms of the wider circuits that surround and inform those industries.

WHAT IS THE INDUSTRY AS A 'TEXT'?

It is therefore important to conceptualise a methodology for doing media industry studies in such terms. Eva Van Passel (2015) suggests that methodologies of media industry studies typically come from many different fields and disciplines (such as cultural studies, business studies, film studies, etc.), and yet none of these other fields or disciplines provide sufficient methodologies given the shifting and specific concerns of media industry studies. Indeed, media industry studies is in some ways a combined methodology of these cultural, business, and film studies approaches—taking the strengths and affordances of particular approaches so as to enhance and contextualise the others. And taking such a multiperspectival approach is necessarily largely because of changes taking place in the media industry itself. Consider the following comment made by the CEO of Hearst Magazines UK to describe the fundamental operation of their company: 'We are not a publisher [...] Our job is to create a business which is diversified and will enable a connection with our audience around our different brands' (Siegert et al. 2011: 57). Shifts towards the digital have revolutionised the production, distribution, and consumption practices of most media industries today, not just the publishing sector. And one of the key impacts of digitisation has been the diversified spreading of media into a whole host of multimedia platforms and outlets. What Henry Jenkins (2006) famously called convergence culture has epitomised a contemporary media landscape that is characterised by an increased sense of participation, a heightened exposure of media content, and a cross-platform dispersal of that content. Almost as a response, it seems, we have the words of Hearst Magazine UK's CEO; the noted emphasis on 'diversification' over a single media platform, on global understandings of media audiences, and on 'brand' rather than the specificities of a media text, all point to one overriding idea—that the *doing* of media industry studies in this contemporary setting requires what Gillian Doyle (2015) calls a 'multi-method analysis design' in order to successfully navigate the complexities of these industries.

Media industry studies is thus partly about understanding the relationships between structure (social hierarchies, political forces, economic motives, policies, etc.) and agency (how people create and produce, how teams are forms, how media and audiences are conceptualised, etc.). But it is also about understanding the wider cultural climates where media industries communicate meanings, messages, and values that shape our understanding of those industries. And this means thinking about media industries—and the practitioners they employ—as the centre of a proverbial spider web, with larger socio-political forces and more local cultural manifestations working to inform those media industries in ever-complex ways.

Consider, for instance, the concept of brand. Most simply, branding is an industrial practice of differentiation, intended to stamp a unifying identity onto a product (or a series of products) in the hope of establishing a bond with audiences. Branding, on the grandest level, can be understood as a response to larger economic and capitalist forces in society, one triggered by our dominant consumerist society and manifested as the precise strategy of branding. But brand is in fact an industrial practice, one designed, shaped, orchestrated, and managed by agents working for organisations. In other words, branding may be a product of deep economic forces, but much of what we define to be branding comes from corporations and people. And yet on another level, branding is nothing if not the product of cultural meanings; all brands are infused with ideologies, attitudes, ideals, trends, and fads that enable them to speak to consumers and carry economic potential. In other words, branding is in fact a cultural phenomenon that manifests as a product of discursive communications.

I point to branding as just one example of what might be the object of study in media industry studies, but I use it to demonstrate the idea that in the media landscape—particularly in the twenty-first century, a time when media spreads and migrates across multiple screens, digital replications, multi-media and multi-national media conglomerates around the world—the study of media industries is decidedly complex and requires consideration of social, economic, corporate, and even cultural factors. As Caldwell (2008) shows us, cultural production is a site of sprawling struggle, contestation, and negotiation between a range of stakeholders—be it practitioners or audiences. Emily Caston (2012), in this same vein, points out how the UK music video industry is itself a 'hybrid production culture', one built from the fusions of graphic design, portrait photography, live concert performance, fine art, and film.

Contemporarily, indeed, media work becomes even more expansive, if only because of the very nature of digitised systems, compartmentalisation, and casualised labour. Consider the ways in which the BBC produces content for one of its flagship shows: *Doctor Who*. Much of what we might actually consider to be *Doctor Who*—its television episodes, its advertisements, its web series, its online prequels, its games, its DVDs, and so on—is produced across not only multiple divisions within the BBC itself but also across intermediary and freelance agencies that work to support and extend the brands of major television series in the UK. The role of an intermediary practitioner, working to produce a *Doctor Who*-branded web game, for instance, would be to develop such content in a way that remains true to the BBC's values, approval, and integrity—ensuring their own creativity is in line with that of the BBC's. Paul Grainge and Catherine Johnson (2015) argue that the relationship between the intermediary and the main creative at the BBC is in fact one of negotiation, and not simply one of supervision and enforcement, especially when considered from the perspective of the intermediary agency. In fact, according to Grainge and Johnson, many of these intermediary practitioners, at least in the UK, see the act of collaboration—receiving notes, guidelines, briefs, revision requirements, etc.—as part and parcel of their daily working processes; individual creativity does not necessarily even come into it. And this is not to consider the political and ideological pressures placed on the BBC by the UK government. With its status as a public service broadcaster, funded by license fee, the BBC is driven by long-standing political regulation, shaping aforementioned working practices. Equally, much of what is communicated about how *Doctor Who* is produced industrially, and thus the meanings and values of its production, comes from the cultural discourses around and alongside the BBC's communicative powers. This means that if studying something such as the production of *Doctor Who* in an industrial context—an example that I use randomly to show how any media text exists as part of an expansive sprawl in and across multiple contexts—one is required to consider multiple sites of study, researching multiple disciplinary perspectives.

And this sense of expansive sprawl creates particular challenges for the researcher. One needs to decide on the specific parameters of the research, the specific focus, before locating that focus within a wider context of study. For example, what are the political policies that underpin the production practices of the BBC's television programmes? What characterises the BBC's production processes when developing its television programmes across platforms? And how do cultural perceptions of the BBC's television programmes inform the company's productions?

The way that contemporary media industries operate within vast social, corporate, and cultural spheres thereby creates a truly rapidly moving, morphing research target. Caldwell (2015) suggests that media industry studies is rather like looking over the shoulders of people who are in turn looking over the shoulders of others. There is the slightly ironic sense that media industry studies actually means examining all sorts of peripheral processes, practices, and communications around industry before one even gets to the actual industry that one wishes to interrogate.

Thinking About Media Industries Socially

It is precisely because media industries exist in and across so many terrains—their very existence as industries is defined by their power and their communication across borders—that it is useful to turn towards sociological theory. Indeed, social theory can be useful for conceptualising the goals and critical orientations of media industry research, and for conceptualising media industries as an object of study. Anthony Giddens' (1984) structuration theory is particularly useful as a theoretical framework for conceptualising media industries in this way.

Giddens' structuration theory represents an attempt to bridge the gulf between notions of structure and agency in social life. It is based on the analysis of both large-scale (or macro) structures and the smaller-scale (or micro) work of individuals, without giving primacy to either. Giddens uses concepts from both objectivist and subjectivist social theories—simultaneously critiquing objectivism's focus on detached large-scale structures, which can be seen to lack close regard for human elements, while equally critiquing subjectivism's exclusive attention to individual or group agency without greater consideration for socio-structural context. In this way, structuration theory argues that neither macro- nor micro-focused analyses are alone sufficient for understanding the complexities of social order; instead, researchers should adopt and unite both perspectives equally.

Giddens may have been discussing social theory specifically, but in actual fact his structuration theory has much continued relevance to conceptualising the study of media industries. What Giddens called large-scale (or macro) structures in society might typically be characterised as the political economy approach in media and mass communication studies, since in this context political economy similarly aims to understand how grand underpinning social structures such as economics and political policies shape media. And what Giddens called the smaller-scale (or micro) work of individual agency shares considerable overlap with the perspectives of many cultural studies scholars, who—in opposition to political economists—prefer to understand the workings of culture as localised relationships between people and communities.

Giddens understands the idea of structure as one of duality, not simply between micro and macro, but also between structure as *medium* and structure as *outcome*. For Giddens, structures can be both the product of the deep economic and political systems that govern a society (thus, an outcome), and equally as the local operations of agents within a particular society that afford actions to be carried out (thus, a medium). This duality is the very core of structuration theory, and in Giddens' social theory the duality of structure works to emphasise that they are merely different sides to the same central question of how social order is created. Structuration theory is thereby rooted in the central assumption that social order is not a linear or vertical process, i.e., where all macro forces 'drip down' to dictate operations of micro actions below. Instead, it acknowledges that the duality of structure is a feedback–feedforward process where agents and structures mutually enact social systems as a reciprocal cycle.

Conceiving of media industries in this way—that is, as social structures—allows us to consider industrial spaces as workflows whose influence reaches inwards and outwards, both to the powers of governments, policy-makers, economic forces, etc. as well as to cultural attitudes, expectations, and of course audiences. The media, in its simplest definition, is *communication*—and so it makes sense that studies of media industries understand those industries as contextual vessels of communication, tracing links, relationship, impacts, and influences between the work of the media industries and their communicative implications around and outside industry.

Specifically and perhaps most usefully for our purposes, structuration theory conceptualises the workings of this feedback–feedforward relationships by examining three processes: (1) *structure* (2) *interaction* and (3) *modality*. Structure, in this instance, refers to the deep systems that govern a social system, i.e., economics and politics; interaction is the agent's activity within the social system; and modality is the means by which structures are translated into values, actions, and meanings.

Now, if I were to apply this social thinking to the study of media industries, one can quite similarly say that media industries—themselves like mini social systems complete with a critical mass of agents, each driven by both overlapping yet diverse aims—can be conceptualised as a 'structure' (i.e., the deep political and economic forces in society that underpin how media industries function), as an 'interaction' (i.e., the actual practices of production within the media industries), and as a 'modality' (i.e., the wider social and cultural arenas of the media industries where these economic and political forces are communicated as discursive sets of meanings and values).

So, the first of these principles can be called the *societal context*, where the operations of the media industries emerge as the outcome of deep structures in society. The second of these can be called the *corporate context*, which concerns the working practices that make up production cultures within the media industries. And the third of these can be called the *discursive context*, which concerns not actual practice but the discourses communicated by media industry practitioners, and thus the ways in which media practitioners narrativise the transformation of deep social structures into clear sets of meanings and understandings about the media industries.

THINKING ABOUT MEDIA INDUSTRIES AUTHORIALLY

In other words, one might say that part of the sense-making process that researchers must attempt when studying and theorising the media industries is about identifying patterns of authorship and voiced communication amidst webs of social, political, economic, corporate, and cultural forces. Studies of the media industries now investigate the operation of power within production communities and the impact of this power on the media texts produced. This growing body of research has examined, amongst other themes, a wide range of considerations: the lived experiences of production workers, the working cultures in which they operate, the identity of the production worker and its influence on their production decisions, the creative agency of actors, the influence of wider economic and political forces, the impact of new technologies, and the formal and informal institutional hierarchies which have shaped working practices in the media industries. All of which can be understood as questions of understanding the mode of creative authorship within, between, and across industrial structures.

Usefully, and as briefly indicated earlier in this book, Michele Hilmes (2014) defines media industry studies as itself 'the study of authorship—authorship in the way that it might have been defined in more traditional media, such as in literature and in film studies.' Of course, fields such as film studies have been preoccupied with issues of creative authorship for a long time. Traditional film studies might have worked to identify authorship within the likes of films as a single creative vision—typically via the director. And although the authorship debate played a crucial role in legitimising film studies scholarship, as McDonald (2013: 147) explains it also

> placed a double obstacle in the way of attending to matters of industry: By situating the individual as the agent of production, authorship neglected attention to the broader industrial, institutional, and market contexts in which film exists; and subsequently, the critical dismissal of authorship in favour of attention to the meanings and politics of texts or discourses blocked attention to the circumstances in which those very texts or discourses were produced.

Importantly, however, where Hilmes' (2014) comprehension of industrial authorship differs is in the way she argues that 'media industry studies is picking up the postmodern flag, you might say, by expanding studies of authorship into a much wider range of activities that allows us to contextualise the act of creativity, or of creative authorship, and of production in a far wider range of contexts.'

Caldwell, too, specifically discusses the production cultures of the media industries as an 'industrial auteur theory'. For Caldwell (2008: 199), 'negotiated and collective authorship is an almost avoidable and determining reality in contemporary film/television.' Caldwell (2008: 199) argues that 'a systematic struggle over control still very much determines authorship', hailing this 'controller-as-author status' as some-thing that varies from medium to medium, from role to role, and even from corporation to corporation. Importantly, Caldwell's emphasis on the relationship between a struggle for control and authorship in the media industries goes straight to the heart of my sociological approach to under-standing media industry studies. In short, the societal context strongly shapes patterns of authorship within the corporate context, with those authorship patterns and values communicated via the discursive context, wherein media practitioners are able to narrativise the remarkably messy transformation of social, political, and economic forces into corporate agency as clear sets of authored values, meanings, and messages about the media industries. Authorship, when viewed in this way, thus remains a highly useful concept for analysing and understanding how and why media industries operate contextually.

Before I offer some more specific examples of how this authorial approach to researching different contexts of media industries might map on to particular objects of study, allow Hilmes to first demonstrate this thinking in her case study below. Here, she conceptualises the study of the historical US radio industry according to three distinct but interconnected levels of authorship: first, the nation author; second, the individual author; and third; the network author. These three levels of authorship in the radio industry all work to demonstrate the societal context, the corporate context, and the discursive context, respectively.

CASE STUDY: INDUSTRY AS AUTHOR: DECONSTRUCTING CREATIVITY

Michele Hilmes

Long before poststructuralists began to deconstruct the figure of the individual author as solitary genius (Barthes 1978; Foucault 1977), both media theorists and media industries themselves had been forced to grap-ple with the problem of shared, complex authorship. Historically, creativ-ity has always been a messy affair, full of mash-ups and borrowing, as any student of Shakespeare or of hip-hop knows. The romantic notion of the autonomous individual author was as much a construct of eighteenth cen-tury industrial imperatives as it was a reflection of reality (Charvat 1974). Once intellectual property rights became legally enforced, lines had to be drawn. Authorship claims in twentieth century mass media industries proved particularly difficult to pin down, even as creative roles burgeoned across a range of professions and arts.

When film critics and scholars in the 1960s proclaimed the director to be the primary *auteur* of the feature film, they paved the way for film to be treated as an art and for text-driven scholarship to thrive (Sarris 1962). Yet this assertion flew directly in the face of how films were actually made: No matter how important the director, other artistic input—writing, acting, design, editing, music direction, special effects—had an enormous impact on the expressive qualities of the film, and its ownership, most likely by a studio, typically diverged from all of those roles. So, alongside the many critical reviews and academic studies that look at films through the lens of the all-powerful director, an alternative version gives equal credit to the creative efforts of other professions, even those formerly considered 'below the line' (Caldwell 2008). And an important strain of media studies, beginning with Adorno and Horkheimer's scathing critique of the 'culture industry', places equal weight on the larger industrial forces that shape creative conditions and set the terms for key decisions—from studio management to theatre owners, censors, courts of law, regulatory bodies, national policies, and international treaties (Horkheimer and Adorno 1944; Holt and Perren 2009; Gray and Johnson 2013).

Here I will use three case studies to explore the idea of industry as *auteur*. All of them are based in the broadcasting industry, since broadcasting has been an even slipperier object of analysis than film, for reasons that I hope will become clear. First, I will look into the increasingly prevalent contemporary practice of international television co-production in order to examine the *nation* as author. Next, I will examine the trials (literally) and tribulations of an early radio writer, Irna Philips, as she sought to establish just what *individual* authorship and originality meant in early US radio. Finally I will explore the idea of the broadcasting *network* as author, contrasting the authorial status of the BBC with US networks across the twentieth century. Each focus demands a different set of questions and points to divergent methodologies.

THE NATION AS AUTHOR

More than any other medium, broadcasting has been closely associated with the programmes and policies of its national governments, from the very beginning when the first regulatory decisions were made, to the present controversies over global media flows. Broadcasting was seen as a medium specifically called upon to unify nations, during peace and war, and whether taken under direct supervision of the state, held at arms-length, or regulated as private enterprise, radio and television received far more direct state intervention into their operations than other media.

Thus the nation took on a strong authorial role, shaping industry structures, regulating content and operations, and frequently initiating investigations into broadcasting's political and cultural effects. This can still be seen in the case of international co-production, now becoming one of most ubiquitous forms of television thanks to digital distribution. Many countries, particularly those with strong public broadcasters, exercise strict control over what can be considered a national production, and the intrusion of too much 'foreign' investment or influence can be a source of conflict.[1] Public broadcasters in particular operate under a mandate to promote and reflect their national culture, written into mission statements and worked out in restrictions on the percentage of 'imported' programs permissible in their schedules and strict rules as to when a co-produced program can be counted as 'national' (and thus qualified for national subsidy and grants).

Britain and the United States have had a long history of television co-production, as can be seen in the case of the American public television program, *Masterpiece,* which has featured British/American co-produced drama since the 1970s. With American public television providing a certain percentage of up-front funding for the high-budget literary adaptations that make up most of *Masterpiece*'s schedule, which are produced in Britain by British broadcasting companies and studios, the net result has been positive for both sides in terms of audiences and support of their general mission, but has often become a target of criticism along national lines. How much influence do American co-producers exercise on productions funded by the British public? How British are these programmes prominently featured on American public television? Such questions come up persistently both in industry discourse and in government investigations. Both sides are required by national mandates to assert their primary, or at least substantial, authorship over the dramas, while downplaying financial and creative detail that might throw those contentions into dispute. This makes for tricky terrain for the researcher, where assertions of creative control cannot be taken at face value. Now that more direct industry investment is flowing both ways—BBC America flourishes on most US cable systems, and Netflix pushes into the British market—the role of nation as author become more diffuse and perhaps even harder to discern, but it is clear that national policies and industrial interests still matter, once again circling around the issues of ownership and originality inherent in industrial cultural production.

IRNA PHILLIPS AND INDIVIDUAL AUTHORSHIP

These issues of ownership and originality inherent in industrial cultural production highlight another important source of authorial influence in the broadcasting industry—the role and definition of the individual author. Irna Phillips was an American radio innovator who is frequently referred to as 'the mother of soap opera' for pioneering the long-running daily serial drama, a form that came to dominate daytime radio schedules in the US. Both the nature of radio itself—invisible, broadcast 'live', often semi-improvised, with no visible lists of screen credits or any other permanent record of who did what—and the particular demands of the highly serialised style of program that became the hallmark of American radio and television created unique problems for establishing authorship in broadcasting, including Phillips' own. It led to a ground-breaking lawsuit file by Phillips against her employer, Chicago radio station WGN, that contributed to the formation of the Radio Writers Guild and to the contractual negotiations of authorial status that remain extremely central to media industries today (Hilmes 2013).

First, the backstory: A former schoolteacher trained in speech and theatre at Northwestern University, Phillips was hired in June 1930 by Henry Selinger, the manager of Chicago station WGN, to perform in a variety program. In September 1930, Phillips began writing what is remembered today as the first US soap opera, *Painted Dreams,* featuring the lives and loves of an immigrant Irish woman, her daughter Irene, and their lodger Sue Morton. Philips wrote all the scripts herself, as well as performing the role of the main character, Mother Moynihan. She was paid $25 a week for her efforts, as an employee of WGN.

The show was a success with audiences. Almost a year later, in September 1931, the station succeeded in selling the show to a sponsor; this prompted Phillips to take the unprecedented step of registering her first ten program scripts with the Copyright division of the US Patent Office 'claiming to be the author and owner [...] without notice or knowledge' of her employers at WGN.[2] The following April, for reasons never fully disclosed,

WGN fired Phillips, but the station went on producing *Painted Dreams*, using other writers. Phillips immediately filed a lawsuit against the station claiming that she had created the work and that it was her property, not the station's. Her petition was denied on two grounds: First, that as an employee of WGN, the serial was 'work for hire' and hence owned by the employer that paid her salary; second, that the basic concept for the series had been given to her by the station manager, Henry Selinger, making him the original author if anyone was. These were the two fundamental issues—ownership and originality—around which debates over broadcasting authorship would revolve in the years to come, and still does.

Phillips appealed this decision. Her rebuttal rested on the crucial link between originality and ownership, arguing that it was her detailed scripts and months-long elaboration and enactment of them that had created the show, not the basic, bare-bones concept given to her by Selinger. In response to her appeal, WGN developed at great length Selinger's claim to authorship of the show, stating that not only the basic idea—'a homely daytime serial involving an Irish mother, her daughter, and the daughter's friend'—but also a considerable amount of the setting, plot, and characterisation had been his.[3] The legal document compares Selinger's outline and Phillips' early scripts point by point, making a fascinating study of the complexities of determining what constitutes originality in a serial medium.

The case dragged on through the decade, ending in 1941 with a final defeat for Phillips—by this time herself a highly successful serial drama entrepreneur with her own production house, where she asserted ownership over other writers' work the way WGN had over hers. The lawsuit's tortuous deliberations reveal all the complexities of authorship in a medium like radio where storylines could go on for years, changing enormously over time, and where elements like performance, pacing, and aural style cannot be fully captured in a written script. Phillips' case set off alarms across the broadcasting industry, leading to the formation of important industry organisations still operating today whose task is explicitly to negotiate the status of authorship under conditions of mass production, such as the Writers' Guild of America and the Writers' Guild of Great Britain. These are key sites of authorial power in the contemporary media industry, all too often neglected by researchers but crucial to understanding the relationship between creative workers and an increasingly dispersed industry.

THE NETWORK AS AUTHOR

In the broadcasting industry, networks stand as the largest, most visible entities in terms of commissioning and distributing programmes and organising the broadcast flow into a daily and weekly schedule. Even in this era of online streaming and mobile viewing, the network retains its prominence as a sort of virtual venue (a 'place' where one can go, day after day, to connect with one's programs), despite the disruptive effects of various technologies going back to the DVD, which for the first time disassociated the program viewing experience from its 'authoring' network. Today we are more likely to refer to this function as 'branding', where some kind of unifying identity is imposed by all manner of paratextual discourses experienced both during and outside of the viewing experience: IDs, graphics, logos, memes, advertising, publicity, and so on (Johnson 2011).

But to consider the range of authorship positions available to networks across history, it is interesting to compare the dramatically different authorial status of the British Broadcasting Corporation (BBC) over most of its existence with that of the major American networks. For the first thirty-five years of its life, the BBC was Britain's only broadcaster, and even after competition was introduced in the 1950s it remained the primary source of British radio and television, garnering the majority of the viewing and listening audience. Crucial to its mission as the dominant public service broadcaster was a strong authorial stance, exercising highly centralised control over its programmes and schedules. It functioned somewhat like a Hollywood movie studio in its level of vertical integration, employing thousands of staff to write, direct, produce, perform, manage, publicise, and support these activities, as well as taking responsibility for its programmes in the eyes of the public and of the UK government.

Not until the deregulatory decades of the 1980s and 90s did the old BBC system begin to break apart, reducing the numbers of in-house creative staff under a new requirement for increased outsourcing of production. Though the BBC continues to produce many of its own programmes, not only for its home audiences but for viewers around the world, it is now far more likely to act as a commissioner of programmes from other producers, both domestic and foreign. Yet the BBC 'brand' is still strong and in fact quite valuable internationally, pointing to the persistent strength of its authorial function, which at many points it has gone to great length to protect. Thus it is difficult to imagine conducting research into television—or radio—in Britain without having to account for the authorial presence and influence of the BBC, even as it comes under various challenges.

In the United States, broadcasting networks formed under very different social and political conditions, as private commercial entities. Though originally taking a central creative role in the production of the programs sent out over owned or affiliated stations, by the early 1930s the networks' primary business had become the selling of airtime to outside producers, mainly commercial sponsors, who used radio and later television to advertise goods and services. The programmes themselves were largely produced by advertising agencies on behalf of their clients, and thus authorship in US broadcasting became highly diffuse, divided amongst thousands of different originating institutions—sponsors, agencies, independent production companies, individual stations, Hollywood studios, educational institutions, religious organisations—who retained ownership and creative control over their programs. Though as social and economic institutions the two early major networks, the National Broadcasting Company (NBC) and the Columbia Broadcasting System (CBS), were very strong and influential, their authorial standing and creative control remained weak, in direct contrast to the BBC (Hilmes and VanCour 2011).

By the late 1940s, however, the networks began to take steps to assert a stronger authorial presence, originating more 'sustaining' or non-sponsored programmes and attempting to build up a sense of coherent identity. Television increased the networks' desire to consolidate their control over the industry, and by the late 1960s they succeeded. For a period from the 1960s through the 1990s, the three major national networks[4] achieved a nearly BBC-like status in their ownership of and control over television programmes, even though most were produced by the television arms of Hollywood studios and a host of so-called independents—all highly dependent on the commissioning, investment, and promotion of the commercial network oligarchy. And while the 1980s and 1990s saw the intervention of new terrestrial networks (Fox, the CW, Univision) as well as hundreds of cable networks, many of them consolidated under conglomerate owners drawn from other arms of the media business (Disney, Universal, News Corporation), the broadcast networks remain a key site of identity, aggregation, and creative decision making. No single US network can match the domestic dominance of the BBC in Britain, but the network as *auteur* remains a powerful force (Hilmes 2007).

The assertion of authorship is essentially an assertion of responsibility: Who is primarily responsible for the creation of this text or practice? Therefore, where should an analysis of a particular media studies problem or phenomenon begin? For literature in the eighteenth century, the answer was the individual author. For some film scholars in the mid twentieth century, the answer was the film director. In the twenty-first century media industries, we look to analytical approaches that reflect the complexity of the media itself, such as production studies, brand analysis, cultural policy, convergence culture, transmedia and transnational perspectives. Yet authorship remains a crucial analytic, both as a concept and as a practice, to help us sort through the deconstructed landscape of media industry studies today.

THE THEORETICAL TAPESTRY OF MEDIA INDUSTRY RESEARCH

Hilmes' conceptualisations of the nation author, the individual author, and the network author may have been in direct reference to the broadcast industries, but the approaches taken here map on to my aforementioned three-fold model of conceiving of media industry studies: Hilmes' discussion of the nation as author, for instance, delves into political and social impacts, national policies, and regulatory economic power on shaping industry structures—*the societal context of the media industries*. Hilmes' exploration of what she calls the individual author, meanwhile, is most pointedly about identifying the ownership patterns, originality claims, and creative development strategies of individual agents within the media—*the corporate context of the media industries*. And Hilmes' consideration of the network author, finally, is essentially an exploration of how the media industries are positioned as meaningful across wider circuits such as agencies, sponsors, and educational institutions, as well as via the public domains of brand—*the discursive context of the media industries*.

In other words, Hilmes' contribution serves as a highly useful case study for demonstrating what sociologists might call the 'theoretical tapestry' of media industry research—that is, the overarching conceptual framework of this book, signalling just how these ideas of political economic, corporate, and discursive contexts of study might actually materialise in media industry research.[5] There are, in effect, multiple stages of production and multiple processes of industry workings, making it more important than ever to adopt more contextualised and holistic research methodologies.

Yet thinking so expansively does raise important methodological challenges for the researcher, many of which will be considered in the ensuing chapters where I focus on appropriate methodological tools for examining each of the three contexts of study in turn. But the very fact that the media industries are so sprawling and indeed so messy means that as researchers we cannot think in finite terms and in terms of clear boundaries. Instead, it is important to take a somewhat transmedial approach to the study of media industries—that is to say, to look across borders, to acknowledge the borderlines, to consider interconnected organisations and the cultural climates of their vast geographic differences, and so on. After all, today the media industries operate within a complex, convergent, multi-platform, digitised, trans- and inter-medial status of industrial operation, and so studying their workings within the ethos of contextualisation effectively means looking across these vast social thresholds.

And it is in that sense that we can claim that media industry studies is indeed about processes of understanding *contextualisation*. As Hilmes (2014) puts it, doing this kind of contextualised media industry research will 'bring us into examining structures, workings, and policies'—things that go beyond the text and place media within this very vital context of political economics, corporations, and discourse.

Looking across multiple thresholds also means adopting multiple methodological tools—making strategic use of *particular* methodologies for understanding *particular* aspects of a given media industry research question. Thus, as will be laid out across the next three chapters, I propose that political economy analysis continues to operate as a key framework for tracing connections between deep social structures and their impacts on media industry workings in ways that allow for insights into the media industries as an outcome of societal structures; interviews and ethnographic analysis, meanwhile, are crucial for understanding the corporate context of the media industries in ways that position media industries as a medium for shaping creative cultures via agency and collaboration; and, lastly, gathering ephemeral documentation—i.e., analysis of trade papers, magazines, promos, websites, social media, and other paratexts produced by industry practitioners—can provide important insights into the discursive context of the media industries and their wider culturalist functions.

And together, these three methodological approaches—in turn forging layers of contextualisation between the media industry's creative, productive, and cultural sites of operation—can enable the researcher to theorise complex authorial workings of anything from production to distribution, from branding to policymaking, from organisational management to professional ideologies, and so on and so forth. For as Hilmes (2014) has signalled, it may well be that authorship is a fundamental means of conceptualising the grand theoretical focus of what media industry studies actually is. The next chapter then examines the first of these three methodological approaches—ephemeral documentation analysis—theorising its value and potential applications.

NOTES

1. The Canadian content rules provide a particularly explicit system of national authorship guidelines.
2. *Irna Phillips vs. WGN Inc.* 'Petition for Leave to Appeal', Supreme Court of Illinois, February 1941: 3. B63, Irna Phillips collection, Wisconsin Historical Society (WHS).
3. 'Answer to Petition for Leave to Appeal', *Irna Phillips vs. WGN*, Supreme Court of Illinois, February 1941: 5–6. Irna Phillips collection, Wisconsin Historical Society (WHS).
4. NBC and CBS were joined by the American Broadcasting Company (ABC) in 1943.
5. Robert E. Park and Ernest W. Burgess famously used the term 'theoretical tapestry' in reference to the sociological work produced by doctoral students as part of the thinking behind the Chicago School of Ethnography in the twentieth century.

BIBLIOGRAPHY

Alasuutari, P. (1995). *Researching Culture: Qualitative Method and Cultural Studies*. London: SAGE.
Ashton, D., & Noonan, C. (Eds.). (2013). *Cultural Work and Higher Education*. Basingstoke: Palgrave Macmillan.
Barthes, R. (1978). The Death of the Author, in *Image, Music, Text*. Ed. and trans. by Stephen Heath. New York: Hill and Wang, pp. 142–148.
Bertrand, I., & Hughes, P. (2005). *Media Research Methods: Audiences, Institutions, Texts*. Basingstoke: Palgrave Macmillan.
Burke, P. (1980). *Sociology and History*. Boston: George Allen & Unwin Ltd..
Caldwell, J. T. (2008). *Production Culture: Industrial Reflexivity and Critical Practice in Film and Television*. Durham and London: Duke University Press.
Caldwell, J. T. (2015). Production Studies: Where Do We Go From Here?, Panel Presentation at the Conference of *New Directions in Film and Television Production Studies* (Bristol, April 14–15).

Caston, E. (2012). "Kick, Bollocks and Scramble": An Examination of Power and Creative Decision-Making in the Production Process During the Golden Era of British Music Videos 1995–2001. *Journal of British Cinema and Television,* 9(1), 96–110.

Caston, E. (2014). The Fine Art of Commercial Freedom: British Music Videos and Film Culture. *Scope: An Online Journal of Film and Television Studies, 26,* 1–18.

Caston, E. (2015). Equalities, Human Rights, and Heritage: The Need For an Industry-Academia Forum, Panel Presentation at the Conference of *New Directions in Film and Television Production Studies* (Bristol, April 14–15).

Caston, E. (2016). Not Another Article on the Author! God and Auteurs in Moving Image Analysis: Last Call for a Long Overdue Paradigm Shift. *Music Sound and the Moving Image.* Special Issue 'Musical Screens: Musical Inventions, Digital Transitions, Cultural Critique' (forthcoming).

Caston, E., Parti, N., Walker, N., & Sutton, C. (2000). Report on the Music Video Industry in 1998 and 1999. *Promo* (April).

Charvat, W. (1974). Literature as Business. In R. E. Spiller et al. (Eds.), *Literary History of the United States* (4th ed., pp. 960–968). New York: Macmillan.

Curran, J., Morley, D., & Walkerdine, V. (1996). *Cultural Studies and Communications.* New York: Arnold.

Doyle, G. (2015). PhD Workshop on Researching Media at a Time of Transition, presentation at the University of Glasgow (Glasgow, June 10).

Dwyer, P. (2015). Theorising Media Production: The Poverty of Political Economy, Panel Presentation at the Conference of *New Directions in Film and Television Production Studies* (Bristol, April 14–15).

Foucault, M. (1977). 'What is an Author?' Trans. Donald F. Bouchard and Sherry Simon. In Donald F. Bouchard (Ed.), *Language, Counter-Memory, Practice* (pp. 124–127). Ithaca, New York: Cornell University Press.

Giddens, A. (1984). *The Constitution of Society: Outline of the Theory of Structuration.* Cambridge: Polity Press.

Gilbert, N. (2001). *Researching Social Life.* London: SAGE.

Grainge, P., & Johnson, C. (2015). *Promotional screen industries.* New York: Routledge.

Gray, J., & Johnson, D. (Eds.) (2013). *A Companion to Media Authorship.* Chichester: Wiley-Blackwell.

Hilmes, M. (1999). *Hollywood and Broadcasting: From Radio to Cable.* Urbana: University of Illinois Press.

Hilmes, M. (Ed.) (2007). *NBC: America's Network.* Berkeley: University of California Press.

Hilmes, M. (2013). Never Ending Story: Authorship, Seriality, and the Radio Writers Guild. In J. Gray & D. Johnson (Eds.), *A Companion to Media Authorship* (pp. 181–199). Chichester: Wiley-Blackwell.

Hilmes, M. (2014). An Interview with Professor Michele Hilmes. *Industrial Approaches to Media – The University of Nottingham.* Available at: http://www.

nottingham.ac.uk/research/groups/isir/projects/industrial-approaches-to-media/index.aspx

Hilmes, M., & VanCour, S. (2007). Network nation: Writing broadcasting history as cultural history. In M. Hilmes (Ed.), *NBC: America's network* (pp. 308–322). Berkley: University of California Press.

Hobday, M. (1998). Product Complexity, Innovation and Industrial Organization. *Research Policy, 26,* 689–710.

Hobday, M., Rush, H., & Tidd, J. (2000). Innovation in Complex Products and System. *Research Policy, 29,* 793–804.

Holt, J., & Perren, A. (Eds.) (2009). *Media Industries: History, Theory, Method.* Chichester: Wiley Blackwell.

Horkheimer, M., & Adorno, T. (1944). The Culture Industry: Enlightenment as Mass Deception. In *The Dialectic of Enlightenment* (pp. 120–149). Trans. J. Cumming. New York: Continuum.

Jenkins, H. (2006). *Convergence Culture: Where Old and New Media Collide.* New York: New York University Press.

Johnson, C. (2011). *Branding Television.* New York and London: Routledge.

Johnson, C. (2013). The Mutual Benefits of Engaging with Industry. *CST Online.* Accessed December 3, 2015, from http://cstonline.tv/mutual-benefits

Johnson, R., Chambers, D., Raghuram, P., & Tincknell, E. (2004). *The Practice of Cultural Studies.* London: SAGE.

McDonald, P. (2013). Introduction: In focus—media industries studies. *Cinema Journal, 52*(3), 145–149.

Newsinger, J. (2015). The Infrapolitics of Cultural Practice: Uncovering Hidden Transcripts in Production Studies, Panel Presentation at the Conference of *New Directions in Film and Television Production Studies* (Bristol, April 14–15).

Passel, E. V. (2015). Film and Television in Flanders: Analysing Remuneration for Screenwriters, Directors and Actors, Panel Presentation at the Conference of *New Directions in Film and Television Production Studies* (Bristol, April 14–15).

Sarris, A. (1962). Notes on the Auteur Theory in 1962. *Film Culture, 27,* 1–8.

Seale, C. (1998). *Researching Society and Culture.* London: SAGE.

Siegert, G., Gerth, M., & Rademacher, P. (2011). Brand identity-driven decision making by journalists and media managers—The MBAC model as a theoretical framework. *The International Journal on Media Management, 13*(1), 53–70.

CHAPTER 5

Media Industries as Structure: Objectivism and the Societal Context

Matthew Freeman

What are the broader social, economic, and political factors at work in shaping the creative impetus of the media industries and the media they ultimately produce? This chapter focuses on answering this question by building on what Giddens called the structure (i.e., the deep political and economic forces in society that, for our purposes, can be seen to underpin how media industries function). This allows us to consider how the study of such deep political and economic forces in society remains key to considering the larger workings of media industries as outcomes of larger societal forces. I begin by exploring the first of my three contexts of media industry study—the *societal context*, which I have defined previously as where the operations of the media industries emerge as the outcome of deep structures in society.

This chapter first considers some of the conceptual considerations of embarking on media industry research where this societal context is the primary object of study—looking at the relevance of what Mosco (1996: 46) famously identified as 'the study of [...] power relations that mutually constitute the production, distribution, and consumption of resources'

M. Freeman (✉)
Bath Spa University, Bath, UK
e-mail: m.freeman@bathspa.ac.uk

on contemporary media industry studies. In so doing, I also consider the idea of what is known as 'objectivism' in business and management studies, linking this ontological notion to political economy in media industry studies. Second, the link to more ontological ideas of objectivism allows me to consider a sociology of media industry studies, pointing to the value of economic sociology and methods such as social network analysis to particular aspects of media industry studies. Third, and to demonstrate the study of the societal context via political economy, Petros Iosifidis provides a case study looking at the political economy of television sports rights. Lastly, I conceptualise studying media industries within a historical–societal context. Ultimately, this chapter will showcase how these methodological and ontological approaches—drawn from the likes of business and management, economic, law, and indeed aspects of sociology—can allow for a crucial understanding of the underpinning *societal context* of the media industries.

POLITICAL ECONOMY: CONCEPTUALISING STUDIES OF SOCIAL CONTEXT

Media industries are so pervasive in terms of their communicative influence, their social standing, their economic imperatives, and their artistic functions that it makes considerable sense to consider *a sociology of media industries*. There are many ways of seeing the media industries, and one of these would be to understand media industries as what sociologists might call a 'structure'—that is, as macroeconomic entities that operate as an outcome of existing and notably deep forces in society.

As has been shown earlier in this book, doing media industry studies most basically means *contextualisation*—looking at industry as the object of study around which the researcher tries to explore how larger economic, historical, social, cultural, or political variables may shape or impact more concrete industrial practices and policies. Hanne Bruun (2015) agrees, arguing that 'as scholars we need to understand media's cultural–political role in a profoundly changing media landscape.' For Bruun (2015), 'a productive way to do this is to do research that actually involves the producers and the industries as organisations and cultural–political agents in specific contexts in order to do research on an informed level.' While interviewing may be a means of engaging with media producers and practitioners, as I explore in Chap. 6, how exactly can these contexts of socio-economic-political specificity be analysed?

In spite of Bruun's merging of culture and politics, for a long time the latter was segmented—alongside economy and mass-market forces—as a methodological study of relationships between the media and wider concerns. The *political economy* approach is to understand how the way that media organisations operate (and the products they provide) is shaped by the economic and political context in which they operate. Or as Havens et al. (2009: 235) elaborate, the analysis of political economy of the media concerns a 'focus on the larger level operations of media institutions', with 'a general inattention [paid] to entertainment programming [and] the role of human agents.' As Petros Iosifidis explains in his case study, political economy is occasionally tied up with Adorno and Horkheimer's critique of the 'culture industry' as a political and economic behemoth designed to manipulate the masses into submission. Janet Wasko and Eileen R. Meehan (2013: 150) note that many political economists have been 'denounced as economic reductionists, accused of ignoring media workers, artefacts, and audiences [...] misrepresenting the blame of "evil capitalists" for the media's content and operations.'[1]

Similarly, political economy might be argued to imply an over-emphasis on aspects of the media that carry associations of the purely mechanical. Words such as 'production', 'mass-market', 'distribution', and even 'industry' itself imply a move away from studying the artistry and creativity of the media in favour of a more 'business-like' analysis. And this is not untrue. But as Paul Dwyer (2015) discusses, conceptualising the media industries in terms of production lines, manufacturing, and deep social structures risks minimising the complex differences between the production of a piece of media and the production of any other mass-market consumer product, such as a car. Dwyer (2015) acknowledges that while the Hollywood studio system of the mid-twentieth century once worked on a system of management and assembly line construction where bits of production (scriptwriting, directing, editing, etc.) were divided up across the studio (much like production on a car would be divided up across a factory), it can be argued that talking about mass production in the context of cars makes more sense than if talking about films, for example. After all, with a car, one design is used to make millions of products over and over again. With films, however, one design (i.e., a script) makes just one product. Even in the Classical Hollywood age and its highly structured studio system of the past, when a new film was green-lit a whole new assembly line was formed. In other words, while it remains problematic to take an all-encompassing attitude, the media industry, singular conceived, is the result of unifying social structures; political economy nevertheless considers factors like economic structures, political policies, and societal influence in ways that, if conceived as multiplicities, make its focus highly useful for doing media industry studies.

TAKING AN OBJECTIVISM APPROACH

Alleviating such claims of reductionism and simplification perhaps means considering the approaches and perspectives taken by disciplines besides media industries studies—most notably those of both business and management studies and sociology. Bryman and Bell (2011: 7) note that 'business research methods tend on the whole to be more eclectic and explained in less detail than in some other social sciences such as sociology.' Yet conceptualising the societal context of media industries via a combined use of business studies and sociology has much merit. In one sense, the philosophy of studying the societal context of the media industries—focusing, that is, on the how macroeconomic considerations enable media industries to operate the way they do—shares much in common with what is sometimes called 'critical realism' in philosophy, business studies, and other disciplines. As Bhaskar (1989: 2) discusses, 'we will only be able to understand—and so change—the social world if we identify the structures at work that generate those events and discourses [...] These structures are not spontaneously apparent in the observable patterns of events; they can only be identified through the practical and theoretical work of society.'

Moreover, in identifying an ontological approach to dealing with a focus such as this, in another sense to return to the discipline of business and management studies is particularly useful—in this case, specifically, its concept of 'objectivism'. As Bryman and Bell (2011: 21) explain, 'objectivism is an ontological position that asserts that social phenomena and their meanings have an existence that is *independent of social actors*. It implies that social phenomena and the categories that we use in everyday discourse have an existence that is independent or separate from actors' [emphasis added]. In other words, and to apply this ontological position to the study of media industries, the views of objectivism are akin to those of political economy discussed previously and would assume that the workings of all media industries are ultimately driven by the far larger structures that govern society.

Before I consider methods for examining this societal context, let's now briefly consider what the objects of study within this particular context might be.

POLITICAL ECONOMY: OBJECTS OF STUDY

Though media industry studies seeks to examine a wide array of questions and concerns, be they policymaking, production, distribution, creative labour, marketing, etc., the question of power is one that has informed much thinking. As Schlesinger indicated previously, much media-based research once typically focused on the idea of gatekeeping, studying ownership and communicative power in news organisations, for example. Ina Bertrand and Peter Hughes (2005) also focus on media organisations in their methodology of studying industrial aspects of the media, privileging the ways in which media 'institutions are codified, like law and religion' (2005: 109). For Bertrand and Hughes (2005), a study of media institutions affords an understanding of change, ownership, censorship, and indeed the power of industrial gatekeeping.

Concepts such as gatekeeping—that is, exploring who makes decisions as to what goes into a media product and what does not—has become important in terms of understanding media production, not to mention in terms of understanding the economic workings of media companies and industries. But the study of media industries in this way has also lent itself to examining broader questions of industry practices and decisions, of power structures and operational routines and work habits in the media industries. When studying media industries in the societal context we might map the connections and relationships between societal forces such as ideology, regulation, politics, education, and economics, and specifically how such forces inform the divisions, departments, control, staffing, and functions—with these latter institutional manifestations here emerging as the outcome of the former societal pressures. The mapping of media industries in such a way can, at its best, work to reveal important insights into production hierarchies, into questions of priority, into corporate synergy, and into commercial imperatives, as Petros Iosifidis now explains.

CASE STUDY: THE POLITICAL ECONOMY OF TELEVISION SPORTS RIGHTS

Petros Iosifidis
The following case study as a whole will offer an outline of how political economy has come to operate across different aspects of media, cultural, and communication studies, and I will attempt to outline a methodology for how best to implement this approach for research. My contribution

sits alongside this, offering a case study where I reflect quite openly about how I myself use political economy in my own research, how exactly I went about doing this from a methodological standpoint, and also how effective it has been as a method of research. I therefore frame my contribution around a piece of research where I took a political economy approach. More specifically, this case study contribution aims to think about the how's and why's of using this approach for television sports rights. I have also used a political economy theory for the analysis of public service broadcasting (see Iosifidis 2007, 2010), media ownership (Iosifidis 1997, 2011), and social media (Iosifidis and Wheeler 2016).

POLITICAL ECONOMY PARADIGM

Let me start by summarising the main aspects of the political economy paradigm. Within the domain of political economy, *critical political economy* is taking a different stance than *classical political economy*, with the former providing a critique of the impact of market mechanisms and the economy on society and the latter considering market forces as a positive trend, offering enhanced choice for consumers (Harrison 2006). Since its inception in the 1970s, the critical political economy approach has been concerned with the structural development of the media under capitalism. It focuses on themes such as media growth and power, the expansion of corporate reach and influence, and the trends toward media privatisation, commercialisation, and reregulation. The central thesis of the theory is that there exist economic structures of dominance in the media and communication sectors that impact negatively on the range of views and opinions disseminated by the media. As a result, what prevails in a given society is a hegemonic set of ideas, or a 'dominant ideology'.

Critical political economy asserts that privately owned media can be viewed as instruments of class domination in order to maintain the status quo. A key text illustrating the arguments for this stance is Herman and Chomsky's *Manufacturing Consent* (1988), which discusses a 'propaganda model' in the American news media, incorporating five filters that determine news content, ownership, funding, flak, sources, and ideologies. Some scholars have criticised this model on grounds that ownership, as a dominant factor, does not necessarily determine news content as owners, advertisers, and key political personnel 'cannot always do as they wish [because] they operate within structures which constrain as well as facilitate, imposing limits as well as offering opportunities [and] analyzing the nature and sources of these limits is a key task for a critical political economy of the future' (Golding and Murdock 1991: 16).

Herman and Chomsky (1988) have defended the validity of their model by arguing that it focuses on media *behavior*, rather than media *effects*. On a broader perspective, critical political economy attempts to incorporate historical and contextual aspects, without however underestimating the significance of vested interests and other commercial considerations in media production and consumption. According to Flew (2007: 31), the political economy critique of mass communication theory relates to the rediscovery of the Marxist stance towards capitalism, which connected this critique of media in liberal democratic societies to a wider conceptual understanding of the bases of social order in class-divided societies. From this perspective, the theory asserts that developments in global media could be understood as one dimension of the transformation of contemporary capitalism.

In his classic study in the field, *The Political Economy of Communication*, Mosco (1996) argued that the tradition of political economy pays emphasis on three aspects: an analysis of the historical transformation and social shifts; an examination of the social world as a whole, in which the media occupy a large part; and a critical interest in promoting social values and the democratisation of media systems. Thus from a critical political economy perspective, the role of the media in global capitalism needs to be viewed from an angle which combines historical, structural, political, and cultural criticism.

First, the media could be assessed in the context of broad developments and processes of capitalism—systemic crises (for example, the recession of the mid-1970s or the 2008–09 economic slowdown); the production of new types of commodities and endless commercialisation; the growth of multinational corporations; advances in technology, marketing, and advertising which reduce the time between production and consumption.

Second, a structural analysis of the media—political economy's core theme—is needed to get a grasp of the changing institutional arrangements of the media sectors as a result of mergers, acquisitions, joint ventures, and other types of integration and amalgamation that could lead to high levels of concentration of media ownership and a threat to political pluralism and cultural diversity. Garnham (1990) referred to structures of domination based upon class relations and argued that political economy views class (the structure of access to the means of production and distribution) as the main reason for the structure of domination. Political economists called for a transformation of the media and their underlying structures to make them more open and accountable. Murdock and Golding (2000) provided a critique of the changing balance between public and commercial media, the reduction of government regulation, and the 1980's/1990's privatisation of state-owned media and telecommunications enterprises.

Third, critical political economy is informed by an understanding of the cultural issues that result from the economic logic of media commercialisation. This, according to Ampuja (2004: 73–4), requires a renewed focus on commodification and consumerism, two phenomena that formed the main target of the Frankfurt School's critique of the 'culture industry'. Strange (1988) and Flew (2007: 32) have added another element—that is, the understanding that critical political economy must be *global*, as the insistence upon a global perspective has been central to the continued and renewed development of the theory.

There are, however, limitations to the political economy approach, expressed mainly by cultural studies scholars. In fact, cultural studies and political economy have frequently considered each other as a competitor, rather than an ally. The differences between the two paradigms have revolved around the question of articulating developments in the economic and cultural spheres. The debates between scholars representing the two disciplines have been fierce and focused on whether one theory over-emphasises the economic sphere (which is cultural studies' key criticism of political economy) or whether the other theory over-emphasises the cultural sphere (which is political economy's key criticism of cultural studies) (Grossberg 1991, 1996; Garnham 1990).

THE POLITICAL ECONOMY OF TELEVISION SPORTS RIGHTS

I will now turn to the rationale of using political economy for analysing television sports rights, demonstrating how this approach might actually manifest. There is a symbiotic relationship between media and sports organisations. On the one hand, sport provides a valuable source of content for media organisations. Whilst on the other, the media (mainly television broadcasters) provide an increasingly important source of revenue for sports organisations (either directly from the purchase of broadcast rights, or indirectly via exposure for sponsors). As with actual sporting contests, however, within the bounds of this relationship, all of the participants are 'playing to win'. Broadcasters compete against one another for lucrative sports rights contracts, as well as against sporting organisations in a contest to secure the 'best' price for the rights on offer. Sports organisations also compete to promote their sport in a contest for public attention with other sporting events and organisations. And finally, at risk of stretching the analogy, there is also an ongoing contest between politicians, regulators, sporting organisations, and broadcasters over the legal and regulatory framework for sports broadcasting. My co-authored book *The Political Economy of Television Sports Rights* (Evens et al. 2013) and subsequent article (Evens et al. 2015) were concerned with understanding how these contests and, in particular, the relationship between media and sports organisations has been (and is) shaped by a combination of economic, political, socio-cultural, and technological forces.

The focus of the above publications is on market and regulatory issues (rather than issues of representation and/or audience behaviour) and as a result these texts adopted an analytical approach focused on what is often termed the 'political economy of the media'. As already mentioned, the political economy approach to understanding the media is concerned with how the way that media organisations behave (and the content they provide) is shaped by the economic and political context in which they operate. More specifically, my analysis of the relationship between media and sports organisations took place against the backdrop of two key developments. First, the last couple of decades have witnessed a period of almost constant technological change within the media industries, which has seen the development of new broadcast delivery technologies, such as satellite and digital television, as well as the growth of new media technologies, chiefly the Internet. To date at least, the former has had a more significant impact on sports broadcasting than the latter, and therefore the book serves to highlight the continued primacy of television broadcasting. Whilst not seeking to understate the potential impact of new media technologies on sports broadcasting markets and their regulation, the book emphasises the unrivalled capacity of live television broadcasting to provide a focal point for national and global audiences (for example, the Olympic Games; FIFA World Cup finals; the NFL Super Bowl), as well as a major source of revenue for both broadcasters and sports organisations (for example, rights to English Premier League football, US Major League Baseball rights, Indian Premier League cricket).

Secondly, digital technologies and market developments have also been shaped by a general shift towards the 'marketisation' of broadcasting, particularly in Europe and the US, but also throughout much of the rest of the world (Murdock 2000; Murdock and Wasko 2007; Freedman 2008: 50–2; Hesmondhalgh 2007: 105–36). Inspired by neoliberal ideas, over the last three decades marketisation has been pursued through four major policy and/or regulatory interventions, employed in various combinations (Evens et al. 2013: 5–6):

- Privatisation (the sale of public assets to private investors). Whereas in the US there were relatively few public assets to be sold in the first place, numerous European governments have overseen the complete or partial privatisation of publicly owned broadcasters (for example, TF1 in France) and telecommunications operators (for example, Deutsch Telekom in Germany).
- Liberalisation (opening previously restricted markets to new entrants). For example, the 1996 US Telecommunications Act allowed for cable and telecommunications companies to enter each others' markets and relaxed restrictions on cross-media ownership. Similarly, during the late 1980s and 1990s, EU directives facilitated the opening up to competition of both European broadcasting (Television without Frontiers, renamed Audiovisual Media Services) and telecommunications markets.
- Reorienting of regulation (away from the defence of the public interest, to the promotion of 'fair' competition). In Europe, this trend is best illustrated by the increased influence of the European Commission's Competition directorate over key areas of media regulation, such as mergers and the definition of 'state aid' with regards to public service broadcasters (Wheeler 2004). In the US, the removal of long-standing public interest regulations during the late 1980s and 1990s, such as the Fairness Doctrine and Financial Interest and Syndication (Fin-Syn) rules, could also be seen to represent the prioritisation of competition (and free speech) concerns over any wider interpretation of the public interest.
- Corporatisation (urging or obliging publicly financed organisations to seek additional sources of income and to maximise their market value). For example, successive British governments have urged the BBC to pursue commercial opportunities (mostly overseas) via its commercial arm, BBC Worldwide, and also to reduce its operating costs (Born 2004). Alongside new developments in broadcasting technology, such as encryption and digitalisation, these political initiatives have facilitated the growing 'commodification'

of broadcasting. Perhaps most notably, throughout Europe the universality of broadcasting traditionally offered by public service broadcasters has been eroded by the growth of pay TV, and even in the US the main free-to-air commercial networks face increased competitive pressure from pay TV services available via cable and satellite. All of which means that 'more and more television services are offered for sale at a price and [are] available only to those who can afford to pay' (Murdock 2000: 43).

By adopting a political economy approach my work has highlighted how professional sport has developed into a highly valuable global industry. The main focus has been on the role played by the media, and particularly television broadcasting, in the development of sport in both economic and cultural terms. Specifically, on the one hand, sports organisations and television broadcasters have built a synergetic relationship that has allowed both to further their commercial interests. In this sense, it could be argued that the commodification of sport has served the interests of all the main participants within the sports–media–business complex, including media conglomerates, marketing agencies, brands and sponsors, sports event organisers, sports associations, and even professional athletes (although perhaps not always sports fans). Just as significantly, on the other hand, in many countries free-to-air television coverage of sports events and competitions, most notably by public service broadcasters and terrestrial commercial networks, has facilitated shared viewing experiences, which have fostered a sense of national identity and cultural citizenship. To begin with at least, the broadcasting of major sporting events played a key role in the development of sport into a key part of popular culture. Paradoxically, then, free-to-air sports broadcasting provided the foundation on which the highly commercialised sports industry of today is built. Following the marketisation of broadcasting from around the 1980s onwards, in many countries the availability of at least some key sports competitions and events on free-to-air television has been eroded and as a result the contribution of sports broadcasting to cultural citizenship has been partially undermined. Policy intervention is therefore required to preserve live free-to-air television coverage of major sporting events. At the same time, across the world, pay TV broadcasters have used exclusive deals for the television rights to premium sporting events as a means to establish a dominant market position. In such cases, regulatory intervention is also required to ensure improved competition in the broadcasting market.

One of the key parts of my research examined how the contrasting perspectives on television and sport—economic and cultural—have been reflected in different approaches to the regulation of sports broadcasting. First, competition policy aims to facilitate free, fair, and effective competition (both the upstream and downstream) in the sports broadcasting market. And, secondly, sector-specific media regulation, in this case, major events legislation (also commonly referred to as 'listed events' or 'anti-siphoning' legislation) aims to guarantee the public's right to information and preserve free access to television coverage of major national or international sporting events. There have been repeated calls from pay TV broadcasters and some sports organisations to relax both of these strands of regulation. In the book we have made the case for a regulatory approach that seeks to balance the commercial priorities of broadcasters and sports organisations with the wider social and cultural benefits citizens gain from free-to-air sports broadcasting. Based on the findings presented in eight country reports, we concluded that in many cases the balance between commerce and culture in sports broadcasting has shifted too far in favour of the commercial interests of dominant pay TV broadcasters and sports organisations seeking to maximise their income from the sale of broadcast rights. As a result, citizens often face either the loss of access to television coverage of key sporting events and competitions and/or rising bills from pay TV and pay-per-view services. Against this background, we contend that national governments, as well as supranational regulatory bodies (such as the EU) should undertake the following actions: first, resist pressure from pay TV broadcasters and/or sporting organisations to relax or abolish existing legislation designed to preserve free-to-air coverage of major sporting events; and secondly, apply the existing competition rules more vigorously and with more emphasis on the economic and cultural specificities of the sports broadcasting markets.

To summarise, my research adopted a political economy approach that provided a comparative analysis of the regulation of television sports broadcasting, examining how contrasting perspectives on television and sport—economic and socio-cultural—have been reflected in two main approaches to the regulation of sports broadcasting: competition law and major events legislation. The results of this analysis suggest that in many cases, the balance between commerce and culture in sports broadcasting has shifted too far in favour of the commercial interests of dominant pay TV operators and sports organisations. In effect, I made a case for the pursuit of an approach to sports broadcasting regulation that seeks to balance the commercial priorities of broadcasters and sports organisations with the wider cultural benefits citizens gain from free-to-air sports broadcasting.

ECONOMIC SOCIOLOGY: NETWORK ANALYSIS

To clarify, Iosifidis' demonstration shows how a political economy of the media concerns the larger-level operations of media institutions, focusing on how these operations are shaped by economic and political forces. And it is in that sense that political economy remains a highly valuable tool for understanding the *societal context* of the media industries, despite political economy often seen as the opposite of cultural studies, as Iosifidis explained above. As Alisa Perren (2013) also states, 'media industry studies, at least as Jennifer Holt and I conceptualized it, was a useful frame because it enabled us [...] a means of moving past well-worn debates about political economy 'versus' cultural studies once and for all. Media industry studies, from our perspective, is both. It does both.'

But if political economy emphasises the embeddedness of economic activity within larger institutions, tracing how economic and political institutions have affected the behaviours of those institutions beneath them, then the subfield of economic sociology—emerging within sociology around the 1970s—shares important methodological facets important for this more nuanced study of the media industries. As has been hinted throughout this book, sociology is useful for conceptualising the study of media industries because as a discipline it thinks both top-down and bottom-up: Sociological thinking would consider the deep structures of economics, say, and the actions of small communities, not as opposing ideological perspectives or bodies of knowledge but rather as the shared social workings of human agency. Sociology considers social behaviour through the lens of history, networks, and institutions. Also significant is the way that sociology opts not to carve out simple categories separating the likes of politics, economics, law, and anthropology from one another. As Bauman and May (2001: 4) put it, 'there is no natural division of the human world.'

All of which is to say that, when studying the media industries, tracing how economic and political forces in society shape industrial operations means focusing on specific networks and relationships between macro and micro elements—between, say, the global media industry and professional sport rights. Or as another example, while assessing the impact of UK politics on the UK film industry would likely lead to an unwieldy research project, studying the networks between the policymakers in a regulatory body and the stakeholders within a film organisation would allow for a clearer understanding of how societal forces can shape media industry operations.

And it is in that sense that *network analysis*—a methodology derived from sociology in the 1930s and typically taught in business schools—becomes a key methodology for actually doing media industry studies. Mark S. Mizruchi (2007: 3) describes network analysis as being best suited to thinking about deep sociological structures but from a far more micro perspective, and so with individual actors or organisations being its primary focus. As Mizruchi (2007: 8) explains at length:

> Network analysis is based on the idea that the most important components of social life rest neither in the formal institutions under which actors operate nor in the individual attributes and traits with which they are identified. Rather, the most important aspect of social life, according to network theorists, is the nature of the relations that actors have with one another. These relations can be mapped into a structure, network analysts suggest, and the structure of the resulting network determines to a great extent the nature of the relations within it. It is less important to know that an actor is a white, middle-class, Protestant male, for example, than to know the specific constellation of relations within which the person is situated.

Mizruchi (2007) demonstrates how network analysis is useful for addressing the debates in political economy over the relation between corporations and the state, for instance. And lest we forget, media industries are themselves networks—networks of communication, of creativity, and production, closely intertwined as they are with audience consumption habits and larger societal functions and regulatory patterns. Importantly, Mizruchi (2007: 12) bases his rationale to make use of network analysis within a political economy framework on the fact that, historically, ever since large corporations were consolidated in the United States, 'these firms were connected with one another through what were termed "corporate interlock networks".' As has been noted earlier in this book, the rise of what many would call 'convergences' in the media industries means that acknowledging these networks of corporate interlocks makes considerable sense, and also provides researchers with a clearer trajectory through which to examine influences and impacts between macro forces and micro workings. Taking this sociological approach to political economy, as Mizruchi (2007: 15) has shown, provides a means of examining behavioural consequences of interfirm network ties, and can indeed be applied to the subfield of media industries in ways that may afford insight and interpretation into what I have defined as the *societal context* of media industries—allowing for opportunities to understand the operations of the media industries as emerging from deep structures in society.

POLITICAL ECONOMY: CONCEPTUALISING MEDIA INDUSTRY HISTORY

Given this particular focus in media industries on examining wider societal contexts and tracing connections between the macro and the micro, Wasko and Meehan (2013: 156) have questioned whether the turn to this more holistic political economy approach to analysing contextual impacts on media industries is really an 'attempt to create a stripped-down, more acceptable, apolitical economy or a meaner, broader, more relevant cultural studies', especially given the calls for media industry studies to be both *for* and *about* the media industries. Wasko and Meehan may well be correct in this thinking, for, as Caston (2015) has stressed, the media industries see the real value of media academics as being able to fully contextualise their work.

Thinking more 'apolitically' is in line with the work of the historian, whose job is to study human societies but is 'concerned with the particular, the unrepeatable, the unique' (Burke 1980: 33). Studying the societal context of the media industries in historical circles seems entirely in line with the more sociological approach of this book, since social systems have patterns of social relation that naturally change over time; the changing nature of space and time determines the interaction of social relations and therefore structure in much the same way that the changing nature of societal forces such as politics and economics will naturally reshape the workings of media industries over time. And yet a notable concern of media industry studies—one closely tied to the political economy approach of tracing connections between wider contexts and media industry practice—is the question of whether the shift towards impacting and even changing the current working conditions and strategies of the media industries will make historical research far more marginalised in favour of contemporary studies. As McDonald (2013: 146) notes, 'in the interests of timeliness, much work on media industries has focused on contemporary developments, and although this work is undoubtedly essential, it does invite the question—How can the historiography of media industries be developed to situate the now and the new within longer term patterns of continuity and change?' Elinor Groom (2014) also touches on this issue, arguing that 'no matter how many times historians reiterate that anything and everything that happens is historical, history continues to be seen as something different to contemporary media industry studies. Often this is because the experience of researching the past is different to the experience of researching the present.' Explains Groom (2014),

> [e]ven when the methods are the same, analysing something that has already happened is different to studying phenomena in the moment that it is happening. Archives are viewed primarily as repositories of historical evidence, and by "historical" I mean the received understanding of the *word*, meaning "from the past". So it might be argued that the use of archives is irrelevant for media industry research, which is concerned with understanding how the media works and operates, which implies "in the present". Yet the archives do provide evidence of industry, and if you are lucky that evidence will be preserved so that you can understand how that industry worked when it was in operation.

Let us also not forget that studies of history have been crucial to the emergence of media industry studies as a subfield in recent years. McDonald (2013: 147–148) explains how 'it was through the revisionist "historical turn" that Film Studies first began any concerted engagement with industry, [as] the workings, practices, and pleasures of film became situated within wider contextual circumstances, including the industrial conditions of film's very existence.' Yet from a methodological standpoint, part of the problem in doing historical media industry research is the difficulty of openly acknowledging—and often battling—with the incongruent, incoherent, indecisive pull of history itself. David Hesmondhalgh (2007) famously identifies that media industries operate in a complex struggle between continuity and change. Some industry practices, he says, remain the same over time, while some are new, and many others are a fraught combination of the old and the new. As media industry researchers, therefore, we must often theorise entirely different conceptual models for examining what it is to be a historical form or precedent of media industry activity during the contexts and structures of the past, rather than simply trying to apply the media industry's present incarnations to the contexts and structures of the past.

But from a methodological standpoint, one question still remains: Why do media industry history? If this subfield of research is being conceptualised as that which becomes both *about* and potentially *for* media industries, then what is the value of such historical research? Bertrand and Hughes (2005: 114) show how historical studies of the media industries can reveal new narratives about impacts and catalysts of change over time, further noting how such research might often cross the cultural studies/ media studies disciplinary border. More than providing stories though, and as if in direct response to McDonald's earlier query, Caldwell (2015) points out that the histories of media industries are something that we, as scholars, can *give* to the media industries, because knowledge of the histories of media is something that industry personnel are not likely to have the time to go and look into themselves, despite this knowledge of the past being incredibly important and helpful to current practices.

And as these kinds of new narratives about impacts and catalysts of change over time are identified, it is useful to return to what sociologists would call the 'structure'—that is, the deep societal systems or 'entities composed of mutually dependent parts' (Burke 1980: 42). Explains Burke (1980: 42),

> [t]o speak of the "social structure" of seventeenth-century England, say, is to suggest that the major institutions (king, church, Parliament, guilds, manors, and so on), and the major groups in society (peers, gentry, yeomen, craftsmen, and so on) depended on one another, in the sense that a change in one group or institution would be followed by changes in others.

As stated in Chap. 4, media industry studies is partly about understanding the relationships between structure (social hierarchies, political forces, economic motives, policies, etc.) and agency (how people create and produce, how teams are formed, how media and audiences are conceptualised, etc.). Thus the role of the historical media industry researcher—at least when looking through the lens of the societal context of study—is to interrogate how macro components of a social structure (industrialisation, consumerism, shifts in regulation policy, and so on) impact changes in more local media industry workings (professional practices, corporate policies, distribution strategies, and so on), with a sociologically thinking methodology, such as network analysis which is a useful tool for conceptualising these links.

POLITICAL ECONOMY: DOING MEDIA INDUSTRY HISTORY

What, though, does such a historical political economy approach look like? Precisely *which* histories are we talking about exactly? How do we decide to piece together fragments of a historical moment (i.e., via which political movements, which cultural trends, which social activities, etc.?), and why should certain fragments be understood as integral to particular narratives of media industry histories? Broadly speaking, does the social structure inform the media industries, or do the media industries inform the social structure? Indeed, what is 'context' in the context of media industry history? And, perhaps most significantly of all, how can we begin to conduct applied scholarly research about media industries when those industries in question exist in the distant past, out of date and very often out of reach?

Allow me to demonstrate an answer to these questions via reference to my own research into the industrial history of transmedia storytelling. Here, my aim was to understand how the social, economic, cultural, and even political moments of the early twentieth century all worked to inform the way that media industries told fictional stories across multiple media forms. And achieving this aim meant using a kind of network analysis, in the broadest sense, to make sense of macro-historical social developments as that which informed more micro-storytelling capabilities.

Consider this example. Advertising at the turn of the twentieth century—a fast-developing industry and system of social and commercial communication—provides us with a source of early transmedia storytelling (Freeman 2014a). Fiction writers such as *The Wonderful Wizard of Oz*'s L. Frank Baum made use of the emerging advertising tools of the early twentieth century, including newspaper comic strips, printed maps, paper booklets, and newspaper adverts as a means of narrating parts of the *Wizard of Oz* story across multiple media forms. Of course, this implies that transmedia storytelling, as a specifically historical practice of the emerging media industries, was constantly changing form and was, essentially, everywhere within US society at that time—transcending everything from the giant billboards on the side of buildings to the artistic arrangements in shop windows, from the media forms of newspaper comic strips to, eventually, the cinema and the radio. Each of the various forms served to attract an audience's attention with storytelling before steering them elsewhere, across additional platforms to other related narratives in consumer and media products in ways that would now be called transmediality (Freeman 2014a, 2015). In other words, transmedia storytelling, at this time at least, was a direct product of the early twentieth century's emerging social climate—namely, industrialisation and consumer culture—and simultaneously of the economic and political ideologies that underpinned and exemplified modern advertising in this time.

In other words, thinking sociologically about the media industries—applying frameworks of social structure with a network analysis in line with political economic approaches of media industries—afforded in this case a direct multiperspectival understanding of how marketing, mass communication, consumer culture, branding, and so on—provided a social catalyst for the emergence of particular storytelling strategies in and across the American media industries of the early twentieth century. When engaging with the possible history—or histories—of media industries we must therefore work harder than ever to identify the connections between industry and its societal context. Understanding the past activities of the media industries means comprehending those industries not simply through the study of their outputs, but also through the broader activities of surrounding socio-political-economic developments.

A logical line of questioning then might ask the following: What does it mean to understand an industrial media practice as a historical social system? What did this practice look like as part of the economy and culture of a specific historical setting—and what economic, political, social, and/or cultural role(s) did it have within that historical setting? Yet part of the real value of historicising the practices of the media industries can be to re-understand those practices as simultaneously emerging from very different social-historical forces, whilst also operating as the social blueprints that would later inform the decisive components of our contemporary media landscape.

Hanne Bruun (2015) agrees with this line of questioning, arguing that 'historical approaches are very productive, not media history proper, but media development approaches trying to grasp the multi-factor and deeply contextual reasons for industry change.' Bruun's distinction between 'media history proper' and 'media development approaches' is highly significant, for while traditional media history may wish to take a more inward-looking approach to its research focus, using a historical developmental approach affords a richly outward-looking, contextualised view of how the cultural, political, social, and economic trends of history impacted technological changes, media production policies, audience segmentation, and so on.

Indeed, many of the practices and activities that dominate the work of the media industries today are built from much older processes of industrialisation and consumer culture, amongst any number of other socialised factors. Present media practices are embedded as part of a tangled social web that includes the economic and cultural fabric of the past. We might even say that one of our jobs as media industry researchers is therefore to untangle that social fabric, and as media industry historians to trace how media industries have evolved across the face of history. Doing so can reveal ever-changing media industry developments as more of a traceable dialogue, and thus more specifically revealing how the past can influence the present—and in turn potentially carve the path for the future of many media industry developments.

NOTE

1. See, also, Roberta Pearson, 'What Will You Learn That You Don't Already Know? An Interrogation of Industrial Television Studies', panel presentation at the conference of the *Society for Cinema and Media Studies* (Boston, March 24 2012).

BIBLIOGRAPHY

Ampuja, M. (2004). Critical Media Research, Globalisation Theory and Commercialisation. *Javnost/The Public, 11*(3), 59–76.

Balio, T. (1995). *Grand Design: Hollywood as a Modern Business Enterprise, 1930–1939*. Berkeley: University Of California Press.

Balio, T. (2013). *Hollywood in the New Millennium*. London: BFI Publishing.

Baum, L. F. (1900). *The Wonderful Wizard of Oz*. Chicago: The George M. Hill Company.

Bauman, Z., & May, M. (1990). *Thinking Sociologically*. Malden MA: Blackwell Publishing.

Bertrand, I., & Hughes, P. (2005). *Media Research Methods: Audiences, Institutions, Texts*. Basingstoke: Palgrave Macmillan.

Bhaskar, R. (1989). *Reclaiming reality: A critical introduction to contemporary philosophy*. New York: Routlege.

Born, G. (2004). *Uncertain Vision: Birt, Dyke and the Reinvention of the BBC*. London: Secker & Warburg.

Boyd-Barrett, O., & Newbold, C. (1995). *Approaches to Media: A Reader*. New York: Arnold.

Bruun, H. (2015). Author Interview: *Industrial Approaches to Media*. 22 June.

Bryman, A., & Bell, E. (2003). *Business Research Methods*. Oxford: Oxford University Press.

Bryman, A., & Bell, E. (2011). *Business Research Methods*. Oxford: Oxford University Press.

Caldwell, J. T. (2015). Production Studies: Where Do We Go From Here?, Panel Presentation at the Conference of *New Directions in Film and Television Production Studies* (Bristol, April 14–15).

Caston, E. (2015). Author Interview: *Industrial Approaches to Media*. 20 June.

Du Gay, P., & Pryke, M. (2002). *Cultural Economy: Cultural Analysis and Commercial Life*. London: SAGE.

Dwyer, P. (2015, April 14–15). *Theorising media production: The poverty of political economy*. Panel presentation at the conference of New Directions in Film and Television Production Studies, Bristol.

Evens, T., Iosifids, P., & Smith, P. (2013). *The Political Economy of Television Sports Rights*. Basingstoke: Palgrave Macmillan.

Evens, T., Iosifids, P., & Smith, P. (2015). The Regulation of Television Sports Broadcasting: A Comparative Analysis. *Media, Culture & Society, 37*(5), 720–736.

Flew, T. (2007). *Understanding Global Media*. London: Palgrave Macmillan.

Freedman, D. (2008). *The Politics of Media Policy*. Cambridge: Polity Press.

Freeman, M. (2014a). Advertising the Yellow Brick Road: Historicizing the Industrial Emergence of Transmedia Storytelling. *International Journal of Communication, 8*, 2362–2381.

Freeman, M. (2014b). The Wonderful Game of Oz and Tarzan Jigsaws: Commodifying Transmedia in Earth 20th Century Consumer Culture. *Intensities: The Journal of Cult Media, 7*, 44–54.

Freeman, M. (2015). Branding Consumerism: Cross-media Characters and Story-worlds at the Turn of the 20th Century. *The International Journal of Cultural Studies, 18*(6), 629–644.

Garnham, N. (1990). *Capitalism and Communication*. London: SAGE.

Giddens, A. (1984). *The Constitution of Society: Outline of the Theory of Structuration*. Cambridge: Polity Press.

Golding, P., & Murdock, G. (1991). Culture, Communications and Political Economy. In J. Curran & M. Gurevitch (Eds.), *Mass Media and Society* (pp. 15–31). London: Edward Arnold.

Groom, E. (2014). It's All On Paper: Archiving the Media Industries, and Studying Archive Collections. *Industrial Approaches to Media – The University of Nottingham*. Available at: http://www.nottingham.ac.uk/research/groups/isir/projects/industrial-approaches-to-media/elinor-groom.aspx

Grossberg, L. (1991). Strategies of Marxist Cultural Interpretation. In R. K. Avery & D. Eason (Eds.), *Critical Perspectives on Media and Society* (pp. 126–159). New York: Guilford Press.

Grossberg, L. (1996). Cultural Studies v. Political Economy: Is Anyone Else Bored with this Debate? *Critical Studies in Mass Communication, 12*(1), 72–81.

Harrison, J. (2006). The Political-Economy of Blair's "New Regional Policy". *Geoforum, 37*(6), 932–943.

Havens, T., & Lotz, A. D. (2011). *Understanding Media Industries.* Oxford: Oxford University Press.

Havens, T., Lotz, A. D., & Tinic, S. (2009). Critical Media Industries Studies: A Research Approach. *Communication, Culture & Critique* 2:2(June): 234–253.

Herman, E., & Chomsky, N. (1988). *Manufacturing Consent: The Political Economy of the Mass Media.* London: Vintage.

Hesmondhalgh, D. (2007). *The Cultural Industries* (2nd ed.). London: SAGE.

Hesmondhalgh, D. (2014). The Menace of Instrumentalism in Media Industries Research and Education. *Media Industries Journal, 1*(1), 21–26.

Hesmondhalgh, D., & Baker, S. (2011). *Creative Labour: Media Work in Three Cultural Industries.* Abingdon, Oxon: Routledge.

Hilmes, M. (1999). *Hollywood and Broadcasting: From Radio to Cable.* Urbana: University of Illinois Press.

Holt, J. (2011). *Empires of Entertainment: Media Industries and the Politics of Deregulation, 1980–1996.* New Brunswick: Rutgers University Press.

Holt, J. (2013a). The Future of Media Industry Studies – Academic-Industry Collaboration. *Media Commons* (May 30). Available at: http://mediacommons.futureofthebook.org/imr/2013/05/30/future-media-industry-studies-academic-industry-collaboration

Holt, J. (2013b). Two-Way Mirrors: Looking at the Future of Academic-Industry Engagement. *Cinema Journal, 52*(3), 183–188.

Holt, J., & Perren, A. (Eds.) (2009). *Media Industries: History, Theory, and Method.* Malden: Wiley-Blackwell.

Iosifidis, P. (1997). 'Methods of Measuring Media Concentration. *Media, Culture & Society, 19*(3), 643–663.

Iosifidis, P. (2007). *Public Television in the Digital Era: Technological Challenges and New Strategies for Europe.* Basingstoke: Palgrave Macmillan.

Iosifidis, P. (2010). *Reinventing Public Service Communication: European Broadcasters and Beyond.* Basingstoke: Palgrave Macmillan.

Iosifidis, P. (2011). *Global Media and Communication Policy.* Basingstoke: Palgrave Macmillan.

Iosifidis, P., & Wheeler, M. (2016). *Public Spheres and Mediated Social Networks.* Basingstoke: Palgrave Macmillan.

Mayer, V., Banks, M. J., & Caldwell, J. T. (2009). *Production Studies: Cultural Studies of Media Industries.* New York: Routledge.

McChesney, R. (2004). *The Problem of the Media: U.S. Communication Politics in the 21st Century.* New York: Monthly Review Press.

McDonald, P. (2013). Introduction: In Focus – Media Industries Studies. *Cinema Journal, 52*(3), 145–149.

Mizruchi, M. (2007). Political Economy and Network Analysis: An Untapped Convergence. *Sociologica* (April). Available at: http://www-personal.umich. edu/~mizruchi/vvpub.pdf

Mosco, V. (1996). *The Political Economy of Communication*. London: SAGE.

Mulgan, G. (1997). *Life After Politics: New Ideas for the 21st Century*. London: Fontana Press.

Murdock, G. (2000). Digital futures: European television in the age of convergence. In J. Wieten, G. Murdock, & P. Dahlgren (Eds.), *Television across Europe: A comparative introduction* (pp. 35–57). London: Sage.

Murdock, G., & Golding, P. (2000). Culture, Communications and Political Economy. In J. Curran & M. Gurevitch (Eds.), *Mass Media and Society* (3rd ed., pp. 70–92). London: Edward Arnold.

Murdock, G., & Wasko, J. (2007). Introduction. In G. Murdock & J. Wasko (Eds.), *Media in the Age of Marketization* (pp. 1–7). Cresskill: Hampton Press.

Pearson, R. (2012). What Will You Learn That You Don't Already Know? An Interrogation of Industrial Television Studies, Panel Presentation at the Conference of the *Society for Cinema and Media Studies* (Boston, March 24).

Perren, A. (2013). Dissecting Distribution: The Potential Role(s) of Media Industry Studies Scholars. *In Media Res* (May 31). Available at: http://media-commons.futureofthebook.org/imr/2013/05/31/dissecting-distribution-potential-roles-media-industry-studies-scholars

Presence, S. (2014). The ethics and politics of media engagement. Industrial Approaches to Media—The University of Nottingham. Available at: http://www.nottingham.ac.uk/research/groups/isir/projects/industrial-approaches-to-media/industrial-approaches-to-media-inaugural-event.aspx

Saunders, M., & Lewis, P. (2012). *Doing Research in Business & Management: An Essential Guide to Planning Your Project*. New York: Pearson.

Scolari, C., Bertetti, P., & Freeman, M. (2014). *Transmedia Archaeology: Storytelling in the Borderlines of Science Fiction, Comics and Pulp Magazines*. Basingstoke: Palgrave Pivot.

Seale, C. (1998). *Researching Society and Culture*. London: SAGE.

Strange, S. (1988). *States and Markets: An Introduction to International Political Economy*. London: Pinter.

Szczepanik, P., & Vonderau, P. (Eds.) (2013). *Behind the Screen: Inside European Production Cultures*. New York: Palgrave Macmillan.

Wasko, J., & Meehan, E. I. (2013). Critical Crossroads or Parallel Routes? Political Economy and New Approaches to Studying Media Industries and Cultural Products. *Cinema Journal, 52*(3), 150–156.

Wheeler, M. (2004). Supranational Regulation: Television and the European Union. *European Journal of Communication, 19*(3), 349–369.

CHAPTER 6

Media Industries as Interaction: Constructivism and the Corporate Context

Matthew Freeman

Back in Chap. 4 I suggested that conceiving of the study of media industries in the way that Giddens (1984) understood social structures allows for a consideration of the feedback-feedforward communication processes that underpin everyday media industry workings. And specifically, if what Giddens called the structure (i.e., the deep political and economic forces in society that underpin how media industries function) remains key to considering the workings of media industries as outcomes of larger societal forces, then this chapter will delve deeper into what it means to understand media industries as an 'interaction' (i.e., the actual practices of production within the media industries). I explore the second of my three contexts of media industry study—that being the *corporate context*, which I have defined previously as the study of the working practices that make up production cultures within the media industries.

This chapter will first consider some of the conceptual considerations of embarking on media industry research where this corporate context is the primary object of study—discussing the key methodological role of cultural studies and its humanist focus on the study of people. Second, in exploring the practical processes involved in studying people, I will then outline ways to overcome the issue of gaining access to media industry

M. Freeman (✉)
Bath Spa University, Bath, UK
e-mail: m.freeman@bathspa.ac.uk

© The Editor(s) (if applicable) and The Author(s) 2016
M. Freeman, *Industrial Approaches to Media*,
DOI 10.1057/978-1-137-55176-4_6

practitioners before considering theoretical dimensions of interviewing these media industry practitioners. This extends to outlining a set how-to principles for making contact with media industry professionals in the first place, looking at how to get the best out of an academic–industry interview. Importantly, this leads me to theorising a methodological shift in media industry studies—that is, from seeing interviewing as a process of data transfer exercises from subjects to observers, to instead conceiving of interviewing as sustained dialogues between mutual partners. Third, the chapter reflects on the extent to which media industry practitioners should be studied in a different way to studying media audiences, and what those different strategies or approaches might be, while also considering what media audience studies can potentially teach media industry studies. It is here that I go on to examine the role of ethnography in the context of media industry studies, and offer some examples of the kind of critical insights that this method of study might provide.

Lastly, Sarah Ralph ends the chapter with a case study that offers her own reflections about the importance of being 'creative' when doing interviews with media industry practitioners, offering further guidance. Ultimately, this chapter will showcase how interviewing and ethnography can allow for a crucial understanding of the *corporate context* of the media industries, diverging while also building on the understandings provided by the societal context examined previously.

The Trouble with Mass Production

As noted in the previous chapter, Paul Dwyer (2015) has pointed out that conceptualising the media industries in terms of deep societal influences and grand manufacturing lines risks minimising the complex differences between the productions of media and the productions of any other mass-market consumer product, such as a car. Instead, media production more accurately works on the basis of individual projects—or 'complex products', to borrow Hobday's (1998) expression, principally on account of the many complex factors such as unit cost, product volume, system architecture, design paths, variety of knowledge bases, skill and engineering inputs involved in the corporate process, which all go into defining any given media product. Methodologically then it is important to stress that one should not over-simplify the idea of media production by theorising it in 'standardised' or 'mass-produced' terms perhaps more common of the business world. Rather, it is equally as important to approach media production as being about cultures of creativity and innovation across a range of people, policies, divisions, and institutions. In other words, researching media industries also means taking a micro—rather than a strictly macro—approach to studying media industries.

Specifically, and as was hinted back in the introduction to this book, it is crucial with media industry research to find ways of harmonising one's understanding of both the media's economic and its symbolic status, for all works of the media (be they films, television programmes, radio podcasts, video games, etc.) are at once texts that are designed to articulate cultural meanings and substance and enjoyment to audiences, and equally commodities that are intended to generate profits. For the study of media industries we must therefore adopt methodologies that afford an understanding of both media's business and artistry simultaneously, for both are the bedrock of what I call the corporate context of media industry studies.

So, before I consider methods for examining this corporate context, let's first briefly conceptualise what the objects of study within this particular context might be.

TAKING A CONSTRUCTIVISM APPROACH

If the corporate context of study in media industry research is indeed the study of the working practices that make up production cultures within the media industries, then clearly it is important to take a very different methodological approach than that used to study the societal context. One of the most pressing questions within the growing subfield of media industry studies is the role of the individual as agent within contemporary media industries. For Perren (2016), 'this has been a welcome corrective to the prolonged dominance of political economic frameworks in media and mass communication research that de-emphasize or marginalize individual agency in favor of the structuring role of macro-level economic conditions within certain industries.' While also acknowledging the importance of political economic considerations, media industry scholars often focus on the innovative ways that individuals working within these industries exert individual agency through their creative negotiation of norms and practices within certain fields (see Banks 2014; Mayer 2012; Havens and Lotz 2011). How do workflows and decisions move across these corporate hierarchies and structures? Are authorship models based on pre-conglomerate Hollywood still relevant? How does the departmentalisation and compartmentalisation of media industries suggest appropriate analytical models?

In identifying a methodological approach to answering questions such as these, in one sense it is helpful to return to the social sciences—

in this case, its concept of 'constructivism'. As Bryman and Bell (2011: 22) explain, 'constructivism is an ontological position that asserts that social phenomena and their meanings are constantly being accomplished by social actors. It implies that social phenomena and categories are not only produced through social interaction but that they are in a constant state of revision.' The views of constructivism echo those of what I call the corporate context of study in media industry studies, which tends to assume that power lies with the agency of the media practitioners within the industry, and that the power of agency can in turn shape larger social and industrial structures.

This concept of constructivism can be extremely useful for our purposes, hinting as it does at the role of cultural perspectives on the work of people. Whereas political economy seeks to understand 'the deep structural changes in national and global political, economic and media systems through its eschewing of economic, social or political analysis' (Ferguson and Golding 1997: xiii), cultural studies explores the forces within and through which people conduct and participate in the construction of their everyday lives—thus observing the narrower or more personal cultures that people create every day. Despite this emphasis on making sense of a sort of 'social vastness', cultural studies sees communities—or in this case, media organisations—as unique communities that while still part of larger systems, operate independently. And understanding those unique communities means talking to individual agents—that is, media practitioners—which itself can be a difficult hurdle to overcome.

Getting Access to Industry

It can certainly be difficult to see and understand the corporate context of the media industries, not least of all because of the scepticism that Mateer identified in Chap. 2 as a barrier standing between academia and the media industries. While this barrier may exist, Mateer argues it is a barrier that *can* be broken down, most notably via trust:

> It is hard to get access to the right people in industry. What I have often told my research students is to find someone related in some way to the "target" person's area and try to work from that person to be introduced to a more relevant person and so forth until the "target" person is reached—referrals are golden. Many in industry are actually very willing to help and give time (when they have it) to people they trust. The key is to find a way to gain

that trust. There is no one solution, but being scrupulous about ethics, being transparent about process and, most importantly, respecting and valuing the input and time of industry people will go a long way in helping the researcher achieve the desired goals. As the business adage goes, "make it easy for someone to say 'yes' and hard to say 'no'" (Mateer 2015).

As for exactly *how*, methodologically, emerging media industry researchers might go about making it easy for their future media industry partners to start saying 'yes' to the offer of conducting interviews, in turn allowing researchers to better understand the corporate context of the media industries and their practices, Mateer (2015) points to the importance of both *networking* and *ethical awareness*:

> The fundamental goal has to be for the researchers to identify key players in the specific areas they wish to examine; from that point forward it is a question of tenacity. Practitioners are busy and obviously their first priority is their work. For the reasons I previously cited, many practitioners are sceptical of academics so the researchers need to gain their trust. Part of this comes down to the need for very clear communication between the researcher and industry partner to show that the research undertaken is being properly conducted and actually seeks to recognise the input of the practitioner directly. In other words, there is a fear among many in industry of being misquoted or having their comments misrepresented. Accordingly, following proper procedures with regard to reviewing interviews and handling of data gathered and making them clear to subjects are of paramount importance.

FORGING A SHARED INTEREST

Paul Grainge (2014) reinforces the importance of networking when attempting to both establish and to maintain connections with media industry professionals. Reflecting on this issue of access, Grainge (2014) suggests that the vast number of interviews conducted for his own research are often achieved by persistence: 'I phoned a media company cold and was just extremely lucky that the person who picked up the phone was not any kind of gatekeeper.' But beyond such notions of chance and luck, Grainge (2014) argues that, in his experience, media industry practitioners can often be highly interested—or at least highly intrigued—about the prospect of being the focus of an academic interview: 'As a researcher you are asking them certain types of questions that they don't get asked a lot, and they quite enjoyed the process of talking about their work in ways that didn't have some kind of corporate business agenda or contractual dimension to it.' Grainge (2014) also suggests that, in his own research about the more neglected media sectors in the UK, such as film marketers and intermediary advertising agencies, it was his decision to pitch his academic status as a sort of scholarly or even public champion of a media sector that was once more colloquially seen as 'the bad side of screen studies' that helped those media industry practitioners under examination revel in the prospect of being interviewed.

Grainge's strategy hints at the importance of finding a shared interest for both yourself as an academic and for media industry partners, who are perhaps not likely to be as fascinated in theoretical reflections and academic journal articles as you. Relating to this same issue of networking and forging access, Catherine Johnson (2014) stresses that when approaching media organisations and industry practitioners with a request for collaboration of some kind, it is key to consider what might be in the process for them. For instance, Johnson (2014a, b) notes that effective techniques here might include an offer to a company for their brand name to be 'represented' in a piece of scholarship that itself comes with a certain inherent prestige on account of the journal in which it will appear; there is even a possibility that the core readership of the scholarship will overlap with the media organisation's core demographic, in which case a mutual commercial interest can be stressed when making contact.

A Paradigm Shift: Subject-Observer to Partner

Philip Drake (2015) reinforces this same point, arguing that forging mutual interests represents a larger shift in how academia now sees interview participants—a shift from subject–observer status to partnership status: 'We should collaborate with, and not just about, the media industries. [...] We need to respect partners as well as focusing on one's own research objectives.' While a subject–observer model implies a sense of distance and an unequal power status between interviewer and interviewee, a partnership model implies equality and far more mutual and long-standing dialogues.

John Ellis (2015) discusses this shift to a partnership-based model of engaging with media industry practitioners specifically: 'Are single-person interviews without a second encounter an adequate research method? We need sustained dialogue, surely?' Ashton (2015), reflecting on his own experiences of studying industry, agrees:

> If I were to offer any advice on researching with media industry practitioners, it would be to take as the starting point a shared interest. I am reminded of a visit from an industry speaker and the response from a student at the end. The speaker presented a lively and fascinating account of transformations in publishing. At the end a student directly asked, "how can I get a job?" By instead engaging with anything from the talk, one would think a more natural conversation and rapport might blossom from which the "give me a job" angle might have had more meaning. The same goes for developing relationships with people for researching media industries—have a shared and common interest and let this move things onwards (not a pre-conceived set of outcomes to be achieved solely for your own benefit).

Catherine Johnson (2014) makes much the same point even more simply and concisely, arguing that when approaching media industry practitioners in the hope of forging a shared interest, it is crucial to pitch the benefits to be gained from the interview experience very clearly as a collaboration, one that comes with mutual benefits to both academia and to industry. It is the creation of *shared research*. And on a practical basis, Grainge (2014) reinforces my assertion from Chap. 2 that many of today's UK media organisations pride themselves on their 'thought leadership' and on their abilities as organisations to fully understand and even theorise the ever-changing media landscape in ways that can be seen to be providing an excellent experience for their audiences. In other words, *knowledge economy* can be utilised as the benefit to industry of collaborating with academia, for knowledge economy has the potential to aid the industry's own working practices and production cultures.

APPROACHING COLLABORATIVE INTERVIEWS

It is in the production of shared research, too—as opposed to thinking of media industry practitioners purely as subjects to be observed—that best demonstrates one of the clearest ways in which media industry research differs to research about media audiences. With the latter, audiences are traditionally conceived of as subjects to be studied, with any remarks offered taken and theorised by the researcher after the fact. Hanne Bruun (2015) elaborates on this difference between interviewing media industry practitioners compared to media audiences, arguing that the difference is primarily to do with the *exclusivity* that surrounds the interviewee:

> First, [industry practitioners] are irreplaceable informants, and if you do not get access to them as informants your whole research project might crumble. In an audience study it will always be possible to find a new informant if someone does not want to participate. Second, industry people are powerful professionals with a career to maintain working within an organisation context in a competitive media system. Third, they possess objective power and interpersonal power, and strategies and tactics need to be considered also if access is granted. The researcher is interested in getting access to the professional knowledge, and not in understanding the life world of the informant like with audience research [...]. All of this will affect your research questions, and the kind of research possible to do.[1]

Moreover, in media industry research, and in contrast to audience research, the aim of producing shared research with mutual benefits allows us to conceptualise the potential benefits to both academia and to industry. In the broadest sense, as Ashton (2015) argues, 'the contribution of media industries to media studies is "industry insight", and the contribution of media studies to media industries is "critical space".'

And conceiving of mutual, if differing, benefits to industry and to academia is particularly crucial given the very different ways that academia and industry actually understand the word 'research', and indeed the fact that the media industries can have a hard time understanding exactly why its day-to-day workings might themselves be of value and of interest to academics. Catherine Johnson (2013) reinforces this point, noting that in her experience of contacting media organisations in the hope of securing interviews, '[f]or industry, 'research' refers specifically to audience research—questionnaires and focus groups used to develop and test new and ongoing projects. As an established part of their business, the media industries have little need of external academics to undertake such work.' Media practitioners are generally used to being the ones who ask the questions—conducting research into audience tastes and consumption habits via test screenings, focus groups, surveys, and so on.

Addressing clearly and upfront then how a conversation between industry and academia can be relevant and of interest to those you are contacting is a must, but the also question of exactly *what* to study in such a context remains an important one.

DOING COLLABORATIVE INTERVIEWS: STUDYING UP OR STUDYING DOWN

In the first instance, when taking an interview approach to studying media industries it can be useful to identify one of two approaches—*studying up or studying down*. Channelling Vicky Mayer, Paul Grainge (2014) acknowledges the typically hierarchical nature of media organisations, meaning that researchers can either opt to 'study up' these organisations or to 'study down' them. Both of these approaches still concern the corporate context, of course, but whereas 'studying up' might mean engaging with the more senior media workforce within a particular organisation—managers, producers, senior executives, etc.—'studying down' would see the researcher focusing on interns, personal assistants, social media posters, and lower-level creatives. This 'studying up' verses 'studying down' model could well dictate the direction of any given research question, affording as it might very different research interests: Studying up is likely to be best suited to studies interested in the likes of management strategy and other 'above-the-line' creative production processes. Studying down, in contrast, could be more suited to studies that seek to understand the professional ideologies of media workers and all 'below-the-line' industry attitudes that characterise practitioners' approaches to media making.

While John Thornton Caldwell (2008) somewhat flippantly suggests that, as a rule of thumb, when conducting interviews with media professionals and companies, 'the higher up you go, the less you learn', Grainge (2014) suggests that the complex hierarchical nature of many media organisations can be both a blessing and a curse for the prospective researcher. While chains of command can arguably make it easier for a researcher to move through multiple employees, Grainge (2014) warns that one wrong word or inappropriate line of questioning might lead to a shutting down of communication between said researcher and the media organisation being studied.

DOING COLLABORATIVE INTERVIEWS: LINE OF QUESTIONING

In fact, there are many anecdotal stories of academics being guilty of major mishaps when conducting interviews with media industry practitioners. Says Grainge (2014), '[w]hen talking to a Hollywood-based producer, something as easily done as phrasing an interview question badly can lead to the whole interview closing down—and not only that, the producer then tells everyone in the studio *not* to talk to you.'

Such stories of interviewer relationships 'shutting down' may be extreme examples, but there are certainly lessons to be learned from the process of actually doing media industry interviews. The first lesson is to ensure that, as researchers, it is clear what the overall objective of the study is and why each question is being asked. Most generally, the researcher may thus wish to envisage research questions such as:

- How do production companies structure themselves?
- How do people work together?
- What kinds of partnerships work, both creatively and in a business sense?
- What are the best ways of making teams?
- What are the processes involved in producing media?

Notice that all of the above research interests characterise a focus on the corporate context of media industries—all allowing for an understanding of not only the working practices that make up production cultures within the media industries, but also an understanding that acknowledges both the creative agency of people and the corporate practices of business. There have been a number of important studies of cultural labour recently, many of which seek to describe and analyse the lives, dispositions, attitudes, and professional ideologies of those who work in the media industries, and on the professional organisations and informal networks that form communities of shared understandings, and which, as John Caldwell has shown, generate their own cultural and interpretative frameworks.

One such academic whose research examines the nature of *work* within the media industries is the aforementioned Ashton (2015a), who has pointed to the overall importance of researching people because, as he puts it, 'it is people that remain the unchanging anchor of the media industries, even amidst the substantial changes to industry brought about by technology and digital platforms.' For Ashton (2015b), 'interview and focus group exchanges at industry events are often key points in establishing research and investigation pathways. On this, I found George Marcus' multi-sited ethnography approach particularly helpful for my research design—quite literally following connections, associations and putative relationships' (see Marcus 1995: 105). Once again, Ashton's people-focused methodology is squarely concerned with relationships amidst the corporate context, seeing people as the agents of power that construct the media industries as an 'interaction' via the practices of production. Says Ashton (2015b), '[b]y following connections, associations and relationships there is a continual prompt to bring together practices, people, ideas and methods.'

DOING COLLABORATIVE INTERVIEWS: CULTURAL PERSPECTIVES

Bringing together practices, people, and ideas epitomises the more sociological approach of this book, or at least the turn towards cultural studies that has become prominent in media industry studies in recent years. In *Production Studies: Cultural Studies of Media Industries*, Vicki Mayer, Miranda J. Banks, and John Thornton Caldwell sought to 'dig deeper into this notion of production as a culture', looking at 'how media producers make culture' (2009: 2). Here, Mayer et al. (2009: 2) conceived that 'the off-screen production of media is itself a cultural production, mythologized and branded much like the onscreen textual culture that media industries produce.' Conceptualising of corporate contexts of media production in this way is crucial to our understanding of media industry studies methodology, for it points to ideas that media industry workings can be analysed, textually, in much the same way that a film might be analysed textually. It also points to the ways in which media industry studies can be theorised using the methodological tools of cultural studies, with the ethnographic turn towards social spaces such as shopping centres and museums equally useful for analysing the cultural mappings of industrial zones.

In line with these ideas of cultural perspectives of media industries and collaborative methodologies, Sam Ward (2014) points to the importance of *place* when doing media industry interviews, not least of all because the space and place in which an interview occurs can be highly important in terms of fostering more 'open means of making contact between academia and industry.' Hilmes (2014) has suggested that having media industry practitioners visit university departments for periods of time in the same vein as the 'Artist in Residence' is one method of forging more collaborative working arrangements between academia and industry; in this model, the rigid nature of interviewing might become more open and revealing.

For Ward (2014), conversely, 'the re-fashioning of the observational academic visiting for an hour or two, into something more sustained and mutually beneficial is a crucial possibility.' Ward (2014) notes that ideas such as these 'will probably require a change in some of the expectations and working practices that we have as scholars, whatever our background, and this is worth thinking through carefully.' Yet with the explicit turn towards media industry studies becoming more prominent, perhaps it is now time to start thinking through how such collaborations could work in the UK.

Eva Novrup Redvall (2015) agrees with these more ethnographic notions, arguing that 'if one wants to study behind-the-scenes processes such as development and screenwriting processes, it seems crucial to me to not only let practitioners explain these processes from their own point of view, but to actually observe them to be able to ask questions about tacit knowledge, conflicts of interest, diverging ideas of how to proceed and work ways that are maybe no longer even questioned.' Redvall's preference for ethnography—essentially 'the writing of culture', a method based on the act of observation—stems from the sense that in the media there is a fundamental difference between what people tell you and what people actually do.

Interviewing, however, remains a key strategy for doing media industry studies, enabling as it can a means to trace connections between modes of production and larger corporate agendas, which may also be shaped by the operations of industry practitioners. Media industries are complex in their organisational structures, and so again this interest in *agency*—how, say, individual screenwriters collaborate with producers, how advertising agencies create marketing materials in line with the creative intentions of a director, or how multiple sites of authorship all function together across expansive sites of production—emerges as an overriding critical concern for the corporate context of media industry studies and its researchers. Exploring these complex modes of agency amidst industrial webs can, in turn, lead to new and highly innovative understandings of authorship, creativity, productivity, and entrepreneurship, amongst many, many other notable areas of scholarly concern.

And so in the context of media industry studies more broadly, the so-called incompatibility of political economy and cultural studies indicated in Chap. 5 need not be a problem. Instead, both of these approaches can be understood as useful to interrogating the wider circuits of society that interact with media industries, with each of these approaches best suited to investigating opposing directions of these circuits. Whereas political economy affords overarching understandings of the impact of deep economic and political social systems on media industry workings, taking a cultural approach to studies of the corporate context and the practitioners within it can offer rich and valuable insights into how the workings of the media industries impact local cultures of production and unique practitioner communities within industry.

Thus in some ways, doing interviews in media industry studies—taking more of a collaborative perspective by seeing the interviewee less as a subject and more as an equal partner—actually means taking what Sarah Ralph calls a creative approach, as she will now demonstrate in the following case study, via interviews which sought to understand local cultures of production in the UK television industry.

CASE STUDY: GETTING MORE CREATIVE WITH INTERVIEWS

Sarah Ralph

At the end of a research interview conducted with an established British television comedy producer he compared our encounter to being 'like therapy', and at subsequent meetings took to calling me 'Dr Sarah', a light-hearted play off both my academic title and various celebrity psychologists who have become known simply by their professional title and mononym. This producer's observation about the experience of being interviewed for a research study was echoed by many of the TV comedy professionals I spoke with in my role as Research Associate on the Arts and Humanities Research Council-funded project *Make Me Laugh: Creativity in the British Television Comedy.*[2]

While most had been interviewed by journalists or commentators from a range of media outlets before, the purpose of those interviews had been to glean information about particular programmes they had been working on—plot and casting details, behind-the-scenes knowledge, etc.—rather than to learn about their everyday working lives and creative processes. Therefore, with little frame of reference or expectation as to what the research interview I had requested would entail, it is interesting to consider what reasons the writers, directors, producers, and other creative workers I spoke with had for agreeing to participate in an academic research project of this kind. As Brett Mills (2008) has found in his earlier series of interviews with people who make television sitcoms, creative professionals' astonishment that academics would be interested in hearing what they had to say about their working practices was seemingly overcome by a mixture of curiosity, the potential for academy–industry collaboration, and the rare chance to discuss their work in a reflexive way. Yet my

'Dr Sarah' moniker also hints at the complexity of the relationship that develops between the media industry researcher and the project participant, one where a researcher needs to simultaneously gain the trust and confidence of participants in order to achieve the access they require, while at the same time trying to maintain a professional and objective 'distance' from those participants in order to draw broader conclusions about the potential shortcomings of the industry and its institutional frameworks.

The *Make Me Laugh* project aimed to follow the working practices of British television comedy industry personnel by means of semi-structured interviews (over 80 of these were conducted between August 2012 and October 2014), and also by using a range of ethnographic techniques to map the creative production processes of specific projects and programmes people were working on. This meant making an approach to people for a preliminary interview, and then during that first meeting attempting to secure their on-going participation. It is a daunting task for a researcher to know where to begin when approaching media professionals within a particular industry for an interview.

Yet a simple first step can be to collate a list of those people you would *ideally* like to speak to, and the reason why that person would make a significant contribution to the research study (for example: they have a key gatekeeper position, they have worked across various roles both in-house at a broadcaster as well as freelance, they are responsible for a recent high profile programme, etc.). Having drawn up such a list with the project's Principal Investigator, Brett Mills, I then worked through this list endeavouring to find contact details for people in order to make an approach. Most often such details could be found easily: for example, through the website of the production company where an individual works, or a basic Internet search using relevant key terms. However, often an approach by email was not immediately, or sometimes ever, successful for making that first contact. The nature of the media and creative industries is such that an email can get lost or buried among the volumes of other correspondence that is daily received by people's inboxes.

An alternative approach that I discovered to be surprisingly more effective was writing a formal letter. Receiving a traditional letter is a rarer occurrence within the sector, and it also meant that I was able to use both the Research Council and host University logos to demonstrate the legitimacy of the project. I structured the letter into three straightforward paragraphs: who I was and the project I was working on, how the materials from the project would be used to achieve its wider aims, and finally the reason why the individual was a particularly important person to speak to. The rationale behind this final paragraph is not persuasive flattery—though it certainly has a secondary purpose of reassuring people that they do have something significant to say—but to make evident that you as a researcher 'know your stuff', both about their work and the wider industry.

Yet beyond these 'cold' approaches, there are of course other ways of gaining introductions or making contact with professionals within a media industry. It is of course useful to draw on any personal contacts that you already have, or those of family or friends. A former school friend of mine had been working on a theatre show with a TV comedy writer, and kindly put me in touch with them early on in the project. This contact proved invaluable not only because the writer agreed to be the subject of a pilot interview in which I tested out the project's interview question schedule, but also because the writer was part of a wider network of television comedy writers in London and was happy to provide email introductions to a number of them. I also made more tailored and inventive approaches to individuals where their high profile within the industry meant a non-supported first approach would most likely not yield a response. For example, I attended a Q&A session with a Head of Comedy that was organised by the BFI and subsequently wrote an academic blog post about this event and the individual's career in television comedy to date. Having promoted this heavily on social media, and receiving a response from the individual via that format, I only then made an approach to them via email requesting an interview, which was accepted with a mention of how they had 'really enjoyed' the blog post. So it is worthwhile spending time thinking imaginatively and resourcefully about how to make contact with key industry figures, though of course such customised approaches are not always guaranteed to be as effective as in this case and should not be the principle means of approach.

Once an interview had been agreed to, I initially found it was the more practical aspects that preoccupied me in advance of meeting a media professional—travel to the location, the suitability of the venue for voice recording, the appropriate clothing to wear according to the interview's context—rather than theoretical or methodological issues. This, I suspect, was due to having a research background in media audience research and being practiced in techniques such as designing question schedules and conducting individual interviews and focus groups. Approaches to methods in qualitative audience research are often drawn from broader social science writings (Grubium and Holstein 2001; Barbour 2008; Bryman 2012), though there are also works specific to the field (Schrøder 2003), and these offer incredibly useful guidelines for designing the research implement. Thus, well in advance of my first interviews the semi-structured question schedule had been drafted, pilot tested (as noted above), and re-drafted, and I was confident in its design. I was also—I felt—experienced at managing interviews—at allowing participants the space to take the discussion off on a tangent, at carefully bringing them back to topic when necessary, and prompting for more detail if I felt it was required. However, there are a number of ways in which I found interviewing television comedy professionals called for a very different approach to the media audience research I had previously conducted.

In the first instance, prior to an interview with an audience study participant you will know little if anything about them. It is during the interview itself that you make what will likely be your only discoveries about that individual, and in relation to a very particularised topic. Whereas with a media professional there is a great deal of research you can carry out prior to the interview about their career and creative work. For most of the television comedy professionals I interviewed (the exception being a small number of early career writers) there were programmes that I could watch that they had been involved in creating—the *artefacts* of their working life—as well as websites charting the timeline of their careers through their programmes, and published interviews where they talk about their personal backgrounds and how they had begun their professional life. In the first interviews I conducted I had been fairly cursory in exploring these available materials, relying on what I felt was a reasonably solid knowledge of the individual's work and my memory of programmes I had watched in the past. However, it soon became clear that my interviewees' expectations about my familiarity with their work was high, meaning that I was potentially missing significant opportunities to probe them for more information when they mentioned former shows or people they had worked with that were unfamiliar to me.

Correspondingly, I noted that when I *was* able to demonstrate an awareness or appreciation of a programme or long-term colleague, it was evident that this increased rapport and the interviewee's receptiveness to my questions. Thus an important—not to mention time-consuming—part of my preparations for interviews from that point onwards was to research as much as possible about a media professional's career to date, the individuals or production companies they regularly worked with, and the projects that they were rumoured to currently be working on.

A further distinction of interviews with media industry professionals rather than with media audiences is that the parameters of the interview are necessarily less fixed. In audience research the boundaries of the interview are usually set by the researcher: The participants, once they have agreed to be interviewed, are required only to participate for the length of time it takes to answer the questions included in the schedule—which are set by the researcher—and are rarely obliged to further participate or volunteer further information. However, in the *Make Me Laugh* project—as in many media industry studies—additional participants were often recruited by recommendation from those that were first interviewed (through snowballing), and at the end of the main schedule of questions I would ask whether the interviewee would be willing to let me chart the creative progress of a comedy project that they were currently working on. This is where the power dynamic that in audience research is so routinely weighted towards the researcher, in media industry research shifts determinedly towards the interviewee. My preliminary interviewees were important to growing the number of TV comedy professionals participating in the project, and as gatekeepers for access to the production process of their shows. On a number of occasions at the close of interviews, participants would agree to an introduction, or to me attending a production event (a script read-through, rehearsal, recording, or screening), and would propose doing it immediately. At the end of an interview with a television comedy writer in a London cafe, I was invited to attend that evening a special screening of a current sitcom at BBC Comedy, where I would be able to meet the show's director, producer, and executive producer. Thus a media industry researcher needs to be willing to be quite flexible and prepared to take up unforeseen opportunities when they are offered at short notice.

As well as the semi-structured interviews that were conducted with television comedy professionals, the *Make Me Laugh* project also used a range of open-ended ethnographic methods to map the creative production processes particular comedy projects went through. The strategies that were adopted in relation to the followed shows varied according to the *access* that was achieved in each case, this having been found to be a key challenge to researchers conducting fieldwork in the media industries (Ortner 2009). Accessibility often depended upon the creative role of the participants that had agreed to an interview on that project. Commissioners and producers were more easily able to organise for me to attend script read-throughs, or visit production sets and edit suites to observe and write field notes, whereas writers would have to approach these personnel themselves to obtain their permission. However, a good established rapport with a number of writers also proved fruitful following the conception of a research interview technique termed a 'script chat'. On request, writers would send the various numbered drafts that a particular episode of a show had been through, and I would read through these versions noting changes that had been made to elements such as tone, character, structure, dialogue, and so on. These observations would then form the basis of an extended interview with the writer (or writers, if it was a co-written programme), so that they could describe and explain in detail their creative process during the development of that episode's script. In one case this was developed even further into a workshop interview that included the producer—also a project participant—who explained their role in translating that final script of the episode to the screen. Ortner (2009: 182) argues that those doing ethnographic research on quite closed communities, such as a media industry, requires researchers to 'get more creative', and just as trying to be imaginative in my approach to engage participants proved productive, so did being inventive in ethnographic methods, especially when a lack of access might have been restrictive.

However, what the variability in terms of access meant for the ethnographic aspect of the project was an unevenness and inconsistency in research materials, and consequently an inability to compare and evaluate *like with like* in relation to the comedy project case studies. Nevertheless, this susceptibility in media industry studies is perhaps something that researchers in the field must acknowledge in the writing up of their research, while all the time striving to 'get more creative' in thinking of ways that this unevenness and inconsistency might be resolved.

NOTES

1. A comprehensive account of this study is forthcoming in Hanne Bruun, (2015) 'The Qualitative Interview in Media Production Studies', in Paterson, C., Zoellner, A., Saha, A., and Lee, D. (eds.) *Advancing Media Production Research: Shifting Sites, Methods and Politics* (Basingstoke: Palgrave Macmillan), 141–146.
2. This project, *Make Me Laugh: Creativity in the British Television Comedy Industry* (2012–15), was led by Brett Mills, at the University of East Anglia (see www.makemelaugh.org.uk), and was supported by the Arts and Humanities Research Council [project reference AH/I003614/1].

BIBLIOGRAPHY

Ashton, D. (2009a). Making it Professionally: Student Identity and Industry Professionals in Higher Education. *Journal of Education and Work*, 22(4), 283–300.

Ashton, D. (2009b). Critical Thinking Across Contexts. *Politics and Culture* 10(4): http://www.politicsandculture.org/issue/2009-issue-4/

Ashton, D. (2009c). Interactions, Delegations and Online Digital Games Players in Communities of Practice. *Participations: Online Journal of Audience Research*, 6(1): http://www.participations.org/documents/ashton.pdf

Ashton, D. (2011). Pathways to Creativity: Self-learning and Customising in/for the Creative Economy. *Journal of Cultural Economy*, 4(2), 189–203.

Ashton, D. (2013a). Creative Contexts: Student Voices and Reflection on Work Placements in the Creative Industries. *Journal of Further and Higher Education*, 39(1), 127–146.

Ashton, D. (2013b). Industry Professionals in Higher Education: Values, Identities and Cultural Work. In D. Ashton & C. Noonan (Eds.), *Cultural Work and Higher Education* (pp. 172–192). Palgrave Macmillan: Basingstoke.

Ashton, D. (2013c). Cultural Workers in-the-Making. *European Journal of Cultural Studies*, 16(4), 468–488.

Ashton, D. (2014). Creative Contexts: Work Placement Subjectivities for the Creative Industries. *British Journal of Sociology of Education*. doi:10.1080/01425692.2014.916602.

Ashton, D. (2015a). Producing Participatory Media: (Crowd)sourcing Content in *Britain/Life in a Day*', *Media International Australia*. Special Issue on 'Making Media Participatory' (154): 101–111.

Ashton, D. (2015b). Author interview: Industrial approaches to media. 17 June.

Ashton, D, & Jeune, N. (2013). Hid(ing) Media Professionals: Constructing and Contesting the 1st AD. *View: Journal of European Television History and Culture*, 2(4): http://journal.euscreen.eu/index.php/view/article/view/JETHC047/85

Ashton, D. & Couzins, M. (2015). Content Curators as Cultural Intermediaries: "My reputation as a curator is based on what I curate, right?". *M/C Journal* 18 (4).

Atkinson, P., Coffey, A., Delamont, S., Lofland, J., & Lofland, L. (2001). *Handbook of Ethnography*. London: SAGE.

Alasuutari, P. (1995). *Researching Culture: Qualitative Method and Cultural Studies*. London: SAGE.

Banks, J. (1996). *Monopoly television: MTV's quest to control the music*. Boulder: Westview Press.

Barbour, R. (2008). *Introducing Qualitative Research: A Student Guide*. London: SAGE.

Bertrand, I., & Hughes, P. (2005). *Media Research Methods: Audiences, Institutions, Texts*. Basingstoke: Palgrave Macmillan.

Bruun, H. (2015). Author Interview: *Industrial Approaches to Media*. 22 June.

Bryman, A. (2012). *Social Research Methods* (4th ed.). Oxford: Oxford University Press.

Bryman, A., & Bell, E. (2011). *Business Research Methods*. Oxford: Oxford University Press.

Burke, P. (1980). *Sociology and History*. Boston: George Allen & Unwin Ltd.

Caldwell, J. T. (2008). *Production Culture: Industrial Reflexivity and Critical Practice in Film and Television*. Durham and London: Duke University Press.

Caldwell, J. T. (2009). "Both Sides of the Fence": Blurred Distinctions in Scholarship and Production (a Portfolio of Interviews). In V. Mayer, M. J. Banks, & J. T. Caldwell (Eds.), *Production Studies: Cultural Studies of Media Industries* (pp. 214–216). New York: Routledge.

Caldwell, J. T. (2013). Para-Industry: Researching Hollywood's Blackwaters. *Cinema Journal, 52*(3), 157–165.

Caldwell, J. T. (2014). Para-Industry, Shadow Academy. *Cultural Studies, 28*(4), 720–740.

Caldwell, J. T. (2015). Production Studies: Where Do We Go From Here?, Panel Presentation at the Conference of *New Directions in Film and Television Production Studies* (Bristol, April 14–15).

Curran, J., Morley, D., & Walkerdine, V. (1996). *Cultural Studies and Communications*. New York: Arnold.

Drake, P. (2015). Production Studies as a Field of Enquiry: Sources, Methods, Approaches, Panel Presentation at the Conference of *New Directions in Film and Television Production Studies* (Bristol, April 14–15).

Dwyer, P. (2015, April 14–15). *Theorising media production: The poverty of political economy*. Panel presentation at the conference of New Directions in Film and Television Production Studies, Bristol.

Ellis, J. (2015). The ADAPT Project, Panel Presentation at the conference of *New Directions in Film and Television Production Studies* (Bristol, April 14–15).

Ferguson, M., & Golding, P. (Eds.) (1997). *Cultural studies in question*. London: SAGE.

Giddens, A. (1984). *The Constitution of Society: Outline of the Theory of Structuration*. Cambridge: Polity Press.

Grainge, P. (2014). Interviewing Media *Professionals. Industrial Approaches to Media – The University of Nottingham*. Available at: http://www.nottingham.ac.uk/research/groups/isir/projects/industrial-approaches-to-media/industrial-approaches-to-media-inaugural-event.aspx

Grubium, J., & Holstein, J. (Eds.) (2001). *Handbook of Interview Research*. London: SAGE.

Havens, T., & Lotz, A. D. (2011). *Understanding media industries*. Oxford: Oxford University Press.

Hilmes, M. (2014). An Interview with Professor Michele Hilmes. *Industrial Approaches to Media – The University of Nottingham*. Available at: http://www.nottingham.ac.uk/research/groups/isir/projects/industrial-approaches-to-media/index.aspx

Hobday, M. (1998). Product complexity, innovation and industrial organization. *Research Policy, 26,* 689–710.

Johnson, C. (2013). The Mutual Benefits of Engaging with Industry. *CST Online*. Accessed December 3, 2015, from http://cstonline.tv/mutual-benefits

Johnson, C. (2014a). Interviewing Media Professionals. *Industrial Approaches to Media – The University of Nottingham*. Available at: http://www.nottingham.ac.uk/research/groups/isir/projects/industrial-approaches-to-media/industrial-approaches-to-media-inaugural-event.aspx

Johnson, D. (2014b). Understanding Media Industries From All Perspectives. *Industrial Approaches to Media – The University of Nottingham*. Available at: http://www.nottingham.ac.uk/research/groups/isir/projects/industrial-approaches-to-media/derek-johnson.aspx

Johnson, R., Chambers, D., Raghuram, P., & Tincknell, E. (2004). *The Practice of Cultural Studies*. London: SAGE.

Marcus, G. E. (1995). Ethnography In/Of the World System. *Annual Review of Anthropology, 24,* 95–117.

Mateer, J. (2015). Author Interview: *Industrial Approaches to Media*. 15 June.

Mayer, V. (2012). Through the darkness: Musings on new media. *Ada: Journal of Gender, New Media and Technology 1*(1). http://adanewmedia.org/2012/11/issue1-mayer/

Mayer, V., Banks, M. J., & Caldwell, J. T. (2009). *Production Studies: Cultural Studies of Media Industries*. New York: Routledge.

Mills, B. (2008). After the Interview. *Cinema Journal* 47:2(Winter): 148–153.

Ortner, S. B. (2009). Studying Sideways: Ethnographic Access in Hollywood. In V. Mayer, M. J. Banks, & J. T. Caldwell (Eds.), *Production Studies: Cultural Studies of Media Industries* (pp. 175–189). New York: Routledge.

Perren, A. (2016). FLOW 2016 roudtable questions. FLOW Journal. Available at: http://www.flowjournal.org/flowconference-2016/flow-2016-panel-questions/

Redvall, E. (2015) Author Interview: *Industrial Approaches to Media*. 1 June.

Schrøder, K., et al. (2003). *Researching audiences*. London: Arnold.

Walvaart, M. (2015). Discussing Power Dynamics of Audience Participation in Television Productions, Panel Presentation at the Conference of *New Directions in Film and Television Production Studies* (Bristol, April 14–15).

Ward, S. (2014). Interviewing Media Professionals: Why? Where? and Whither? *Industrial Approaches to Media – The University of Nottingham*. Available at: http://www.nottingham.ac.uk/research/groups/isir/projects/industrial-approaches-to-media/sam-ward.aspx

CHAPTER 7

Media Industries as Modality: Culturalism and the Discursive Context

Matthew Freeman

How does the media circulate—not to audiences, but *around* audiences? And what are the wider influences of communication on how the media is perceived? Building on Giddens' (1984) seminal notion of structuration even further, it is important to remember that the media industries, like a society, are a complex feedback-feedforward process of communication. The innate communication of the media means that their industrial workings are not vertical, neither top-down nor bottom-up. Rather, the media are *communications*—and, as has been argued previously, it makes sense that studies of media industries understand those industries as contextual vessels of communication, analysing the communication processes and discourses of the media industries and their implications around, between, and outside industry.

That is to say, if media industries are essentially communication, as much about the discourses articulated as they are the inner workings of organisations, then we need to research media industries not simply as a structure (the deep political and economic forces in society that underpin how media industries function), or simply as an interaction (the practices of production within the media industries). In addition to these two binary approaches, we also need to conceptualise media industries

M. Freeman (✉)
Bath Spa University, Bath, UK
e-mail: m.freeman@bathspa.ac.uk

© The Editor(s) (if applicable) and The Author(s) 2016
M. Freeman, *Industrial Approaches to Media*,
DOI 10.1057/978-1-137-55176-4_7

131

as cultural sprawls. It is in that sense that we can apply Giddens' idea of 'modality' to the study of media industries, which I defined in Chap. 4 as the wider cultural arenas of the media industries where larger economic and political forces are communicated as more local and discursive sets of meanings, messages, and values.

Indeed, there is a wide gulf separating the macroeconomic considerations of media conglomerates and the individual scale of creative media decision making. This chapter then will examine how we most effectively theorise and potentially bridge this scalar problem in analysing the media industries. What is the productive middle ground between questions of political economy and human agency? I will examine the broad cultural range in between corporate scale and individual scale media industry studies, identifying a number of appropriate and best practice research methodologies for doing these studies critically. I explore the third of my three contexts of media industry study—that being the *discursive context*, which concerns not actual practice but the discourses communicated by media industry practitioners, and thus the ways in which media practitioners narrativise the transformation of deep social structures into clear sets of meanings and understandings about the media industries.

This chapter, first, will consider some of the conceptual considerations of embarking on media industry research where this discursive context is the primary object of study—further delving into the methodological role of cultural studies. Second, in exploring the methodological processes involved in studying discourse, I will then examine the discursive analysis of more peripheral media artefacts as a methodological approach to studying the media industries. Specifically, I consider the ways through which the researcher can make use of the huge array of publically available documents that are created every day in the course of the media industries' work (such as trade papers, social media, schedules, memos, contracts, protocols, press releases, articles and interviews in the newspapers, and countless more). Lastly, these observations and ideas will then be reinforced and expanded by Dave Harte, who offers an insightful case study at the end of this chapter about the sorts of conclusions one can make about the journalism industry and its highly discursive communications by studying the everyday, seemingly trivial pages of social media. This will showcase how trade paper and social media analysis can allow for a crucial understanding of the *discursive context* of the media industries, showcasing the media industries as cultural processes of feedback-feedforward between society and people.

Taking a Culturalism Approach

So, if the societal context of study in media industry research is the study of how deep structures in society inform media industry operations, and the corporate context is indeed the study of the working practices that make up production cultures within the media industries themselves, then thinking about a sociology of media industries—and specifically as *media industries as authors of society*—offers a useful framework for interrogating the media industries as vessels of meaning-making, as sites of communication that stand between macro and micro forces of production.

And such a framework again requires a different methodological approach than those used to study either the societal context or the corporate context—one that affords an analysis of the media industries as constructions of authorship that allows audiences to be engaged creatively within, between, and across industrial structures.

In identifying a conceptual framework to exploring a focus such as this, it is useful to return to the discipline of cultural studies—in this case, particularly, its long-standing concept of 'culturalism'. Introduced by sociologist Florian Znaniecki in the early twentieth century, culturalism is an ontological approach that ultimately aims to eliminate simple binaries between seemingly opposing phenomena, such as nature and culture. For our purposes, this approach is important for remembering that macro and micro forces of the media industries—such as deep economic impacts and individual professional ideologies—are not opposing factors, but rather opposite sides of the same proverbial coin. Znaniecki proposed that a culturalism approach allowed him to 'define social phenomena in cultural terms' (Halas 2010: 2), noting that our culture shapes our view of the world and our thinking (Dulczewski 1984: 187–188). Importantly, Znaniecki argues that while the world is composed of physical artefacts, such as films, television programmes, corporate offices, policy documents, etc., we are not really capable of studying the physical world other than through the lenses of culture (Dulczewski 1984: 189). And thinking culturally means, as Halas (2010: 52) identifies, acknowledging that 'the subject-observer dualism must be broken down'—thus the in-betweens of the macro societal and the micro corporate contexts should be broken down—and instead these two should be mediated by a study of *language*. For as culturalism suggests, 'reality is not an absolute order but changes in a creative evolution' (Halas 2010: 52). In other words, and for the subfield of media industry studies, the media industries—huge, complex sites of production and communication—should not be studied in a vacuum but rather across the entire fabric of culture.

Moreover, in thinking about media industry studies as webs of language across the entire fabric of culture, Jack Newslinger (2015) argues that we can now begin to conceive of such research not purely in terms of 'the large discourses' of the singular media industry, but more so in terms of the smaller multiplicities of the media industries. For Newslinger (2015), studying these smaller, multiple sites of communication allows us to break up the overarching emphasis on a unified form of production—that is, any underlying assumptions that all aspects of the production are working towards the same goal. In contrast, of course, the media industries are made up of any number of conflicting ideologies, different practices, goals, and so on. And this is important work, for as John Caldwell (2015) asserts, 'we need to identify all of the tangential, ancillary, erased, parallel or invisible units labour or workers connected.'

In fact, a key focus in the subfield of media industry studies of late has been to examine the 'in-betweenness' of the media industries—that is, those smaller, more marginalised, more tangential aspects like independent advertising agencies, freelance creative strategists, and brand consultants. Studying sites such as these, at least in the UK, may well be to do with availability of access and the fact that it can be easier to talk to a small, independent media agency than it is a vast conglomerate, but it also speaks about the ways in which media industries today are to a large extent defined by their spreadability—across subdivisions, media, technologies, countries, audiences, and so on and so forth. In that sense, these smaller, more tangential 'in-betweens' are in fact fundamental to understanding the inner workings of today's media industries.

And studying this innate spreadability of the media industries indeed means focusing explicitly on the role of communication, language, and meaning making. Bauman and May (2001: 3–4) note that, sociologically speaking, our understanding of the workings and structures of a society are often the result of 'the relations between *language* and *experience*.' That is to say, when thinking of media industries as part of a discursive context, it is the way in which media practitioners narrativise the transformation of deep social structures into sets of meanings via discourses about the media industries that plays a key role in shaping our experience of media industries.

THINKING ABOUT LANGUAGE AND EXPERIENCE

If media industries do in fact work behind proverbial curtains, as was noted in the introduction to this book, then how can one go about lifting this curtain and analysing the relationship between the language of the media industries and our experience of the media industries? To some extent, and to re-cite Derek Johnson (2014), 'the industry is already talking to us—via Twitter, in trade articles, and more.' And it is sources such as these—the writings of media practitioners in trade papers, the images of brand logos imposed on corporate social media pages, the choice of words articulated in a press interview and published in magazines and newspapers, etc.—that will be the methodological focus of this chapter. In short, this chapter is about studying *discourses*—the meanings and messages that are communicated by, in, and often through the media industries, and which work to shape our understandings of what those industries actually are and what their role in society really is.

Analysing the discursive context of the media industries means adopting a particular methodological approach, one which requires the researcher to start small in their thinking and allow their focus to gradually get bigger and bigger, tracing the meanings about industry that may be communicated by industry and across a range of that industry's peripheral documentation. When thinking discursively and through the lens of culturalism, moreover, it is likely to be the case that the 'industry' is not actually the focus of study at all but is instead the larger framework through which a different, smaller area of enquiry can then be investigated and analysed. For example, as Lotz (2014) notes of her own research, 'I cannot say that I view "media industries" as my focus as such. Typically there is some phenomenon that I find of interest—whether it be the emergence of female-centered television dramas or the changing nature of US television and discourse about it. Aspects related to media industry operation thus become a lens for trying to make sense of the phenomenon, rather than serving as the site of the study.' Michele Hilmes (2014) elaborates on this general principle:

In terms of how you *do* media industry research, it always begins with a text of some kind—we are first looking at a film, or a television programme, a website, a magazine, etc.; the text is what is preserved and is what you can always get access to. And then you broaden out from there, making use of ancillary sources—such as trade press, policy documents and collections of internal memos perhaps available in archives.

For Hilmes (2014) too there is much value in examining the media industries via this sort of ancillary or peripheral documentation, which means treating trade press materials and any other available documentation produced by, for, or about the media industries as *texts* to be analysed. Doing so can enable the researcher to identify any number of discourses pervading the media industries and any number of their cultural meanings. Derek Johnson (2014) discusses the importance of the trades:

> In the age of media industry studies wherein some researchers have secured access to sites of production, we have come to devalue the trade journal as 'just' the promotional ramblings of public relations offices and their sycophantic friends writing the articles. Yet even if they are puff pieces, these trade stories circulate with Hollywood and other media industries as claims about how those cultures of production work. Compared to my interviews—which were stories that professionals had circulated to an audience of one (me) and equally needed to be taken with a grain of salt—at least trade journal reports circulate throughout a number of different communities working in these media sectors, above and below the line. In the future, therefore, I am particularly interested in reasserting the value of trade discourse as a site of analysis.

For Johnson then, analysing trade papers as texts might mean that the researcher is unable to accurately decipher how the media industries work—lacking in an ability to reveal the corporate context of media industry studies, for instance. But analysing documentation such as industry trade papers can allow for understandings of 'the industrial meanings, identities, and discourses that produce those industries as a tangible phenomenon'—what I have called the discursive context of study. And for Johnson (2014) at least, 'maybe that is even more interesting in some ways.'

MAKING USE OF TRADE PAPERS AND SOCIAL MEDIA

Leora Hadas (2014) agrees with Johnson's interest, noting that 'a huge variety of documents are created every day in the course of the media industries' ongoing work: Schedules, memos, contracts, protocols, press releases, articles and interviews in the trade press and countless more.' For Hadas (2014), 'we are blessed by just how much text the media industries produce beyond their actual products', and she elaborates by identifying some of the precise knowledge bases and areas of focus that any comprehensive analysis of industry trade papers can reveal:

> The more things are recorded, organised and made concrete, the more we have to go on when seeking to understand how cultural products come to be, how their production is managed—who benefits and who loses, who is seen and who remains unseen, how hierarchies are created and maintained, how creativity translates to business, etc.

When analysing trade papers one becomes aware of how each of these peripheral pieces of text tells not only one story, but three—firstly about its content, secondly about the people who produced it, and thirdly about the audience they intend it for. No press release is ever for the press alone. Many documents that would seem intended for circulation only within a film or television studio, for example, such as shooting scripts and series bibles, are often released publically in other contexts.

Thus while observation and interviews might tell us about day-to-day affairs and how creative workers perceive themselves and their environment—as was discussed in Chap. 6—for Hadas (2014) it is 'those official documents that tell us what has been codified and made binding. They represent a permanence in time, as it is documented interactions, accounts and commitments that are kept for posterity and eventually makes up the official history of the media industries.' Offering critical insights into everything from stories of management flows to creative brand identity, trade papers have indeed emerged as crucial artefacts for researchers. And the fact that trade papers are publically available, be it for traditional consumption purposes or not, goes some way to dispelling the myth that media industry studies is all about gaining inside access to media industries. Rather, it is equally about theorising the social, economic, political, and cultural place of the media industries in society.

Furthermore, Alisa Perren (2016: 228) observes that 'trade publications such as *Variety, Hollywood Reporter, Broadcasting & Cable, Billboard, Comic Book Resources, Publisher's Weekly*, and *Advertising Age* are often the "go-to" sources for industry professionals, the means by which media workers keep up with the latest news about their business.' For Perren (2016: 228–229),

[t]he trades have been valuable resources for media industry researchers for a number of reasons. First, they typically cover crucial industrial issues, events, and players in far more detail and with greater regularity than do mainstream publications. Not only can researchers follow the latest news pertaining to a particular issue, but they can also see how discussions about that issue have developed over time. Second, trade publications provide researchers with vital background knowledge, helping them to fill in the blanks before they initiate interviews with industry practitioners. [...] Third, the trades provide a sense of the dominant discourses within the media industries. Different trades speak to different industrial sectors and have their own language (or "slanguage," as *Variety* calls it). By reading these publications, it is possible to get a snapshot of the mindset of "the industry" in the broadest sense—the anxieties, priorities, and achievements of those in power.

Perren is correct, and before anyone can even begin to think about producing scholarly research that provides value for both academia and for media industries, it is first crucial for the researcher to be able to understand something *about* the media industries, something that might equally be learned via analysis from a wider, more contextualised cultural perspective. And for scholars such as Toby Miller (2006: 21), 'cultural studies is a tendency across disciplines, rather than a discipline itself.' In other words, as Pertti Alasuutari (1995: 2) puts it, taking a cultural approach to study means making use of all useful theories in order to gain insight about the phenomena one studies.' Cultural studies methodology has often been described by the concept of *bricolage*: piecing together various items of documentation in culture so to assess the role and manifestation of a chosen object of study across a vast sociological terrain. The likes of Twitter feeds and other social media sites, trade papers, magazine pieces, newspaper articles, etc. are an example of this cultural bricolage—such sources at once communicate about the media industries and are industries unto themselves.

Like trade papers, indeed, social media is another easily accessible 'text' produced by the media industries that shares much the same characteristic of being easily and publically available outputs about the communications of media industries. In terms of methodological function, social media differs to trade papers in the sense that it is much closer to being an actual media product—social media is of course a platform of consumption for media audiences. And yet social media is still no less discursive in its communication than an industry trade paper, and in so far as it revolves around media industry practitioners talking to audiences via a platform, social media is another text that can be analysed to uncover industry discourses.

FROM *How* TO READ TO *What* TO READ

This multifunctionality of trade papers and social media is precisely why such materials remain useful for understanding the ways that media industry practitioners narrativise the transformation of deep social structures into clear sets of meanings and understandings about the media industries. Amanda Lotz argues that such materials articulate a discourse that is important for anyone involved in media industry studies to better understand 'the history, norms of practice, and text of the medium' (Lotz 2007: 34). Before Lotz developed her own theories of the television industry, for instance, she read trade publications such as *Television Week* and *Broadcasting and Cable* for years: 'Part of my training included constant reading of trade press to maintain familiarity with the nuances of industrial practice' (2007: 34).

In this same vein, Jack Newslinger (2015) suggests that looking at online user-generated content—especially that which is produced by media industry personnel—can be enormously useful for analysing the more 'hidden' discourses of the media industries—or rather those discourses that are somewhat more 'personal' to the media industry practitioners creating them compared to the more corporate discourses displayed on a media company's website, for instance. 'Media personnel have blogs and social media, so why not use these for research?', asks Newslinger (2015).

Relatedly, Elinor Groom (2014) adds public libraries, museums, archives, and heritage sites as further opportunities to assess additional media industry discourses:

> Research trips to libraries, museums, archives, heritage sites and other vessels of data involve a different set of rituals and preparations, compared to the process of interviewing working professionals, or conducting audience surveys or consulting Google [...] When I prepare for an archive visit, I am less concerned with cramming everything there is to know about my subject, or with judging whether my outfit is too formal or not formal enough; I am more concerned with jotting down exact reference numbers, checking up on the regulations regarding note-taking and sharpening my pencils accordingly. Researching in archives, libraries and museums does require forethought and preparation, but so long as you've done your due diligence as a researcher, the archives will reward you with a period of focused research with your materials, without the distraction of social interaction. The documents don't answer back.

Such spaces and documentation may not answer back, as Groom puts it, but they do indeed convey much information that manifests culturally. And so the key question, as so often happens when considering aspects of methodology, moves from *how* to read to *what* to read. Internal correspondence—by far the hardest kind of industrial documents to gain access to—could in theory tell you the actual facts of how a particular marketing decision was made, for example, but could it ever really tell you the *whole* story of this marketing decision? Does the decision, as it was made within a studio, for example, and recorded only for that film studio's eyes and ears, have any comprehensible meaning apart from the press release that it resulted in?

It may well be the case that far more publically accessible documentation such as trade papers, newspaper reports, magazines articles, corporate websites, etc. actually reveal more about the media industries as a 'modality', i.e., the wider cultural arenas of the media industries where larger economic and political forces are communicated as more local and discursive sets of narrativised meanings, messages, and values.

CHALLENGES OF USING INDUSTRY TEXTS

However, while studying the discursive context of the media industries can be argued to afford a more contextualised understanding of how media practitioners communicate and translate the complex societal impacts and workings of the media industries into engaging stories and consumable sets of ideas, this is far from the end of the story. For as Groom (2014) concludes, while 'some may feel that paperwork is only supplementary or secondary to "the media"', such sources are only the beginning phase in 'understanding the industries that created the media—not just the individual creators and their creations.' And this dynamic raises methodological challenges.

Perren (2016: 30), for example, adds that 'perhaps the overarching point that industry-oriented researchers should keep in mind is that the trades function *as part of* the media industries in general,' and must therefore be approached with some caution. Building on the drawbacks identified by Kenton T. Wilkinson and Patrick F. Merle (2013) previously, John Thornton Caldwell (2008) argues that the trades frequently function as the public relations arm for the media industries. Caldwell (2008) argues that the trade papers produced by and for the media industries can on occasion be guilty of perpetuating long-standing industrial myths. Caldwell warns against media industry studies scholars using what is presented in the trades as the 'truth' or taking their reports at face value. Instead, it is crucial to remember that published reports are simple discourses, they are communication—neither fact not fiction, not right nor wrong.

So, as a way to demonstrate how best to make use of industry documents such as social media, and to do so in ways that reveal insights into the discursive context, allow Dave Harte to show how he makes use of social media in his own research to reveal the discursive communities and communication of the UK journalism industry.

CASE STUDY: RESEARCHING JOURNALISM THROUGH SOCIAL MEDIA

Dave Harte

The role of the ordinary citizen in making journalism represents a significant challenge to those whose profession it is to produce the news for print, online, or broadcast. The 'citizen journalist' has seemingly entered the profession without the need for formal training and has arrived as newsgatherer, publisher, and curator. Sometimes the citizen as newsgatherer is an altogether accidental affair as they bare witness to a breaking news event and instinctively reach for their smartphones to share images and words with whoever wants to see them. Examples of professional journalists then openly pleading with the citizen for rights to republish these images are easy to find. From a plane landing in the Hudson river (in 2009), to the Glasgow helicopter crash (in 2013) and a bus crash in Coventry (in 2015), the first-on-the-scene images we saw in newspapers and on television were taken by citizens and carefully negotiated from their grasp by canny news picture editors. These examples might feel like exceptions given the events covered are hardly of the everyday. Yet the citizen—equipped as they are, as indeed we all are, with devices capable of taking images, shooting video, publishing to the Internet—makes contributions to news gathering at a more banal, everyday, 'hyper'-local level. Further, as my own research has revealed, some of them make impressive use of social media platforms to develop ad hoc, informal, local news operations that draw on other citizens as their newsgathering resource.

In this case study I will look at how an examination of social media can tell us much about everyday citizen journalism. As part of a UK research council funded project on 'Creative Citizenship'[1] I have been examining the role played by citizen-led news initiatives that cover small local areas. Such 'hyperlocal' media have increasingly attracted the attention of policymakers and commentators in the UK. The UK charity Nesta has been an advocate for the sector and its definition of what a hyperlocal news publisher is remains the most quoted: 'Online news or content services pertaining to a town, village, single postcode or other, small geographically defined community' (Radcliffe 2012: 9). In policy, much is made of hyperlocal media's potential to plug the 'democratic deficit'. In 2009 the then Labour Government, in its Digital Britain report, cited the 'medium-term potential of online hyperlocal news' to contribute to a pending gap in the provision 'between the old and new' (Department for Culture Media and Sport 2009: 150). Ofcom, the UK communications regulator, in its 2009 review of local and regional media in the UK, noted hyperlocal media as being nascent in contrast to a developing US scene. Much of the UK material 'is hard to find, either because it does not attract a lot of traffic, or because it fails to deploy the strategies required to get a high ranking in traditional search engines' (Ofcom 2009: 45). In their 2012 overview of the emerging network of hyperlocal websites Ofcom claimed that these sites have '[t]he potential to support and broaden the range of local media content available to citizens and consumers at a time when traditional local media providers continue to find themselves under financial pressure' (Ofcom 2012: 103).

But claims made for hyperlocal media often go beyond their contribution to news: 'I do think the growing belief in hyperlocal media needs much more thought, especially in Britain. We have fractured communities here and there is an urgent need to find some glue' (Greenslade 2007). Metzgar et al. have noted how 'grant-making organizations have hailed HLMOs [hyperlocal media organisations] as a potential saviour for the struggling news industry. Scholars have proclaimed HLMOs a 21st century breeding ground for civic engagement' (Metzgar et al. 2011: 773). Such scholarly optimism is not new when it comes to discussing the role the Internet plays in reforming journalism. Dan Gillmor lauds the potential democratic benefits that come as a result of us all being '[a]ctive users of news, not mere consumers' (Gillmor 2004: 238). 'Everyone is a journalist,' argues John Hartley (2009: 154) who seems positively delighted at that prospect. Meanwhile, former journalists turned academics Gary Hudson and Mick Temple offer an acerbic critique in their essay 'We Are Not All Journalists' (2010), arguing that many academics are 'stretching the concept of journalism to extremes' (2010: 66) by claiming that any 'user' that generates news content is therefore a journalist.

These tensions in the debate around the role of technology ultimately hinge on the extent to which it allows participation in the process of doing journalism and whether such participation is to the benefit of journalism's normative mission, that is, to enhance democracy. It might be right to surmise that such participation, on whatever terms, may 'not automatically result in, and should therefore not be confused with, increased political participation in the public sphere' (Paulussen and D'Heer 2013: 4). Yet Benkler (2003) makes the point that at the very least we are moving away from the model of a powerful media subjugating its readers 'with the Baywatch effect, the depoliticization of public conversation' (Benkler 2003: 1265). The development of alternative media forms as facilitated by the Internet 'offer[s] substantial outlets for more attractive democratic practices and information flows than we saw in the twentieth century' (Benkler 2003: 1265). Joss Hands puts forward a compelling case for a framework with which to view the role of technology. He describes a 'digital networked technological hegemony, within a horizon of techno-capitalism' (2011: 47)—a framing that allows opportunities for resistance. He contrasts Heidegger's pessimistic view on technology (that it entraps us) with the realities of living in a world with near-ubiquitous take-up of digital devices (in the developed world at least). That is, by putting technology in the hands of the 'multitude' whose everyday use of it may be both ordinary and extraordinary by turns, capitalism is unwittingly opening itself up 'to a new cycle of democratisation and social, economic and political flux' (2011: 47).

B31 VOICES

In my research with the hyperlocal news service 'B31 Voices' it is this 'multitude' that I have been keen to gain insight to. With over 20,000 likes on their Facebook page and 7,500 followers on Twitter (as of October 2015), B31 Voices seems to have a large audience for the few suburbs of south Birmingham it covers. Typical of hyperlocal news operations in the UK (Williams et al. 2014, 2015), it is run by non-professional journalists, in this case a husband and wife team. My interviews with them revealed that what had started as a modest form of place-blogging in 2010 had since morphed into something rather more burdensome: 'I will be walking along the supermarket and I will hear people saying, oh did you see about that on B31 Voices. And I say: "oh that's us. You are aware that there are a lot of readers and they are relying on it […] I would feel bad if I gave up, I would feel guilty. [...] I think now it has got to a point where it has snowballed out of control in a way and people actually rely on it now' (Sas Taylor 2014). Undertaking research within the hyperlocal newsroom inevitably comes up against the fact that the newsroom is also the home, and boundaries between work time and leisure time aren't always clear. As Marty says, 'It is constant. We talk about B31, it is like 24/7 pretty much.' Keeping up with the social media output takes up most of the time and it isn't unusual for the Taylors to find themselves waking in the middle of the night to make contributions to Facebook or Twitter: 'We might have a missing person or a missing pet that's touched everyone, and I will check in the middle of the night to see if there's any news,' says Sas. Marty adds, 'So when we are talking about a dog, it can be about 4 o'clock in the morning, we might wake up, has that dog been found? Yes, it is ridiculous, it really is, it is wrong.'

Undertaking Social Media Analysis

In parallel to my research within B31 Voices' 'newsroom', I wanted to be able to understand the behaviours of its social media network. I decided to focus on a single month (March 2014) and attempt to draw down as much data as possible from its Twitter and Facebook networks. Although I was myself a member of these networks it was clear that I could not keep up with every single post or adequately account for the scale of activity just through observation. Both Twitter and Facebook allow access to posting data through their APIs (Application Programming Interface). The process for acquiring API 'keys' on either platform is quite straightforward providing you have an account yourself. 'Scraping' Twitter data is made even easier through the excellent work of some third party developers, and in this instance I used a resource called TAGS, developed by Martin Hawksey.[2] This allowed an archive of tweets to be collected that made mention of the B31Voices Twitter handle (@B31Voices). In all, there were 1143 mentions of @B31Voices by other accounts on Twitter in March 2014. But those mentions were not dominated by a small number of noisy users: 91 % of users mentioned @B31Voices fives times or less. A similar story emerges on Facebook where the 5,567 likes on the 223 posts were largely from individuals who clicked 'like' five times or less in the month examined. To a degree this suggested that there was a long tail to online participation.

Such statistical analysis is possible because the data accessed via the APIs can be analysed in a package such as Microsoft Excel (thus enabling pivot tables and charts to be created). The Facebook data is particularly rich, or at least it seems so. It can tell the researcher who commented on the original post, who liked it, who liked specific comments, and who shared the post. However, the API does restrict some access to data depending on users' privacy settings. Further, in doing this kind of analysis the researcher is faced with an immediate ethical dilemma given that the downloaded data shows the full name of the commenter, sharer, or 'liker'. Anonymising the data should happen as soon as it is downloaded, and in writing up findings one should be careful in quoting directly from users as this may reveal their identity.

What was clear about the B31 Voices data is that their Twitter and Facebook networks play host to a continuous, noisy conversation about everyday living. Everything from the trivial (a lost dog story gets 132 comments alone) to the more serious concerns of local governance and crime gets covered and acts to bring people together online. Interactions are rich in everyday detail. Car accidents and traffic delays often result in near-live updates from the scene as witnesses and participants come together to offer up their version of events. Indeed, it often seems that Sas and Marty Taylor's role is made redundant as 'the people formerly known as the audience' (Rosen 1999) take control of the online space and offer every possible angle to a story, contributing more than just opinions but vivid detail and eyewitness accounts. At points, Sas and Marty intervene to try and make sense of the networked conversation. So during the 'crisis' of a heavy snowfall they used the same hashtag—#B31Snowwatch—across all their platforms in a demonstration of the potential of the networked impact of the B31 community. Updates from citizens on the ground painted a vivid picture of a suburb slowly grinding to a halt as buses stopped running, schoolchildren were sent home, and supermarket shelves emptied as a result of panic-buying. For Sas Taylor #B31Snowwatch was evidence of the value of their service:

The B31 snowwatch, too, was a big thing that clearly proved how much people relied on it and were interacting with it as well. So then you ask yourself: If B31 Voices had not done that, what would have happened? They would have survived—it was not like a major snowfall, but they nevertheless benefitted from it, and so then you feel that you have got to keep that up, and you have got to keep giving them that. (Sas Taylor 2014) The #B31Positive hashtag is a similar ongoing attempt to manage content but this time to promote good news stories and encourage good deeds in the community rather than simply gather news.

Whilst there is plenty of evidence on B31 Voices' Facebook page of citizen engagement in important issues such as politics and crime, perhaps stubbornly it is the banal that gets most attention. Any mention of pets— lost or found—received the bulk of likes, shares, and comments. Pet stories received 76 % of the total shares for March 2014. By contrast, stories concerning local government were never shared. However, participants in the network include local politicians, public sector workers, police, and other official sources of information that tend to treat B31 Voices, despite the informality of its set up, as they would any other media organisation.

In effect, B31 Voices offers a useful, direct-networked connection through to those in local power, even if the residents of the area are more immediately interested in the banal rather than the political. John Postill has expressed frustration at the lack of attention to the ways in which everyday use of Internet technologies might be used to support change at the local level. There is much value, he claims, in studying 'emerging forms of residential sociality linked to "banal activism"—the activism of seemingly mundane issues such as traffic congestion, waste disposal and petty crime' (2008: 419). He makes the case that, with very few exceptions, 'banal activism has been neglected by Internet scholars' (2008: 419). Yet perhaps it is on the back of such banality that the networked potential of this community comes to the fore, thus revealing what Nick Couldry has called 'new networks of trust' (2004: 48).

MAKING SENSE OF SOCIAL MEDIA DATA

Social media is full of communities of geography or of interest not dissimilar in make-up and levels of activity to B31 Voices. However, for the journalism researcher, examining the Facebook and Twitter activity of such communities offers rich sources of qualitative data through which to engage with current debates around the role of the citizen in the news production process. As tempting as it might be to undertake network analysis to attempt to see relationships between users, this would be to ignore that the bulk of this data set is text, written by hundreds of different citizens who come across B31 Voices as part of their everyday engagement with social media. Much could be gained from a more forensic thematic or discursive analysis of citizens' comments and replies.

Researching through social media potentially bypasses some of the methodological issues that traditionally frustrate the media ethnographer undertaking audience studies. Accessing data through APIs is relatively simple, can be undertaken remotely, and the subject remains unaware of their observation (which raises consent and ethical issues).

It should be said though that both the researcher and the citizen news publisher can be equally frustrated by their engagement with the mechanics of social media. For the researcher, the frustration lies in the vexed question as to whether they are getting everything there is to get. What will the API allow them to access? Is this a full set of status updates or partial? Have the rules governing API access changed since I last carried out my research? Is there anything in the missing data that affects my ability to hypothesise? How do I get data from popular yet seemingly private platforms such as Snapchat? For the citizen journalist there is an ongoing battle with the 'algorithm', particularly on Facebook. Are our updates appearing on people's timelines when I want them to? How often should I post in order to maximise my audience? Both researcher and citizen journalist need to be attentive to the ways in which the corporate owners of these platforms change the rules of the game at will, but for both parties the rewards are a deeper understanding of the everyday use of social media and the ways in which its users create community from the endless news of lost pets and traffic delays.

NOTES

1. Full details of this research project are as follows: Ian Richard Hargreaves et al [should all authors be included here?] (2015) *Media, Community and the Creative Citizen*. Cardiff University [project ref: AH/J005290/1].
2. See https://tags.hawksey.info/.

BIBLIOGRAPHY

Alasuutari, P. (1995). *Researching Culture: Qualitative Method and Cultural Studies*. London: SAGE.

Bauman, Z., & May, M. (2001). *Thinking sociologically*. Malden MA: Blackwell Publishing.

Benkler, Y. (2003). Freedom in the Commons: Towards a Political Economy of Information. *Duke Law Journal, 52*(6), 1245–1276.

Caldwell, J. T. (2008). *Production Culture: Industrial Reflexivity and Critical Practice in Film and Television*. Durham and London: Duke University Press.

Caldwell, J. T. (2015, April 14–15). Production studies: Where do we go from here? Panel presentation at the conference of New Directions in Film and Television Production Studies, Bristol.

Couldry, N. (2004). The Productive 'Consumer' and the Dispersed 'Citizen. *International Journal of Cultural Studies, 7*(1), 21–32.

Department for Culture Media and Sport, D. f. B. I. a. S. (2009). Digital Britain. Series Digital Britain; City: 238.

Dulczewski, Z. (1984). *Florian Znaniecki: życie i dzieło.* Wydawnictwo Poznańskie.

Giddens, A. (1984). *The Constitution of Society: Outline of the Theory of Structuration.* Cambridge: Polity Press.

Gillmor, D. (2004). *We the Media.* O'Reilly Media, Inc.

Greenslade, R. (2007). The Peoples' Papers? A New View of Hyperlocal Media. *The Guardian.* Available at: http://www.guardian.co.uk/media/greenslade/2007/jul/12/thepeoplespapersanewview

Groom, E. (2014). It's All On Paper: Archiving the Media Industries, and Studying Archive Collections. *Industrial Approaches to Media – The University of Nottingham.* Available at: http://www.nottingham.ac.uk/research/groups/isir/projects/industrial-approaches-to-media/elinor-groom.aspx

Hadas, L. (2014). The Trouble With Industry Documents: Reading Text and Context. *Industrial Approaches to Media – The University of Nottingham.* Available at: http://www.nottingham.ac.uk/research/groups/isir/projects/industrial-approaches-to-media/index.aspx

Halas, E. (2010). *Towards the world culture society: Florian Znaniecki's culturalism.* Bern: Peter Lang.

Hands, J. (2011). @ *Is for Activism : Dissent, Resistance and Rebellion in a Digital Culture.* London: Pluto.

Hartley, J. (2009). *The Uses of Digital Literacy.* St Lucia, Qld.: University of Queensland Press.

Hilmes, M. (2014). An Interview with Professor Michele Hilmes. *Industrial Approaches to Media – The University of Nottingham.* Available at: http://www.nottingham.ac.uk/research/groups/isir/projects/industrial-approaches-to-media/index.aspx

Hudson, G., & Temple, M. (2010). We Are Not All Journalists Now. In G. Monaghan & S. Tunney (Eds.), *Web Journalism: A New Form of Citizenship?* (pp. 63–76). Eastbourne: Sussex Academic Press.

Johnson, D. (2014). Understanding media industries from all perspectives. Industrial Approaches to Media—The University of Nottingham. Available at: http://www.nottingham.ac.uk/research/groups/isir/projects/industrialapproaches-to-media/derek-johnson.aspx

Lotz, A. D. (2007). *The Television Will Be Revolutionized.* New York: New York University Press.

Lotz, A. D. (2014). Media Industry Studies: Challenges, Pitfalls, Obstacles. *Industrial Approaches to Media – The University of Nottingham*. Available at: http://www.nottingham.ac.uk/research/groups/isir/projects/industrial-approaches-to-media/amanda-lotz.aspx

Metzgar, E. T., Kurpius, D. D., & Rowley, K. M. (2011). Defining Hyperlocal Media: Proposing a Framework for Discussion. *New Media & Society, 13*(5), 772–787.

Miller, T. (2006). *A Companion to Cultural Studies*. Malden: Blackwell Publishers.

Newsinger, J. (2015, April 14–15). *The infrapolitics of cultural practice: Uncovering hidden transcripts in production studies*. Panel presentation at the conference of New Directions in Film and Television Production Studies, Bristol.

Ofcom (2009). *Local and Regional Media in the UK*. London: Ofcom.

Ofcom (2012). *The Communications Market Report*. London: Ofcom.

Paulussen, S., & D'Heer, E. (2013). Using Citizens for Community Journalism. *Journalism Practice, 7*(5), 1–16.

Perren, A. (2016). The Trick of the Trades: Media Industry Studies and the American Comic Book Industry. In M. Banks, B. Connor, & V. Mayer (Eds.), *Production Studies, the Sequel: Cultural Studies of Global Media Industries* (pp. 227–237). New York: Routledge.

Postill, J. (2008). Localizing the Internet Beyond Communities and Networks. *New Media & Society, 10*(3), 413–431.

Radcliffe, D. (2012). *Here and Now: UK Hyperlocal Media Today*. Nesta.

Rosen, J. (1999). *What Are Journalists for?* Yale: Yale University Press.

Seale, C. (1998). *Researching Society and Culture*. London: SAGE.

Wilkinson, K. T., & Merle, P. F. (2013). The Merits and Challenges of Using Business Press and Trade Journal Reports in Academic Research on the Media Industries. *Communication, Culture & Critique, 6*, 415–431.

Williams, A., Barnett, S., Harte, D., & Townend, J. (2014). *The State of Hyperlocal Community News in the UK: Findings from a Survey of Practitioners*. Available at: https://hyperlocalsurvey.files.wordpress.com/2014/07/hyperlocal-community-news-in-the-uk-2014.pdf

Williams, A., Harte, D., & Turner, J. (2015). The Value of UK Hyperlocal Community News. *Digital Journalism, 3*(5), 680–703.

The Reciprocity and Publishing of Media Industry Studies

If Part II looked at the actual *doing* of media industry studies, then Part III will aim to identify clear pathways for ways of making media studies research that is *about* industry, research that is equally valuable *for* the media industries themselves. Steve Presence (2014) notes that many media companies are unsure of the benefits of engaging with academics, while those that are more open to what academia is about are 'perhaps justifiably nervous about the idea of critical scrutiny and essentially opening up their livelihood to examination.' This section explores ways of deciphering this problem, examining methods of 'translating' academic research in ways that are useful and engaging to industry. Thus as Chap. 8 explores what knowledge exchange has come to mean in the context of media industry studies, ending with a global insight into this topic from Henry Jenkins, Chap. 9 aims to rethink what publishing now means in this same context, with Emily Caston's highly insightful case study examining what publishing means in her experience of working with practitioners from the UK music industry.

BIBLIOGRAPHY

Presence, S. (2014). The ethics and politics of media engagement. Industrial Approaches to Media—The University of Nottingham. Available at: http://www.nottingham.ac.uk/research/groups/isir/projects/industrial-approaches-to-media/industrial-approaches-to-media-inaugural-event.aspx

CHAPTER 8

Approaching Knowledge Exchange

Matthew Freeman

Bringing to a close my theoretical discussion of a methodology of UK-centric media industry studies, this penultimate chapter aims to explore what knowledge exchange now means in the context of media industry studies. I begin by considering an ideal form of knowledge exchange in this setting, before focusing on approaches to implementing models of knowledge exchange in different media industry sectors. This includes an analysis of various academics' personal experiences of conducting knowledge exchange, highlighting tips and insights about methodology in this setting.

Reflecting on these particular approaches to knowledge exchange, this chapter will also reflect on the importance of mutual benefits and reciprocity, identifying how the academic researcher can actually go about articulating the mutual benefits of their scholarship to both academic and industry audiences. I outline some specific ways in which academic research can be made valuable to the media industries, outlining different methods for applying this kind of work. I move on to mapping different approaches to reciprocity between industry and academia according to theme. For example, I have shown already how a number of media-based marketing and promotional companies in the UK value 'thought leadership', so how

M. Freeman (✉)
Bath Spa University, Bath, UK
e-mail: m.freeman@bathspa.ac.uk

© The Editor(s) (if applicable) and The Author(s) 2016
M. Freeman, *Industrial Approaches to Media*,
DOI 10.1057/978-1-137-55176-4_8

might scholarly analyses be applied to map these kinds of changes? In the final part of the chapter, Henry Jenkins offers an invaluable insight into what it means to work across the academia–industry divide, providing a set of clear tips and best practice principles for conceiving of scholarship as valuable to the eyes and ears of the media industries.

What Is Knowledge Exchange?

As was argued in Chap. 6, the ethos of doing media industry studies might be argued to be as much about producing scholarly research that has the potential to be relevant *for* the media industry as it is about producing research that is *about* the media industries. As Johnson (2013a, b) noted previously, media industry studies is about forging a 'shared interest', conceptualising benefits to be gained from collaboration and from conceiving of academia–industry partnerships with mutual benefits.

Another way of phrasing this kind of 'shared interest' is knowledge exchange. A vast proportion of UK academic funding bodies require the generation of impact beyond academia through 'fostering global economic performance, and specifically the economic competitiveness of the United Kingdom' and 'enhancing quality of [...] creative output'.[1] The Arts and Humanities Research Council (AHRC) define knowledge exchange specifically as 'the processes by which new knowledge is co-produced through interactions between academic and non-academic individuals and communities.'[2] Still, this emphasis on impact via knowledge exchange raises many important questions about the potential divergences between the needs and values of commercial businesses and the needs and values of academic research—notably the political and ethical questions that have been considered already in Chap. 3. Besides such ethical dimensions, there is a sense that actually doing knowledge exchange of any kind is incredibly challenging to conceptualise, as Amanda Lotz (2014) discusses:

> Approaching the possibility of pursuing a form of knowledge transfer between media industries and academia is quite difficult. I cannot say that I have succeeded much beyond one case where I was invited to speak to employees of a cable channel after its president saw my book and thought it provided a context that was helpful. There is a tremendous amount to be learned whenever opportunities to engage, observe, or interview those working in media industries can be achieved, but getting an audience with them can be challenging. The very nature of their jobs—of day-to-day

deadlines and extinguishing immediate fires—can make the kinds of issues that typically animate academics impossible to ponder, which makes conversations difficult. [...] It is challenging to write simultaneously for both audiences, and so it is not surprising that those in the industry who have encountered academic conversations are uncertain of our relevance.

Beyond these kinds of practical challenges, the very idea of pursuing a form of knowledge transfer between media industries and academia—in other words, making academic research speak to the media industries—could be read and too easily dismissed as being complicit with an attack on the value of intellectual work. Worse still, calls for knowledge exchange between academia and the media industries could be perceived as ascribing value only to scholarship that has a defined market need. Indeed, I do not wish to ascribe any kind of 'employability agenda'; rather, I wish to re-emphasise the kind of critical possibilities that can emerge from collaboration with the media industries, as was demonstrated by Evans and McDonald in Chap. 3. In particular, it is crucial to distinguish between speaking back to power and working for it—between working *with* or *for* media industries—so to conceptualise a form of knowledge exchange in media industry studies as that which allows researchers to forge a collaborative but adversarial position in between academia and industry.

WHAT IS KNOWLEDGE EXCHANGE IN THE CONTEXT OF MEDIA INDUSTRY STUDIES?

What then might knowledge exchange really mean in the context of media industry studies? Principally, much of this ethos of knowledge exchange between academia and the media industries has itself been 'exchanged' from other disciplines and industry backgrounds. Kate Oakley (2013: 29) argues that 'models of so-called knowledge transfer and collaboration which were being put in practice by government were drawn largely from science and technology, and did not adequately reflect the workings of the cultural sector' (also see Crossick 2006). In some ways, many of the political debates and disputes within media industry studies—namely about its role as a facilitator of collaboration and potential knowledge exchange with industry—seem shaped by some of the same political debates and disputes that have played out in business and management studies for many years. As business scholars Bryman and Bell (2011: 5) note, 'some writers have suggested that business and management research can be understood only as an applied field because it is concerned not only with understanding the nature of organizations but also with solving problems that are related to managerial practice.' Hence, in effect, why ideas of consultancy are so commonplace within the field of business and management studies, with a clear sense of the different roles played by theory and practice articulated: 'Backed by bits and pieces of theory, the consultant contributes to practice, whereas the scholar contributes to theory supported by fragments of practice' (Gummesson 2000: 9).

Despite this neat binary opposition, however, Gummesson, like many within the field of business studies, sees the roles of researchers and consultants as closely tied—reinforcing the view that the perspective of both parties is determined by their ability to convince the business community that their findings are 'relevant' and 'useful'. That being said, other business studies scholars would argue that application is *not* a primary purpose to which business research should be directed (Burnell 2003). For these scholars, making academic research explicitly relevant to managerial practice ought not to be the main aim of academic study (Clegg et al. 2002; Hinings and Greenwood 2002). Such scholars believe that research should not be dictated by non-academic interests, such as professional associations and government agencies, who may seek to influence its focus and guide its development in a way that can be useful to current practice but equally susceptible to the whims of business fads and fashions.

Now, in some sense these kinds of broader debates about the purpose and value of academic research and their application to wider industrial settings speaks directly to the kinds of debates in media industry studies discussed previously. But such debates also reiterate seminal work by Gibbons et al. (1994) who suggests that the process of knowledge production in contemporary society always falls into one of two contrasting categories, described as 'Mode 1' and 'Mode 2'. Mode 1 is what might be seen as the more traditional university model, where knowledge production is driven primarily by an academic agenda. Here, only limited emphasis is placed on the practical dissemination of the knowledge outside of scholarship, with the academic community prioritised. In business studies, Bryman and Bell (2011: 24) call this a *regulatory* form of research, where 'the purpose is to describe what goes on in organizations [...] but not to make any judgment of it.' Mode 2, in contrast, is more about direct application, and knowledge is not specified around academic circles. Instead, it involves academics, policymakers, and practitioners who apply a broad set of skills and experiences in order to tackle a shared problem.

This means knowledge is disseminated more rapidly and findings are more readily exploited in order to achieve practical advantage. Bryman and Bell (2011: 24) call this a radical form of research, where 'the point is to make judgments about the way that organizations ought to be and to make suggestions about how this could be achieved.'

Despite the more cautious claims of Clegg, Hinings, and Greenwood above, however, who suggested that Mode 1 research should exist alongside Mode 2 research, others have suggested that business and management research is ideally suited to this latter mode of study (see, for example, Tranfield and Starkey 1998). Given its ethos towards sustained industry engagement and producing shared research, one might well argue that the subfield of media industry studies is equally ideally suited to the objectives of Mode 2 research. In which case, where are the areas of investigation that perhaps best lend themselves to opportunities of collaboration and aims of direct application to media industries?

In one sense, and as was discussed in Chap. 2, both media-based research in academia and the media industries at large do overlap in their respective interests in understanding how to conceptualise audiences, as well as their preoccupations with questions of work and professionalism, and developments in thought leadership. Both academia and the media industries are partly characterised by their shared desires—commercial or otherwise—to carve out new knowledge about the media landscape and to apply that knowledge strategically going forward. Hanne Bruun (2015) agrees:

> The two knowledge systems are not identical but are deeply intertwined, and a dialogue is important for mutual benefits. To do research on an informed level and regarding the media as a knowledge system is also a prerequisite for so-called critical perspectives and approaches in media studies: If you do not know anything about the media there is no interest in your research and no one will listen to your ever-so-clever contributions. But if your work is based on insights the interest is there.

Jon Hickman, however, based within the Birmingham Centre for Media and Cultural Research (BCMCR) at Birmingham City University, insists that knowledge exchange his something that has perhaps always been a major part of many research centres' strategies in the UK. For Hickman (2016), the BCMCR has 'for a long time strove to take the work and the ideas of our research leaders within the School and apply those things to an industry context' (2016). What then have some of these knowledge exchange projects looked like? 'For example,' Hickman (2016) explains,

[a] number of the projects that I was involved in—such as one with Professor Andrew Dubber—centred on work conducted in relation to the music industries. In one, he was basically going in and teaching either his research, the research of the School, or wider ideas concerning the music industries and trying to process how those ideas manifested—or could manifest—in industry settings. So we started by saying, "well, there's this idea that has grown out of industry thinkers, which is the idea that, as an emerging recording artist, you need to earn X amount of money to start making a living and to get by." So we wanted to test out that idea. And in a way, that question was more of a reflection of the research that was going on in the School, because it started with an idea which then developed into a research question around some of the things that we were already working on.

Indeed, for Hickman (2016), as a general process, knowledge exchange projects most typically begin with the projects already underway within a given School or department. From there, it is then a process of 'looking at your resources and your contacts and then thinking to yourself, "okay, what could I do here that would maximise benefits to everybody?"' Most narrowly, aiming to produce knowledge exchange projects that contribute insights into (1) the commercial or behavioural implications of audiences, (2) issues about and solutions for the employability demands of the media industries, and (3) creative strategies for enhancing the productivity of the media industries based on wider research can be seen as three very broad areas for how to define knowledge exchange in the current context of media industry studies. And much of this definition boils down to questions of value. If academic researchers can provide insights about what media industries do that those industries do not already know, and the researcher can promise to do so without damaging the commercial reputation of the company, then that researcher will have a perceived value to the media industries at large. Still, in what specific contexts and instances can this kind of knowledge exchange occur?

WHAT CAN MEDIA STUDIES CONTRIBUTE TO THE MEDIA INDUSTRIES: AND HOW?

The first, and perhaps most everyday, manifestation of knowledge exchange in media studies comes in the act of teaching—the intention that someday there will be a transfer of knowledge when students exert their agency within the media industries. For Derek Johnson (2014), 'I think this kind of intervention is something we all do when we write about industry and then teach those ideas to students who might one day be in the positions to effect change.' Says Johnson (2014),

> I always tell the students in my media industry courses that they will likely be disappointed if they are expecting a course in "how to make it" in the media industries: I am not producing drones. Instead, what I hope they are getting is a way to imagine other possible forms and futures for industry to take—hopefully, more equal, democratic ones—so that they can be agents of change (rather than just continuity) when they enter that industry. This is of course playing quite a long game, and one with a lot of potential for attrition. So media studies would be wise to start building more relationships with institutions and practitioners working in the here and now, even if we constantly butt heads with existing corporate imperatives, if only to help prepare the way for future innovators less set in their ways.

Johnson seems to reinforce the notion here that academia should become the central hub for developing the media industry personnel of the future. Theorisations of the media industries can indeed be taught to the current generation of media studies students with the aim of fostering creativity in those students so that new conceptions and modes of thinking can then be injected into the future generation of the media industries—and such a process can of course be understood as knowledge exchange. As Hanne Bruun notes (2015), 'we educate a lot of the future employees in the media, and the knowledge exchange between the academia and the industry is going on, and has been going on for many years.'

That being said, knowledge exchange is also about far more than the 'long game' of teaching; more so, and what is most exciting about producing research that is both *about* and *for* the media industries lies in the potential to introduce new, innovative, or even radical ways of thinking into the contemporary media industries. The contributions of researchers might be what help develop the media industries into something other than their present form (to either micro or macro degrees). A number of the knowledge exchange projects mentioned by Hickman (2016), for instance, tend to focus on what might be deemed the peripheral or the educative work of the media industries—functioning as forms of training, in some cases, based on a perceived lack of existing knowledge around a given media industry. For example, Hickman (2016) discusses one particularly successful Knowledge Transfer Project at Birmingham City

University that was framed around publishing practices in the UK music industry. But this project sought not to examine the practice of publishing music per se, but instead 'to develop knowledge and understanding in the form of trade shows for people who were struggling with the new reality of publishing and producing music'.

And yet Laura Marshall (2015), managing director of Icon Films, points out that many UK media industry personnel and organisations do not actually know that they are objects of study in academia: 'A dialogue between academia and the media industries would certainly be valued, but I do believe that there is uncertainty about the logistics and mechanisms of how it all works.' So what might media industry studies' micro or macro contributions to the future of the media industries actually be—and how precisely might they manifest within the industry itself?

As will be discussed further in the next chapter, Emily Caston argues that working with the media industries is primarily about setting goals to try and make some kind of progressive change, arguing that we need to use our skills as academics to make a difference to industry—pointing to the BFI National Archive and the British Library as two places where her own work with the media industries has made a contextualised difference. And contextualisation can yield greater, collaborative insights into the most complex cultural questions and phenomena, such as the creation of a canon, for example, which can—and perhaps should—be determined by both the theoretical work of a scholar and the on-the-ground understandings of a practitioner.

Importantly, however, Hickman (2016) stresses that when working with media industry partners on a defined knowledge exchange or knowledge transfer project, a typical output model would be to propose to develop a 'prototype'—such as a platform, website, film, book, service, and so on. But that prototype should not in itself be positioned within the context of the project as a 'commercial' product. Instead, the work of the academic here is to develop ideas and new ways of thinking that have the potential to maximise benefits to industry, but not to work directly for the industry. In that sense, knowledge exchange between academia and industry is really about idea incubation, not market development—and it is in this sense that we can conceptualise a form of knowledge exchange in media industry studies that sees researchers forging collaborative but adversarial positions in between academia and the media industries.

In other words, we are not talking about 'knowledge exchange' so much as 'knowledge sharing', with both academia and industry working together closely towards many of the same critical goals. Derek Johnson (2014) talks about how, in his research about media licensing, he collaborated with organisations such as Futures of Entertainment in the hope of 'engaging in direct dialogue with industry practitioners to share the ideas I was developing about licensing and world-sharing in the course of writing [my book].' Johnson's industry engagement ultimately hoped to show that there were alternate ways of thinking about the practice and concept of licensing, with his work indicating how more positive uses of licencing might be embedded within industry practice in ways that could, potentially, yield commercial rewards: 'I think I felt there was an opportunity being missed to embrace a wider range of creative voices and let go of the idea that the best idea was the one authorised at the centre of all these new industry strategies' (2014). Johnson's contribution to the logics and understandings of media industry licensing was therefore rooted in the benefits of contextualisation, echoing Caston's point from earlier in the book that contextualisation is in fact the real value of academia to the media industries.

But are there any other ways in which media industry studies can contribute to the media industry? Many of the scholars interviewed for this book also cited the role of consultancy as an important form of knowledge exchange. Just as Evans (2014) discussed the creation of 'the recommendation bit' when working with the media industries, consultancy is a way of translating the insights of one's scholarly research into practical, step-by-step how-to's for media industry practitioners—encouraging scholars to reconceive academic work as applied content. Of course, in a context where collaborative research projects between academia and the media industries are being developed with shared benefits to both sides, consultancy could prove a logical output in line with any media industry partner's public or commercial objectives. By way of example, Hickman (2016) points to questions of duration, taste-making, and cultural uses of the media, and also highlights the long-standing desire to better understand new modes of telling stories—be it about fiction, non-fiction, production processes, or cultural experiences—as something that academics can offer industry.

Meanwhile, other industry practitioners and media organisations have described the value of academia–industry knowledge exchange in terms of adding prestige and credentials to their organisation or work via the affiliation of a university or an academic. What's more, Grainge (2014) discusses how his own collaborations with industry partners led to those partners wanting to then theorise and reflect on their own creative practice much more fully, even going on to write a book of their own. Such a result reinforces Catherine Johnson's earlier claim that both the media industries and media industry studies are in fact asking similar critical questions, all of which revolving around conceptions of audience, creativity, and productivity.

And so exchanging knowledge with the media industries about these similar research questions also means talking a shared language. In fact, Gianluca Sergi (2014) pinpoints language as a key concern for achieving successful—and sustained—knowledge exchange across the academia–industry terrain, arguing that 'the media industries speak their own language; if you go to them speaking your own language and they are speaking their language, the two shall not wed.' Sergi's comments echo Catherine Johnson's earlier example of the different ways that the word 'research' can be understood in the media industries compared to academia. And for Sergi (2014), with media industry studies, it is usually the researcher who approaches the industry, and so 'it is your responsibility to make sure they fully understand what you mean, what you are doing engaging with them, and why they should be interested in you.' Importantly, 'always articulate their advantage: *What is in it for them?*' (Sergi 2014).

This importance of speaking the same language, as it were, also boils down to the ways in which research findings are communicated. Katherine Champion (2015) argues that while the many multi-method approaches examined throughout this book—all of which can be classified broadly as qualitative methodologies—are crucial, more quantitative methodologies might be useful in articulating research findings to a media industry audience. Quantitative approaches, in fact, characterise much business and management studies methodology, crossing over usefully into media studies terrain (see Saunders et al. 2015). There is, of course, an array of quantitative data made freely available in the statistical yearbooks of organisations such as the British Film Institute and the European Audiovisual Observatory, not to mention public resources such as Box Office Mojo, the Internet Movie Database (IMDb), and the Lumiere database.

Content analysis is another example of a quantitative approach, a method that is based—in the most straightforward sense—on the act of counting and analysing frequency of occurrence within a specified object of study. For example, Champion's use of content analysis saw her counting differences in terms of text and image in different article types, comparing and contrasting print and online articles to gauge understandings of differences between print and online magazine production modes. With regards to application to the media industries, furthermore, Champion (2015) points out that content analysis is inherently suited to knowledge exchange principles because it can quantify salient commercial data and manifest an understanding about a wider contextual issue in the form of a practical, straight-talking, and easily digestible set of facts and figures—such as in the form of a research report.

WHAT CAN THE MEDIA INDUSTRIES CONTRIBUTE TO MEDIA STUDIES: AND HOW?

On the flip side, the question of what the media industries can offer media (industry) studies is a little bit easier to answer. As John Thornton Caldwell (2008), amongst others, has pointed out, the media industries are already sites of theorisation and critical practice where practitioners are making sense of the worlds in which they work on an everyday level. Caston (2015) agrees: 'Industry practitioners may be economically minded, but that is not to say that these people are not critical and analytical. If anything, it is that critical edge that has got them where they are in the industry.' As such, for Derek Johnson (2014), 'it makes sense that talking to media professionals, listening to the stories and narratives that they offer for negotiating those worlds, and recognising that they are already contributing to the attempt to make sense of media industries would save us the trouble of having to reinvent the wheel or actually embarrassing ourselves by speaking from a position of ignorance of what is happening on the ground.' But as Johnson (2014) further elaborates,

> [t]hat is not to say we should take practitioner theory at face value—like anything it should be interrogated with a critical lens. But trying to understand industrial production without talking to producers is like trying to make claims about consumption without talking to audiences. So in simply talking to us—whether "us" as scholars or more generally as the public—media industries have the power to give us insight and access to this crucial site of meaning making, community, and practice. Fortunately, the media industries love to talk about themselves. Media professionals are constantly "contributing" to media studies by issuing forth a constant stream of discourses and practices for us to think about.

Here is an example of this kind of constant stream of discourses and practice. Professor Andrew Dubber worked on a project called *Aftershock*, which was most broadly about understanding the human processes of writing and performing music, and how the stories of that process can be mediated online. The project saw musicians coming together to work creatively and collaboratively on music, with each of the musicians asked to film their actions, 'pointing a camera at whatever they thought was interesting, whenever they thought it was appropriate' (Dubber 2010). *Aftershock* benefitted from collaborations and networks based in academia, but it also provided new insights into how stories of production can be communicated digitally, how day-to-day activities, thoughts, and concerns of professional musicians transform into creative works, and hence how the challenges of collaboration work more broadly in the music industry—insights that were translated into academic circles.

Studying the media industries can help practitioners to better reflect on what they do and why they do it, then, but engaging with media industries for research can equally enhance a theoretical understanding of the subject. As Paul Kerr indicated back in Chap. 2, media studies used to be about critiquing the media, whereas more recent interest in media industry studies has shifted the theoretical priority towards developing students to shape and take part in the media. Industry can therefore look to academia, not to find some grand overarching model, but rather to feed and to hone new insights and ideas to do with strategic thinking that might, in turn, enhance some of those overarching models over time. Under such a rubric, however, is our role as academics really to reinforce that proverbial media industries bubble—explaining how and why they work—or to crack that bubble and bring in new knowledge and perspective so as to build a whole new bubble? For Derek Johnson (2014),

> [o]n the one hand, it is hard not to imagine that kind of change as a threat to the industrial status quo; but on the other, that kind of change could be extremely profitable and productive, not only for the people effecting it, but also for whole industries that might learn to operate in ways that are less problematic and maybe even still profitable.

Indeed, though Johnson raises the question of whether or not the mission of scholarship is ultimately compatible with the market needs of media institutions, he acknowledges that 'if we see scholarship as a form of activism, I think that implies some kind of commitment to trying to improve the industrial status quo, rather than throwing up one's hands and declaring the industry a lost cause' (2014). And for Johnson (2014), this kind of commitment 'would count as a "contribution," but it hinges on the specific issues we are seeking to change and the hope that we could arrive at some improved or less objectionable form of industry than we have now.'

Hickman (2016) reflects about a not-too-distant future scenario where, at least in his own institution in the UK, universities will cease chasing industry partners and connections after the fact, as it were, and instead will take what he calls a 'shop front approach', whereby universities will become a place where both academics and media industry practitioners can take classes together, and can incubate new projects via conversations and then agree to push those projects and those conversations in directions that are the most appropriate for the project in question. And such a future would certainly be in line with the methodology of doing media industry studies, at least as has been conceived and theorised within the pages of this book, as that which aims to make a contribution to the continuing development of the media industries as equitable sites of cultural production—or at least conceivable as such. As John Ellis (2015) asserts, 'media industry studies gives us, as researchers, something to trade with the industry.' Or, as Catherine Johnson (2013) so eloquently and conclusively puts it, 'the divergence between the needs of academic research and business in this case emerges less in the shared research questions than in the nature of the answers that are generated to these questions, how those answers are communicated, and the applicability of those answers to a commercial business setting.'

Of course, the ways in which answers can be generated and communicated to the media industries are diverse and take many different forms. By way of examples, in the following case study contribution Henry Jenkins reinforces this chapter's core claims and demonstrates how the knowledge of his own research has been exchanged with the media industries in a variety of ways. To do so, Jenkins further elaborates on the roles of teaching, reciprocity, policy, and ends with invaluable insights into how future generations of media studies researchers might go about conceiving of research projects built on reciprocity, pinpointing the need for multiperspectival work. For Jenkins, it is in the crafting of multiperspectival research—designed with reciprocal benefits for academia and industry— that affords academics the richest opportunities to stake out collaborative but adversarial positions in between academia and industry.

Case Study: The Need for Multiperspectival Work

Henry Jenkins

Over the past several decades, those of us living in the developed world have been in the midst of a phase of dramatic, rapid, and prolonged change, much of which has been ascribed to the invention and dispersion of digital and mobile technologies. These changes have impacted all aspects of our lives and thus have implications across all disciplines and institutions. But since most of these changes have centred around shifts in communication platforms and practices, these changes have been most dramatically felt within programs that centre on media and communications.

As the society around us copes with these changes, our expertise is gaining new value and visibility, and we either rise to those challenges or we demonstrate ourselves to be of limited value to our students and society at large. For us to confront this situation, we need to engage in conversation with others who are also confronting dramatic media change—among them, thought leaders in industry, government, policy advocacy and activism, the arts, and journalism.

For many of us coming from the humanities, these new relationships may be uncomfortable and uncertain: our fields since the 1960s have defined themselves in opposition to dominant institutions, rather than existing in conversation with them, and we may see the only possible terms of such a relationship as those of co-optation and subservience. What I advocate, however, is that we expand the concept of being a public intellectual to include engaging in and facilitating important conversations with other key institutions, often as a means of helping to shape and influence the changes that are taking place. We might think of engaging with industry in terms similar to the way we discuss policy work in relation to government or political parties. In those countries where this is a strong tradition in cultural studies, academics engage in important conversations with policymakers with whom they do not always—indeed, rarely—fully agree, but because they want to influence issues that matter to them. As academics, we can be advocates for under-served populations or for the public at large only if we agree to engage in conversations with those who shape the policies and practices that impact their lives. It is hard to speak truth to power if you are not speaking to power, and in the case of the digital, those decisions are more apt to be made by companies than by governments.

Beyond this, the reality is that there are not going to be enough academic jobs in the future for the students we are pumping through our graduate programs; they are going to need to seek work elsewhere and we either help prepare them for that work or we fail them. I think if we want to make a difference, we need to prepare them for potential work in industry, while helping them to see this work in terms of the theoretical and political commitments we have long fostered through our scholarship and teaching. We have to prepare them to make a difference in those contexts where they are going to be working: that does not mean our graduate programs become trade schools, but it does mean we help them to think through what it would mean to apply our theories to real world contexts where they might be working, and giving them a bigger picture of the media changes that are going to impact their future careers.

To me, all of these factors point to the need for new relationships between academia and industry, including those which involve knowledge sharing and co-production as well as those which involve placing students inside corporate spaces for internships.

ESTABLISHING ACADEMIC–INDUSTRIAL RECIPROCITY

Of course, this flow of knowledge and information should not be one directional. We have things to learn from as well as to teach industry. For example, at Massachusetts Institute of Technology, I helped to establish the Futures of Entertainment conferences, which brought together key thinkers for industry, academia, policy, and journalism, for extended discussions of key trends and developments in the media industries. Over time, these conferences developed a core constituency that got to know each other outside of normal work contexts, developed a shared vocabulary and a shared set of convictions that they brought to the projects they undertook. This Futures of Entertainment community asked hard, thoughtful questions, challenging projects which they felt did not reflect a more empowered conception of consumer relations, for example, and these exchanges have been spread widely—through the video recordings which are posted on the web, through Twitter responses, and through new partnerships which developed amongst people who participated at our events.

Since I moved to the University of Southern California, we have also added a west coast event (originally called *Transmedia Hollywood*, later *Transforming Hollywood*), which has supported similar kinds of exchanges. For example, it is clear that the concept of engagement has a strong grip on the ways the entertainment industry is making decisions, displacing the idea of appointment-based viewing with models which count on the consumer to seek out content. For academics writing about the media landscape, it is important that we understand how the industry is thinking about engagement, which effects programming, distribution, and branding strategies. The insights that emerge from these conversations have helped to shape academic writing on connected viewing, fan engagement, and transmedia entertainment, and have allowed academic writing to better keep pace with the changes taking place in a networked culture. For industry insiders, the fact that there is a well-established academic field focused on critically understanding fans and fan culture has been a revelation, and one which has helped them reform their practices to be more respectful of the traditions and values associated with fandom.

In another sense—and perhaps the best sense—knowledge exchange between academia and the media industries might manifest itself as an industrial 'take-up' of academic concepts as institutional practices within the media industries themselves. The example of 'transmedia' may be the best example to illustrate this process. The word, transmedia, was coined by Marsha Kinder in her book, *Playing with Power in Movies, Television and Video Games: From Muppet Babies to Teenage Mutant Ninja Turtles* (1991), where she was writing about characters, such as the Super Mario Brothers, who were being deployed across a range of different media platforms. I had been teaching and reflecting about this concept for many years, but I began to introduce it via a Creative Leaders Program which my faculty had developed in collaboration with Electronic Arts to help their game designers and our students to think more imaginatively about the future of their media. Through these workshops, I got to know game designers such as Neil Young and Danny Bilson, who were exploring new ways that games might interface with films or television programmes.

Through other outreach efforts with industry, I learned about the work that Sony was doing to create web-based content for *Dawson's Creek*, about the alternate reality games (ARG) being developed around articificial intelligence (A.I.), about the marketing being done for *The Blair Witch Project*, about the ways these ideas were being deployed by BMW in the marketing world, and about the plans to extend *The Matrix* into games, comics, and animation. At one of the EA workshops, a summit between film and games industry leaders, I floated the concept of transmedia storytelling, and it was well received, so I introduced it through a column I wrote for *Technology Review*, and expanded that article into a chapter in *Convergence Culture: Where Old and New Media Collide* (2006).

Some of the industry leaders, among them Mark Warshaw, who had participated in the Futures of Entertainment conferences, read the book, and began passing it along to their friends. The book came out just as the Writer's Guild went on strike over issues of payment for digital content. The Writer's Strike specifically centred on whether what writers created for the web was promotion (in which case it was simply work for hire) or storytelling (in which case they should receive residuals), very much the same question that *Convergence Culture* was asking, so I am told that the book was being passed along the picket lines from one writer to the next. When the strike ended, we saw the emergence of Transmedia departments created on the sets of *Heroes*, *Lost*, and other cult shows. This work also provided language for new companies then emerging which sought to consult on the marketing of entertainment properties or advise them on the extensions and management of their fictional worlds and mythologies. This was academia doing what it does best: offering terms and concepts that had use value in conversations that were already taking place elsewhere in the culture and lending intellectual authority to those fighting to change established practices.

Within short order, transmedia became the preferred word to describe these new storytelling practices. Since then, we have seen the concept get adopted by all kinds of funding agencies, all over the world, including various culture ministries, as they have sought ways to foster greater use of digital and other media to extend the capacities of filmmakers and television producers. Worldwide, there are conferences where artists, industry leaders, academics, and policymakers debate different models of transmedia storytelling, and share and critique each other's work. From the start, this has been a space where academics have a vital voice but where there are also core theoretical insights coming from expert practitioners, and where these exchanges have allowed everyone to do better work. These exchanges have not always been without frictions, however, especially as some find the efforts to refine core concepts tiresome, or where academics sometimes distrust the blurring of commercial and creative interests that shape new production, but there has been enough openness and good will that we have worked through such obstacles to keep the conversation going.

ACADEMIA INFLUENCING MEDIA POLICY

So far, I have focused primarily on the relationship between academics and industry, but I think we need to place those relationships in the broadest possible context. Ultimately, what motivates me is an effort to promote a more participatory culture, one where we dramatically expand who has access to the means of cultural production and circulation, one where we insure widespread access to technologies and skills, and one where we protect the rights of the public to meaningfully participate in the decisions that impact their lives. So far, these are more ideals than realities, but I would argue that we have made significant progress on all of these fronts, at least in the English-speaking world, with an understanding that these trends are being played out in somewhat different terms in different countries depending on their political, cultural, and economic structures.

To achieve these goals, I have been willing to consult, advocate, and engage with many different kinds of institutions which have an impact on these issues or whic have resources that might be deployed to foster desired changes. I have consulted with governments; I have worked with foundations and policy think tanks; I have advised educational institutions, from K–12 to higher education, and cultural institutions, such as museums and libraries, and arts-funding agencies; I have worked with activist groups to insure that we have a better understanding of those practices that can be leveraged to promote social justice.

In my teaching, I try to help my students to develop strategies that will sustain more public-facing work. It starts with the ability to write and speak in a variety of different modes: writing an op-ed or a blog post is different than writing a journal article, speaking to a governmental body is different from speaking to industry or a parents–teacher group. You have to know how to start where your audience is, to identify and address their interests and concerns, to use language that they can understand and which resonates with them.

This focus on accessibility and influence is not about dumbing down; it is about taking ownership over every new term you introduce into the conversation, explaining those things you need to know to follow your argument, and not assuming that everyone comes from the same conceptual background. These values hold for speaking across disciplines within academia and they hold for speaking across sectors in the public sphere.

Beyond this, you have to be ready to shed any preconceptions or stereotypes you have about each other; you may disagree or have conflicting interests, but you have to be able to work with good faith with the other party; you have to be prepared to compromise or accept partial successes as steps forward within a longer process of bringing about meaningful change. You need to have a strong ethical compass and a clear sense of what you want to accomplish, and you have to keep your eye on the prize, know what you are working for, and avoid being distracted by battles you cannot win or that will distract you from your core goals.

JENKINS' CORE ADVICE FOR FORMING ACADEMIC PARTNERSHIPS WITH INDUSTRY

1. The academic needs a core ally or sponsor inside each of the member companies where this work is taking place, someone who advocates for funding to support the project, someone who directs attention within the company to the research, and someone who often translates its findings into something the company can act upon. Ideally, this is actually a core group of people, since the turnover in industry is so rapid, or otherwise, your project is going to get orphaned very quickly.

2. The academic needs to understand what formats for presenting findings are going to be most effective at reaching the industry audience. Is it a white paper, a PowerPoint deck, an executive briefing, a creative leader's training session, a brainstorming meeting with each team, a public talk? For each company, the answer to this may be different, so this is something you need to talk through before starting the project.

3. One of the biggest challenges is going to be the temporalities of academia and industry. Sometimes, industry runs faster than academics can keep up with; sometimes industry runs on a hurry-up-and-wait schedule where they lag just as academics get a head of steam. Both sides need to be transparent about what they can and cannot do and when, and still, this is going to be the biggest source of misunderstanding and friction in both directions.

4. I have found that industry listens better when they are paying you. They value things in economic terms, and they value insights they get when they place economic value on it. Besides, I don't do pro bono work for companies that can pay for my services. I'd rather take a little money from a company and give free services to other groups. I never get rich off of this work, pumping most of what they pay back into student fellowships to support the research, but I also do not want to be treated as a cheap resource by companies, if I can help it.

5. Never be afraid to speak truth to power. The company is often seeking advice for academics they are not hearing from within their organisation and this creates a space where you can pass along critique of what they are doing that they need to hear and that help keep you honest as an academic. Besides, in many cases, you are lending your intellectual support

and institutional authority to people around the table who might have been making these arguments all along and are not being heard. When academics and industry work together, we are lending our credibility to each other, and interesting things can develop under these circumstances.

Looking ahead, what do I see to be some of the broader emerging developments in media industry studies right now? We might identify two core strands in this work: The first would be studies of production that seeks to better understand the factors that shape decisions within the media industries or to analyse the mechanisms through which these industries represent themselves to the world; the second would be new directions in audience or fandom studies, which seek to understand how people engage with and through media industries in the context of their everyday lives.

We might map these two schools broadly in relation to Stuart Hall's classic 'encoding/decoding' model (1980). That is, one helps us to understand how media is produced, the other how media is consumed. But keep in mind that these roles have blurred considerably in a world where more and more of us have access to expanded communication capacity, where the audience often recreates and recirculates media that matters to them, where the voice of the audience may also shape the way the industry and its products are understood, and where there are new relationships between producers and consumers emerging via social media. In such a context, the distinctions between production studies and audience studies needs to break down; we need to understand the decisions which are being made on both sides of that classic divide and the ways they influence each other; we need to understand the conflicting motives in a world where most media producers are also fans of the media they produce and where many fans are also producing media which is being consumed by other fans (even if not necessarily in a commercial context).

This all points towards the need for multiperspectival work. We are not going to be able to understand the industry side of this equation if we are not engaging with industry, but we should be careful about aligning our own interests too closely with industry, because many of the key struggles over democracy and diversity require us to tap into the struggles of popular audiences and grassroots media producers. Academics may be situated to bring all of the parties to the table, as we use the university as a kind of neutral territory, where competing groups can share knowledge, listen to each other's perspectives, and develop approaches which better serve their multiple—sometimes conflicting, sometimes aligned—interests.

NOTES

1. See Research Council UK: http://www.rcuk.ac.uk/innovation/impacts/.
2. See Arts and Humanities Research Council: http://www.ahrc.ac.uk.

BIBLIOGRAPHY

Ashton, D., & Noonan, C. (Eds.) (2013). *Cultural Work and Higher Education.* Basingstoke: Palgrave Macmillan.

Bruun, H. (2015). Author Interview: *Industrial Approaches to Media.* 22 June.

Bryman, A., & Bell, E. (2003). *Business Research Methods.* Oxford: Oxford University Press.

Bryman, A., & Bell, E. (2011). *Business Research Methods.* Oxford: Oxford University Press.

Burnell, P. (Ed.) (2003). *Democratization Through the Looking Glass.* Manchester: Manchester University Press.

Caldwell, J. T. (2008). *Production Culture: Industrial Reflexivity and Critical Practice in Film and Television.* Durham and London: Duke University Press.

Caston, E. (2015). Author Interview: *Industrial Approaches to Media.* 20 June.

Champion, K. (2015). PhD Workshop on Researching Media at a Time of Transition, presentation at the University of Glasgow (Glasgow, June 10).

Clegg, S. R., Pitsis, T. S., Rura-Polley, T., & Marosszeky, M. (2002). Governmentality Matters: Designing an Alliance Culture of Inter-organizational Collaboration for Managing Projects. *Organization Studies, 23*(3), 317–337.

Crossick, G. (2006). *Knowledge Transfer Without Widgets: The Challenge of the Creative Economy.* Available at: http://www.london.ac.uk/fileadmin/documents/about/vicechancellor/Knowledge_transfer_without_widgets.pdf

Dubber, A. (2010). So what exactly is this Aftershock thing? *Andrew Dubber.* Available at: http://andrewdubber.com/2010/02/aftershock-wrap-up/

Ellis, J. (2015). The ADAPT Project, Panel Presentation at the Conference of *New Directions in Film and Television Production Studies* (Bristol, April 14–15).

Evans, E. (2014). Ethics in Industry and Audience Research. *Industrial Approaches to Media – The University of Nottingham.* Available at: http://www.nottingham.ac.uk/research/groups/isir/projects/industrial-approaches-to-media/industrial-approaches-to-media-inaugural-event.aspx

Gibbons, M., Limoges, C., Nowotny, H., Schwartzman, S., Scott, P., & Trow, M. (1994). *The New Production of Knowledge: The Dynamics of Science and Research in Contemporary Societies.* London: SAGE.

Grainge, P. (2014). Interviewing Media Professionals. *Industrial Approaches to Media – The University of Nottingham.* Available at: http://www.nottingham.ac.uk/research/groups/isir/projects/industrial-approaches-to-media/industrial-approaches-to-media-inaugural-event.aspx

Gummesson, E. (2000). *Qualitative methods in management research* (2nd ed.). London: SAGE.

Hall, S. (1980). 'Encoding/decoding', *Culture, Media, Language: Working Papers in Cultural Studies* (pp. 128–138). London: Hutchinson.

Hickman, J. (2016). Author Interview: *Industrial Approaches to Media*. 09 May.

Hinings, C. R., & Greenwood, R. (2002). Disconnects and Consequences in Organization Theory?. *Administrative Science Quarterly* 47(3) (September), 411–421

Jenkins, H. (2006). *Convergence Culture: Where Old and New Media Collide*. New York: New York University Press.

Johnson, C. (2013a). The Mutual Benefits of Engaging with Industry. *CST Online*. Accessed December 3, 2015, from http://cstonline.tv/mutual-benefits

Johnson, D. (2013b). *Media Franchising: Creative License and Collaboration in the Culture Industries*. New York: New York University Press.

Johnson, D. (2014). Understanding Media Industries From All Perspectives. *Industrial Approaches to Media – The University of Nottingham*. Available at: http://www.nottingham.ac.uk/research/groups/isir/projects/industrial-approaches-to-media/derek-johnson.aspx

Kinder, M. (1991). *Playing with Power in Movies, Television and Video Games: From Muppet Babies to Teenage Mutant Ninja Turtles*. California: University of California Press.

Lotz, A. D. (2007). *The Television Will Be Revolutionized*. New York: New York University Press.

Lotz, A. D. (2014). Media Industry Studies: Challenges, Pitfalls, Obstacles. *Industrial Approaches to Media – The University of Nottingham*. Available at: http://www.nottingham.ac.uk/research/groups/isir/projects/industrial-approaches-to-media/amanda-lotz.aspx

Marshall, L. (2015). Production Research: Industry Perspectives, Panel Presentation at the conference of *New Directions in Film and Television Production Studies* (Bristol, April 14–15).

Oakley, K. (2013). Making Workers: High Education and the Cultural Industries Workplace. In D. Ashton & C. Noonan (Eds.), *Cultural Work and Higher Education*. Basingstoke: Palgrave Macmillan.

Saunders, M., Lewis, P., & Thornhill, A. (2015). *Research Methods for Business Students*. Essex: Pearson Education Limited.

Sergi, G. (2014). The ABC of Working with Industry. *Industrial Approaches to Media – The University of Nottingham*. Available at: http://www.nottingham.ac.uk/research/groups/isir/projects/industrial-approaches-to-media/index.aspx

Tranfield, D., & Starkey, K. (1998). The Nature, Social Organisation and Promotion of Management Research: Towards Policy. *British Journal of Management.*, 9(4), 341–353.

CHAPTER 9

Publishing Media Industry Research

Matthew Freeman

This final chapter aims to analyse the changing forms, functions, meanings, and roles of publishing in light of the turn towards media industry studies. Building on the general aims of this section to explore ways of making academic research more valuable to media industry stakeholders, I will examine how research findings have been made meaningful to commercial media partners and 'translated' via more non-academic formats, such as industry reports. Based on data gathered from academics and industry practitioners, I also explore the effectiveness of other methods of making academic research speak to a media industry audience, such as festivals, museum exhibits, and archives. For as Justin Smith (2015) proclaims, 'research that studies the media is one thing, but research that *changes* the media is something else entirely.'

WHAT IS PUBLISHING IN THE CONTEXT OF MEDIA INDUSTRY STUDIES?

For a long time the practice of publishing academic work meant only one thing: writing up scholarly articles and chapters that appeared in disciplinarily defined academic journals or books. Of course, the very concept

M. Freeman (✉)
Bath Spa University, Bath, UK
e-mail: m.freeman@bathspa.ac.uk

© The Editor(s) (if applicable) and The Author(s) 2016
M. Freeman, *Industrial Approaches to Media*,
DOI 10.1057/978-1-137-55176-4_9

of research is synonymous with making that research available to an audience, allowing it to provide new knowledge and understanding about a given topic. And while the definition of publishing is quite plainly to make information available to people, publishing in academia has traditionally been an arguably narrow preoccupation. Academics have always had an audience, much like the media industries have always had an audience. But those audiences are seldom the same, a point that goes back to McDonald's earlier characterisation of the gulf between academic and industry fields.

Chapter 2 indicated previously that themes such as thought leadership and conceptualisations of audiences are just two of the interests shared by both academia and by the media industries, but much more can be done to further break down any so-called gulfs between these two worlds. And alongside the different, if somewhat related, emphases on practice-based research, also crucial to this breaking down of ideological barriers is the domain of publishing—by which I mean the methods and outputs used to showcase research to audiences. In most cases, the articles published in academic journals may be respected and read within the academy, but it is fair to suggest that few tend to be read widely by those in the media industries themselves; such articles are written for the eyes and ears of academics, not for practitioners or the general public, and are often 'hidden' behind paywalls and subscription fees. In some ways, the work of the academic is as much hidden behind closed doors and proverbial curtains as is the work of the media industries. For the latter, in fact, academic scholarship is arguably just as inaccessible, both in terms of how such work is presented and in terms of where such work materialises.

Indeed, one of those aforementioned gulfs standing between academia and industry is their respective modes of publishing. The media industries 'publish' their work all the time, taking the form of films, television programmes, video games, music cover art, posters, marketing campaigns, social media apps, and so on. All of these texts are essentially the fruits of the media industry's labour—the 'findings' of the media's 'research' into the types of content that their audiences tend to like, with these texts being the industry's 'publications', as it were. The problem then is not that academia and media industries are worlds apart in their fundamental use of research and publication, but rather that many more traditional scholarly outputs—such as traditional academic books—rarely cross over into the wider public arena of the media industries in the way that the media's more commercial outputs tend to.

And if media industry studies is in fact about producing scholarly research that is somehow both *about* and *for* the media industries, as has been maintained throughout this book, then clearly the modes of publication adopted need to align rather than diverge. But the idea of publishing research that is both about and for the media industries raises a whole series of other methodological questions—namely, should we publish our research *twice*, once for scholars and once for media industry practitioners? Or should we find alternative means of publishing our research via a portal that engages both parties equally? And if so, what are those portals? How does one go about 'branding' the value of their research findings in the context of industry? If working collaboratively with industry, should our industry partners be co-authors?

Working *with* the Industry

Before I get to examining the above questions more closely, there is one useful tip to begin with: Always ask yourself as a researcher, *who exactly is your audience?* Knowing the answer to this question should always dictate any methodological strategy with regards to publishing. As explored in Chap. 3, Evans and McDonald differentiate between those media industry studies projects that see the academic working *with* or *on* the media industries and those that see the academic working *for* the media industries, with additional implications and obligations to do with publishing requirements and expectations also determined by this difference. The former approach tends to concern the types of research projects that have been initiated by the academic researcher reaching out for collaboration with industry, and it would be fair to say that the vast majority of all media industry studies sit within this particular category. And working *with* rather than *for* the media industries can also bring a greater degree of freedom—though not always complete freedom—in terms of what you can do with that research and where you publish it. Chapter 3 has already examined the ethics and politics of collaborating with media industry partners in depth, so now let us explore some specific methods and approaches for publishing one's media industry research in ways that continues to engage the media industry itself. And for this discussion I use the word 'publishing' in the loosest sense.

Remember, as academics, we are not the media industry, and that is important; we offer something else besides that which is already known in the media industries—something more contextualised. In other words, our publications about studies of the media industries have the potential to be of tremendous value and interest, as long as said publications are presented in a relevant and accessible manner. In the broadest sense, Lucy Brown (2015) notes that academia and the media industries can always be cross-promotional, pointing out that it is certainly possible to make use of industry contacts as a way of raising the profile of one's academic research. If one is working collaboratively and in partnership, for instance, why not develop a mutual system where those industry partners discuss your research on social media—tweeting links to given websites and blogs, for example? Of course, for this simple system to work, the publication needs to be accessible to the wider public. A number of universities in the UK are now teaching their postgraduate research students to publicise their ongoing scholarly research as a form of public engagement, publishing snippets and 'thought pieces' on personal—though professionally presented—blogs and personal websites. It is ultimately about making your research more of a public commodity.

That is not to suggest that your hard-fought academic research should be given away for free, as opposed to being published inside expensive books and subscription-based scholarly journals. On the contrary, I am suggesting that academic publishing can learn a lot from the cross-promotional, buzz-building strategies made use of every day by the contemporary media industries in terms of heightening the industry and even public engagement of one's academic research. For example, think about the marketing campaigns that tend to surround any high-profile Hollywood film in the digital age. Films such as *Star Wars: The Force Awakens* (2015) and *Batman V Superman: Dawn of Justice* (2016) are surrounded by a vast array of companion content or what Paul Grainge (2011) calls 'ephemeral media', i.e., the trailers, websites, fan sites, social media pages, news reports, star interviews, and behind-the-scenes documentaries that exist around and between the actual media products they aim to promote. For some, it is this companion content that actually brings audiences to the main media product—in this case, the films. So, can the academic researcher apply this same method as a means of boosting interest in their own work by reaching the widest possible audience? Is it possible for the academic researcher to produce some equivalent form of 'companion content' for his or her own research outputs, with this companion content dispersed further afield around and between the actual scholarly outputs—in this case, perhaps, journal articles or books?

Adopting this more publicly dispersed, cross-promotional approach to publishing academic research has not only allowed scholars to increase their own public profiles and the public presence of their research, but it has also made it easier for research to find its way into the paths of industry—particularly those that share the same conceptual fascinations with thought leadership and audience engagement, as was discussed in Chap. 2. Publishing academic research online, which is then cross-promoted and hyperlinked across multiple platforms in the way championed by the media industries, is also important to eroding that so-called gulf standing between the worlds of academia and media industries once and for all. It is also a key method for enabling academic research to be made of interest and of relevance to the media industries, given the fact that work published on websites, blogs, and social media will need to be written and presented in far more accessible ways than is common in most scholarly journals. In other words, always re-phrase jargon or overly theoretical discussions as clear, practical assertions written in plain English. Doing so will help substantially with any effort to engage the media industries, which in turn can only increase one's chances of seeing their research impact the workings of industry. Sarah Ralph has already demonstrated how her use of social media and blog posts worked to engage the media industry sector being investigated, as was outlined in Chap. 6.

However, taking such a 'public engagement' approach to publishing one's academic research—or rather, publishing parts of one's research, perhaps the more accessibly written companion content alongside the journal article or book—might well extend to more *offline* forms of publication. There are those academics that might opt to collaborate with practitioners from the media festival sector as a way of then quite easily 'publishing' the findings of such a collaboration as a festival open to the public and to industry, translating any scholarly insights into public-facing events and attractions. Similarly, in 2015 Rachel Moseley and Helen Wheatley made use of a collaboration with the Herbert Gallery and Museum in Coventry to form an exhibition called *The Story of Children's Television from 1946 to Today*.[1] The exhibition was one of many publications about research into the history of children's television, with the exhibition just happening to make use of memorabilia, merchandise, clips, images, and interactive displays, rather than taking the more traditional form of words in a book or a journal article. But that is not to say that a festival or museum exhibition represents the public outputs that stand as separate to the academic output. As some of the promotion for this particular exhibition rightly declared, on the contrary, *The Story of Children's Television from 1946 to Today* published academic scholarship *as* a public attraction, 'look[ing] at the programmes of our childhood and how children's television has helped to shape the way we view the world around us.' Furthermore, Lucy Brown (2015) discusses how television and radio appearances—in news or television documentaries, for example—are essentially forms of publishing for academics, using the screen as a window to map audience or industry engagement.

THE ROLE OF ARCHIVES

Nevertheless, publishing via media appearances or national museum exhibits is easier said than done. Perhaps it is possible for media industry studies researchers to make more of an impact on industry with their research via another, perhaps more accessible source—the archive. As researchers we are blessed by the increasing number of archives available to us—that is, the spaces housing collections of records and documents providing information about a place, institution, or group of people—be it physical archives or online collections. It goes without saying that archives are an invaluable source of research, particularly for historical projects. But archives are far more than a research tool—they are also a means of publishing research findings, as well as shaping and reshaping the wider perceptions and understandings of the media industries. As Elinor Groom (2014) discusses, 'academics have to be cognisant of the ways that our culture implicitly, and almost imperceptibly, curates the past. Nowhere is this more evident than in the process of researching in archives, where only those facets of the media that have survived and been archived are available to researchers.' In fact, researching with archives is perhaps one of the clearest examples of doing media research that is both *about* and *for* the media industries, since archives provide both the data to understand the workings of the media industries and the public infrastructure to publicise new outputs for the media industry's own use.

Groom's research into the history of the regional franchise television, which made extensive use of the BFI National archive, offers a useful example of this dual idea, noting that 'I not only engage with archival material for information; I am in the process of structuring and cataloguing a collection of documents spanning from the late 1950s to the early 1980s—authoring the history of Southern Television in more ways than one' (2014). Groom's use of the word 'authoring' is significant here, for it indeed points to how her research about the industrial history of ITV in the UK via the use of archives has led to her reshaping how that history is now going to be understood by both the public and by the wider media industries themselves. Says Groom (2014), '[a]lthough I only have one single historical case study and one equivalent archive collection under my care, the feelings of responsibility and accountability can be overwhelming. [...] Archiving is an industry, too, after all.'

Thinking of publishing as an extension of collaboration in this way—as something that can result in archival progression or even media products like those produced by the media itself—can thus result in outputs of mutual benefit to both academia and to media industries. As a useful case study into how and where such an approach to academia–industry publishing occurs, consider the following research project. *Fifty Years of British Music Video, 1964–2014: Assessing Innovation, Industry, Influence and Impact* is an AHRC-funded collaboration between Justin Smith, Emily Caston, and a panel of industry executives and creatives from record labels and production companies.[2] The aim of the project was to work with an advisory committee of both academics and media industry practitioners to select a canon of music video titles for conservation within the BFI's National Archive, which will then be distributed to the general public by Soda Pictures as a box set DVD and exhibited across the UK in four national cinema screening sessions with leading music video curator David Knight. The project will also create the first national database of British music videos free to access at the BFI and British Library. Much like *The Story of Children's Television* exhibition, the *Fifty Years of British Music Video* project therefore aims to publish outputs that are simultaneously and equally of academic and of industry/public value and interest. In the below case study contribution, Emily Caston—Co-Investigator of the *Fifty Years of British Music Video* research project—discusses how this approach towards academic–industry publication is underpinned by the notion of what she calls 'intellectual collaboration'.

CASE STUDY: INTELLECTUAL COLLABORATION AND THE MUSIC INDUSTRY

Emily Caston

In 2014, the University of Portsmouth and University of the Arts London were awarded a grant by the Arts and Humanities Research Council to investigate *Fifty Years of British Music Video*. The project was designed as a collaboration between a number of public and private stakeholders including the British Library, the British Film Institute, Soda Pictures (a film distributor), and Video Performance Ltd (the licensing agency for the British recording industry). The project was conceived from the outset as a collaboration with the British music video industry, in the sense of a joint intellectual effort. Here I outline some of the major challenges this has posed as well as some of the myriad benefits it promises to yield.

Music video is one of a number of 'hidden' screen industries that has been neglected in government-funded creative industries research (e.g., Hutton et al. 2007). Apart from my own research (Caston et al. 2000), nothing has been published on the industry or its contribution to the British creative economy. The whereabouts of most video masters is unknown, and the collections of significant recording artists, video directors, and production companies has never been curated in any publicly accessible form, let alone put into a systematic catalogue that enables academic analysis in pursuit of rigorous questions about aesthetics, production, distribution, or audiences. As Carol Vernallis (2013a: 261–264) has argued, the canon of music video, dependent on YouTube, is essentially unstable. The Head of Research and Scholarship at the BFI, and the Lead Curator for Moving Image and Curator for Popular Music at the British Library both agreed that this situation needed to be addressed.

Academic interest in analysis of these hidden industries was emerging (e.g., Grainge and Johnson 2015), but published documentation was still limited, with the exception of Fletcher's rich account of British advertising (2008). Non-academic research focused on distribution (Banks 1996; Denisoff 1991), the USA (Austerlitz 2008; Schwartz 2007), or directors and textual analyses (Aust and Kothenschulte 2011), rather than industry studies. Significant research by Donnelly (2007), Railton and Watson (2011), and Vernallis (2001, 2002, 2004, 2007, 2008, 2013a, b) demonstrated the urgent need for evidenced-based understanding of the production of music videos. The intention of our research project is to address that need, using Keith Negus's pioneering work on the music industry as a culture of production (1991) and his later work on creativity (Negus and Pickering 2004). Drawing additionally on Caldwell's work on production cultures (2008, 2014) and his concept of 'industry intellectuals' (2009), we were keen to draw on sociological and ethnographic approaches to the study of art and culture (Bechky 2006; Born 2004, 2010; Hesmondhalgh 2007; Hesmondhalgh and Baker 2011). We want to identify the distinctive and usual characteristics of music video as a hybrid production culture emerging from the fusion of graphic design (album cover design), portrait photography, live concert performance, and fine art in the highly vibrant art school culture of the late 1960s; this has had had a profound, widespread, but as yet undocumented impact on the wider arts economy and culture of Britain.

Designing project outputs that would be of value to all of our project partners was a crucial early step in securing a cohesive collaboration. At a recent symposium on industry–academic partnerships in London, participants gave voice to reasons for the lack of industry–university collaborations: 'The challenges that surfaced include a lack of trust over issues such as intellectual property, uncertainty about the potential benefits of working together, and the difficulty on both sides of finding the time for initial exploratory conversations. Participants also noted an apparent disparity between universities and businesses in the kinds of outputs that would make such collaborations seem worthwhile' (Jones and Clulow 2012). All the partners in our project agreed that our outputs need to include a book on the 'untold story' of British music video, a DVD box set of selected British music videos 1964–2014, a series of public cinema screenings, a database of music videos to be held at the British Library and BFI, a digitised collection for the National Film Archive, two case studies, and a journal special issue. It was felt these could fulfil the mutually agreed goals of having music video considered as a significant art form that has had a substantial impact on arts and culture in Britain, and could no longer be left ignored at the bottom of a hierarchy of value in the screen arts. Other important goals are to secure preservation of art and furnish a new interdisciplinary framework of analysis for the academic community.

Another challenge was the diffuse decentred character of our industry partner. Unlike two previous significant studies of British film and television (Georgie Born's study of the BBC [2004] and Smith and MacDonald's study of Channel 4 [2014a, b]), ours was not a study of a single institution but of a network of freelancers, micro businesses, SMEs, and multinationals cutting across the financing, commissioning, production, and commercial exploitation and dissemination of music video. The music video industry consists of individuals working at production companies, post-production companies, record companies, digital companies, broadcasters, and licensing agencies. Some are employed in-house; others are freelance. Most of the companies also produce and exploit media content for other industries and sectors (such as music, commercials, digital content, and less often features), so it is not the companies themselves that congeal into a recognisable 'network', but the individuals within the companies who do so, and those networks are invisible to outsiders. As such our project posed very different challenges to those tackled by Born and discussed by her in relation to a proposed post-Bourdieuian theory of cultural production (2010).

In order to manage this, we established a steering committee and an industry panel, and also engaged an influential cultural intermediary as our consultant. The steering committee meets quarterly to guide our research: It comprises academics from popular music studies, fashion film, advertising, film and television studies, along with six figures from the music industry—three production company managing directors, an ex-chair of the British Phonograph Industry (BPI), a music lawyer, and a vice president of a major record label. Our industry panel comprises a number of 'industry intellectuals', to borrow Caldwell's terminology, carefully selected for their experience, authority, articulacy, insight, and engagement with the project goals to advise us on the selection of a canon for the box set and national film archive—video commissioners, managing directors, executive producers, producers, directors, cinematographers, editors, and colourists. The panel additionally assists us to make contact with practitioners to set up interviews. Our consultant is the editor of the primary trade paper for the industry, *Promo News*, which began life as a magazine imprint of *Music Week* in the 1980s and now exists as a website; he also curates the UK Music Video Awards, and together with Adam Buxton co-curates BUG, the BFI Southbank regular music video cinema event. The consultant and panel have enabled us to set up interviews and hold focus groups to investigate specific elements of our research questions. Their role in securing access has been crucial.

Interviews and focus groups are core methods of our research design. But due to the nature of the music video business which I have described elsewhere as 'kick, bollocks and scramble' (Caston 2012), the research team has had to adopt a much more flexible approach to its planning and operational research management. In universities, teaching timetables and meeting dates are generally booked in advance, and academics are likely to know what their schedule in two months' time looks like. In music video, schedules change daily or hourly. A brief will arrive in a producer's inbox with sometimes only a day to pitch, and a few weeks to turn the job around. As a result, industry personnel cannot and do not plan their diaries this far ahead—directors' diaries will consist of light or heavy pencils for possible jobs they are pitching on. Our interview and focus group dates would also be pencilled in, but would legitimately be dropped if a job confirmed, or a pitch meeting confirmed. I estimate that 70 % of my meetings and interviews have been cancelled and rescheduled at least once, some four or five times. Being able to be flexible in our response and being supportive of these commercial necessities has been an essential part of our collaboration management and successful partnership.

Because we planned to use semi-structured interviews to investigate our research questions, another challenge was to set up a method to identify the significant 'unspoken'. As Mary Douglas noted forty years ago, 'every sentence rests on unspoken knowledge for some of its meaning' (1975: 173). Our interest in this research project is squarely on what Douglas describes as 'the dark side of the moon', what needs 'not be put into words because it seems obvious' (Douglas 1975: 173). I had already spent fifteen years working as a music video producer and put myself in the position of a fixer/mediator/translator, familiar with boundaries around what would be taboo and off limits or what was likely to be perceived by interviewees as insignificant to them but highly significant to us. Without an 'insider' figure such as myself, a project would need to have a run-in period of ethnographic fieldwork in order to achieve familiarity with what Geertz (1983) describes as 'local knowledge', or 'the Native's Point of View'. My own position has, of course, carried with it certain risks. I am both a 'native' with an ethical commitment to protect my professional community and an academic with an ethical commitment to research.

There are also subjects that are taboo and off limits in the interviews, and consequently confidentiality has been a further issue. At an early industry panel meeting, we agreed to stop filming the session because the fact that the session was being recorded led some of the participants to feel uncomfortable about contributing, lest anything they said was accidentally construed as a negative comment on another freelancer. Much of what was perceived to be off limits centred on behind-the-scenes local knowledge about the production of videos, particularly disputes about the involvement and input of certain crews. Producers and directors were fearful about revealing information about themselves or others that could damage reputations. I have discussed these problems in relation to an interview with Jamie Thraves in the *Journal of Sound, Music and the Moving Image* (2016).

We have also faced legal challenges. In order to put together our DVD box set of music videos we have had to negotiate a number of licenses.

Before applying for funding, we approached the collecting agency, Video Performance Ltd, with a proposal that was approved by their board for a number of rights and access for a collection to be held on site at the BFI and British Library. For the Soda Pictures box set, we have had to negotiate separate licenses with the MCPS (Mechanical Copyright Protection Society) and PRS (Performing Rights Society), and in many cases negotiate approvals from individual recording artists, because of the historic way music videos were contracted and licensed by record companies and artist managers. In the first instance, the challenge has been to identify the correct rights holders for each video so that our independent media lawyer can ensure we are approaching the relevant agencies. Our AHRC budget includes an allocated sum to cover his legal fees. He has thirty years' experience in the British music industry. We decided that it was necessary to engage a lawyer with this specialist knowledge, rather than rely on the in-house legal teams at our respective universities. Our lawyer works closely with our research assistant; because we knew that the legal work would be a substantial component of the project, we set out to recruit an assistant with prior knowledge, training, or professional experience working in business affairs at a UK label.

A particular output designed to maximise the dissemination of our research findings to the general public has posed financial challenges. A 'behind the scenes documentary' was planned to accompany the box set. Universities are not production companies and, as charities, cannot engage in trade without losing money because VAT cannot be reclaimed as it would on a conventional production. We overcame this problem by facilitating an external production company to produce a documentary for our film distributor; the agreement is that we act as consultants, the AHRC is credited, and income arising from sales of the programme to any overseas territories (broadcasters, for example) will be channelled back into a bursary fund at the University to fund further research on British music videos.

The most intractable problem has been the dearth of theory to guide our relationship with our industry partners. Our industry participants are not 'subjects' in the research design, but collaborators and 'co-investigators'. By working with the industry in designing the project and managing it through our steering committee, we have constructed a different kind of partnership from that used in previous academic research on the industry, even where an ethnographic approach is adopted (for example, Powdermaker [1950] and Born [2004]). The disdain shown by academics for intellectuals within the existing literature on media indus-tries research is striking. The kind of attitude towards industry evident in Hesmondalgh's article on 'the menace of instrumentalism' is as shocking in its naïve construction of the biases of industry research as it is in its claim that academic research, by contrast, should be research for emancipation. This attitude manifests little awareness of the biases and vested inter-ests generated by the Research Excellence Framework (REF), academic research paradigms, and limited disciplinary problematics (Hesmondhalgh 2014).

Thus far, our project has demonstrated the rich capacity of industry intellectuals to attain a critical distance in the pursuit of difficult research questions. Time and again creatives have suggested works other than their own, and have often been to great lengths to track down video masters or interviews or documents relating to other individuals, in order for the larger story of 'their craft' to be told. Our practitioners have been excep-tionally keen to listen to our research questions and to adjust their practice accordingly, asking for clear briefs and often volunteering for 'home-work'. They would suggest research answers that would generate a debate amongst us as we reworked our 'evidence'. Many of our practitioners have been fascinated by the discovery of work from previous decades of which they were never aware, and have studied those works and disseminated them through their networks, in ways and with consequences that are likely to impact and generate new creative ideas, genres, and cycles. They see the work of our research team as stimulating new creative ideas and as helping them to attain higher standards of innovation and creativity.

In their article, cited earlier, about the London symposium on univer-sity–industry collaborations, Jones and Clulow (2012), like Hesmondhalgh (2014), highlight the seemingly irreconcilable goals of industry and research. 'While businesses may be seeking saleable products, academics prize excellent research outputs and publications. One could conclude that therein n'er the twain shall meet.' But our project is demonstrating that the twain can meet. Contrary to Hesmondalgh's assumptions, cer-tainly in the arts and entertainments, many businesses do not primarily seek saleable products, but rather critical acclaim, peer esteem, and cul-tural preservation; they seek to be *understood* and to improve their own practice, because their goal is the creation of memorable work that con-tributes to the human experience. In his book on the British advertising industry, Winston Fletcher (2008) regrets that the reason advertising has been so neglected by academics is the suspicion they hold towards the commercial imperative, the assumption that only those cultural products which do not sell hold cultural value. It is important to recognise and respect that the goals of industry practitioners are not dictated simply by a profit motive, or analysed through a naïve, non-evidenced based, theoretically impoverished political economic determinism. The complicated dynamics touched on by Fletcher in his *Powers of Persuasion* (2008: 2) hint at the fact that when an industry like music video or advertising is 'under siege', constantly lambasted for its excessive social power and low artistic standards, those attacks can motivate the practitioners to achieve ever higher standards of innovation and originality.

We are only one year into the research project, but already it is evident that we are collecting an enormous amount of rich data. We plan to include among our outputs a dedicated chapter on the subject of theorising intellectual collaborations in research that move beyond the subject-object approach. In order to progress, British academics have to develop a more sophisticated understanding of the relationship between commerce and art than has yet been demonstrated.

WORKING FOR THE INDUSTRY

This book's theorisation of a sociology of media industry studies—offering alternative but complimentary modes of researching media industries as a structure, as an interaction, and as a modality across societal, corporate, and discursive contexts—goes some way to addressing Caston's criticism above. But perhaps the overarching conclusion of Caston's case study is that studying and collaborating with the media industries can help media practitioners to better reflect on what they do and why they do it. In Caston's reflection above, she also raises a number of invaluable points that all relate to the importance of retaining critical distance from the media industries of which are being both studied and allied with. Caston observed how designing project outputs that would be of value to each of the project partners—be it academics or industry practitioners—was a crucial step in securing a cohesive collaboration. But Caston also raises the potential issues to do with confidentiality and legality that arise when attempting to do so, and of course there remains certain political questions to do with the status of industry partners as co-investigators, as discussed in Chap. 3.

But political issues such as confidentiality and legality also have implications to do with publishing, too. Publishing research that is based on work conducted *with* or *for* the media industries is difficult because producers have the right to impact what, if not how, the researcher publishes. Chapter 3 showed how there might be challenges to remaining critical and objective in collaborative media industry research, particularly in terms of the types of research questions that can—or should—be asked. Beyond these political considerations, however, Catherine Johnson (2013) observes that collaboration 'raises a further question for academic researchers engaging with industry practitioners, which is the extent to which we should give our research away to industry.' For Johnson (2013),

> [p]roviding [industry] with reports based on my research seems a paltry price to pay for the generosity with which their staff have given their time to us. Similarly, when I have interviewed industry practitioners as part of my research I have happily shared the results of that research with them. Over and above that, I do my research as part of my day job, and for me, the value of that research is enhanced if I can communicate it to the broadest audience possible. As such, I am less concerned about potentially devaluing, in commercial terms, my own research, and believe that the more that we can demonstrate the value of our research to the industry, the more the industry will be interested in sharing and engaging with us—and this can only be to our mutual benefit.

Johnson is here reinforcing the overall importance of trust and collaboration that has been argued throughout this book. Nevertheless, the more open approach to publication discussed by Johnson here—and indeed identified earlier in this chapter—tends most often to be saved for those cases of research best characterised as academics working *with* the media industries, allowing as it is might for far more flexibility in terms of how outputs are designed, managed, and distributed.

In certain cases, however—namely those described by Evans as 'working *for* the industry'—ideas of publication may be far stricter. For instance, Evans (2014) discusses how some cases of her own media industry research have come ingrained with one particular output specified—for example, an industry report about the productive application potential of the research findings. Evans (2014) calls this 'the recommendation part: You write a report to your industry partner where you are required to give a recommendation for what the industry should do with your research.' The skill of such a recommendation, Evans (2014) explains, is in considering how the ideas, concepts, and theorisations of an academic argument can be clearly and very specifically embedded—and not just acknowledged—

within 'a concrete strategy decision for the company or practitioners in question.' The actual recommendation here is therefore about posing external, research-informed solutions to internal, everyday media industry problems and commercial briefs.

This sense of everyday is significant, for it speaks to the broader public audience of which the most 'utopic'—by which I really mean impactful and industry-engaged—of media industry studies seeks to reach and influence. This sense of everyday also echoes my earlier claims to do with the value of 'publishing' academic research about the media industries in the form of public spaces such as online ephemera, archives, museums, and festivals. Such outputs are indeed within the reach of scholars, and perhaps the only gulf now standing between the scholar and the effective use of industry-engaged publications is confidence. Says Steve Presence (2014), '[t]here is an inferiority complex that we have as academics, and thus there is certainly a process involved in proving to [the media industries] that our research is valuable, but there is also a certain proving to ourselves that what we are doing is actually useful to them.' Projects such as the earlier discussed *The Story of Children's Television* and *Fifty Years of British Music Video*, however, showcase precisely how valuable, appealing, and impactful academic research can be to the contemporary media industries, especially when designed with such clear intentions of knowledge exchange-based outputs from the start. As was explored in the previous chapter, knowledge exchange is a crucial component of UK academic funding schemes, with its ideas of contextualisation and collaboration the bedrock of media industry studies.

Notes

1. See http://www.theherbert.org/sites/default/files/The%20Story%20of%20Children's%20Television%20Tour%20Pack.pdf.
2. See http://gtr.rcuk.ac.uk/projects?ref=AH/M003515/1.

Bibliography

Abrahams, L. (2010). *Oral History Theory*. Abington & New York: Routledge.
Aust, M. P., & Kothenschulte, D. (2011). *The Art of the Pop Video*. Koln: Distanz.
Austerlitz, S. (2008). *Money for Nothing: A History of the Music Video from the "Beatles" to the "White Stripes"*. London: Continuum.
Banks, J. (1996). *Monopoly Television: MTV's Quest To Control The Music*. Boulder, CO: Westview Press.

Bechky, B. A. (2006). Gaffers, Gofers, and Grips: Role-Based Coordination in Temporary Organizations. *Organization Science, 17*(1), 3–12.

Born, G. (2010). The Social and the Aesthetic: For a Post-Bourdieuian Theory of Cultural Production. *Cultural Sociology, 4*(2), 171–208.

Borne, G. (2004). *Uncertain Vision: Birt, Dyke and the Reinvention of the BBC.* London: Secker & Warburg.

Brown, L. (2015). Television Production in the Academy: Bringing Commercial Practices into the Classroom. Panel Presentation at the Conference of *New Directions in Film and Television Production Studies* (Bristol, April 14–15).

Caldwell, J. T. (2008). *Production Culture: Industrial Reflexivity and Critical Practice in Film and Television.* Durham and London: Duke University Press.

Caldwell, J. T. (2009). "Both Sides of the Fence": Blurred Distinctions in Scholarship and Production (a Portfolio of Interviews). In V. Mayer, M. J. Banks, & J. T. Caldwell (Eds.), *Studies: Cultural Studies of Media Industries* (pp. 214–216). New York: Routledge.

Caldwell, J. T. (2013). Para-Industry: Researching Hollywood's Blackwaters. *Cinema Journal, 52*(3), 157–165.

Caston, E. (2012). "Kick, Bollocks and Scramble": An Examination of Power and Creative Decision-Making in the Production Process During the Golden Era of British Music Videos 1995–2001. *Journal of British Cinema and Television, 9*(1), 96–110.

Caston, E. (2014). The Fine Art of Commercial Freedom: British Music Videos and Film Culture. *Scope: An Online Journal of Film and Television Studies, 26,* 1–18.

Caston, E. (2015). Equalities, Human Rights, and Heritage: The Need For an Industry-Academia Forum. Panel Presentation at the Conference of *New Directions in Film and Television Production Studies* (Bristol, April 14–15).

Caston, E. (2016). 'Not Another Article on the Author! God and Auteurs in Moving Image Analysis: Last Call for a Long Overdue Paradigm Shift', *Music Sound and the Moving Image.* Special Issue 'Musical Screens: Musical Inventions, Digital Transitions, Cultural Critique (forthcoming).

Caston, E., Parti, N., Walker, N., & Sutton, C. (2000). Report on the Music Video Industry in 1998 and 1999. *Promo* (April).

Dawson, A., & Holmes, S. P. (2012). *Working the Global Film and Television Industries.* London: Bloomsbury Academic.

Denisoff, R. S. (1991). *Inside MTV.* New Brunswick: Transaction Publishers.

Donnelly, K. (2007). Experimental Music Video and Television. In L. Mulvey & J. Sexton (Eds.), *Experimental British Television* (pp. 166–179). Manchester: Manchester University Press.

Douglas, M. (1975). *Implicit Meanings.* London: Routledge & Kegan Paul.

Evans, E. (2014). Ethics in Industry and Audience Research. *Industrial Approaches to Media—The University of Nottingham.* Available at: http://www.nottingham.ac.uk/research/groups/isir/projects/industrial-approaches-to-media/industrial-approaches-to-media-inaugural-event.aspx

Fletcher, W. (2008). *Powers of Persuasion: The Inside Story of British Advertising.* Oxford: Oxford University Press.

Frith, S., Goodwin, A., & Grossberg, L. (1993). *Sound & Vision: The Music Video Reader.* London: Routledge.

Gambetta, D. (Ed.) (1990). *Trust: Making and Breaking Cooperative Relations.* New Jersey: Wiley-Basil Blackwell.

Gaut, B. (1997). Film Authorship and Collaboration. In R. Allen & M. Smith (Eds.), *Film Theory and Philosophy* (pp. 149–173). Oxford: Oxford University Press.

Geertz, C. (1973). *The Interpretation of Cultures.* New York: Basic Books.

Geertz, C. (1983). *Local Knowledge: Further Essays in Interpretive Sociology.* New York: Basic Books.

Goodwin, A. (1992). *Dancing in the Distribution Factory: Music Television and Popular Culture.* Minnesota: University of Minnesota Press.

Grainge, P. (Ed.) (2011). *Ephemeral Media: Transitory Screen Culture From Television to YouTube.* Basingstoke: Palgrave Macmillan.

Grainge, P., & Johnson, C. (2015). *Promotional Screen Industries.* London and New York: Routledge.

Greenfield, S., & Osborn, G. (1998). *Contract and Control in the Entertainment Industry: Dancing on the Edge of Heaven.* Aldershot: Dartmouth.

Grice, J. (2013). *Sorrow Might Come in the End: Legal Cases in the Music and Entertainment Industries.* London: CreateSpace Independent Publishing.

Groom, E. (2014). It's All on Paper: Archiving the Media Industries, and Studying Archive Collections. *Industrial Approaches to Media—The University of Nottingham.* Available at: http://www.nottingham.ac.uk/research/groups/isir/projects/industrial-approaches-to-media/elinor-groom.aspx

Gunkel, D. J. (2012). What Does it Matter Who is Speaking? Authorship, Authority, and the Mashup. *Popular Music and Society, 35*(1), 71–91.

Handel, L. (1950). *Hollywood Looks at Its Audience: A Report of Film Audience Research.* Urbana: University of Illinois.

Hearsum, P., & Inglis, I. (2013). The Emancipation of Music Video: YouTube and the Cultural Politics of Supply and Demand. In J. Richardson, C. Gorbman, & C. Vernallis (Eds.), *The Oxford Handbook of New Audio-Visual Aesthetics* (pp. 483–500). Oxford: Oxford University Press.

Hesmondhalgh, D. (2007). *The Cultural Industries* (2nd ed.). London: SAGE.

Hesmondhalgh, D. (2014). The Menace of Instrumentalism in Media Industries Research and Education. *Media Industries Journal, 1*(1), 21–26.

Hesmondhalgh, D., & Baker, S. (2011). *Creative Labour: Media Work in Three Cultural Industries.* Abingdon, Oxon: Routledge.

Holt, J., & Perren, A. (Eds.) (2009). *Media Industries: History, Theory, and Method.* Malden: Wiley-Blackwell.

Howkins, J. (2007). *The Creative Economy: How People Make Money From Ideas*. London: Penguin.
Hutton, W., O'Keeffe, A., Schneider, P., Andari, R., & Bakhshi, H. (2007). *Staying Ahead: The Economic Performance of the UK's Creative Industries*. London: DCMS.
Johnson, C. (2013). The Mutual Benefits of Engaging with Industry. *CST Online*. Accessed December 3, 2015, from http://cstonline.tv/mutual-benefits
Jones, S., & Clulow S. (2012). How to Foster a Culture of Collaboration Between Universities and Industry. *The Guardian* (August 2). Available at: http://www.theguardian.com/higher-education-network/blog/2012/aug/02/the-value-of-research-collaborations
Kaplan, E. A. (1987). *Rocking Around the Clock. Music Television, Postmodernism, and Consumer Culture*. London and New York: Routledge.
Korsgaard, M. B. (2013). Music Video Transformed. In J. Richardson, C. Gorbman, & C. Vernallis (Eds.), *The Oxford Handbook of New Audio-Visual Aesthetics* (pp. 501–524). Oxford: Oxford University Press.
Livingston, P. (1997). Cinematic Authorship. In R. Allen & M. Smith (Eds.), *Film Theory and Philosophy* (pp. 132–148). Oxford: Oxford University Press.
Mayer, V., Banks, M. J., & Caldwell, J. T. (2009). *Production Studies: Cultural Studies of Media Industries*. New York: Routledge.
McDonald, P. (2014). An Interview with Professor Paul McDonald. *Industrial Approaches to Media—The University of Nottingham*. Available at: http://www.nottingham.ac.uk/research/groups/isir/projects/industrial-approaches-to-media/index.aspx
Moy, R. (2015). *Authorship Roles in Popular Music: Issues and Debates*. New York: Routledge.
Mundy, J. (1999). *Popular Music on Screen: From Hollywood Musical to Music Video*. Manchester: Manchester University Press.
Murray, V. S. (2014). 'Collaborative Authorship in Film Production: Walter Murch and Film Editing, *International Journal of New Media. Technology and the Arts, 8*(2), 9–19.
Negus, K. (1997). The Production of Culture. In P. Du Gay (Ed.), *Production of Culture/Cultures of Production* (pp. 67–118). London: SAGE.
Negus, K. (2011). Authorship and the Popular Song. *Music and Letters, 92*(4), 607–629.
Negus, K., & Pickering, M. J. (2004). *Creativity, Communication and Cultural Value*. London: SAGE.
Ortner, S. B. (2009). Studying Sideways: Ethnographic Access in Hollywood. In V. Mayer, M. J. Banks, & J. T. Caldwell (Eds.), *Production Studies: Cultural Studies of Media Industries* (pp. 175–189). New York: Routledge.
Powdermaker, H. (2013). *Hollywood: The Dream Factory: An Anthropologist Looks at the Movie-Makers*. Eastford: Martino Publishing.

Presence, S (2014). The Ethics and Politics of Media Engagment. *Industrial Approaches to Media—The University of Nottingham*. Available at: http://www.nottingham.ac.uk/research/groups/isir/projects/industrial-approaches-to-media/industrial-approaches-to-media-inaugural-event.aspx

Railton, D., & Watson, P. (2011). *Music Video and the Politics of Representation*. Edinburgh: Edinburgh University Press.

Reiss, S., & Feineman, N. (2000). Thirty Frames Per Second: The Visionary Art of the Music Video. In H. N. Abrams, J. Richardson, C. Gorbman, & C. Vernallis (Eds.), *The Oxford Handbook of New Audiovisual Aesthetics (2013)*. Oxford: Oxford University Press.

Richardson, J., Gorbman, C., & Vernallis, C. (Eds.) (2013). *The Oxford Handbook of New Audiovisual Aesthetics*. Oxford: Oxford University Press.

Schwartz, L. M. (2007). *Making Music Videos: Everything You Need to Know from the Best in the Business*. New York: Watson-Guptill.

Smith, J. (2015). Plenary. Panel discussion at the conference of *New Directions in Film and Television Production Studies* (Bristol, April 14–15).

Smith, J. and McDonald, Paul (2014). Channel 4 and British Film Culture. *Journal of British Cinema and Television* 11:4 (October): 413–417.

Vernallis, C. (2001). The Kindest Cut: Functions and Meanings of Music Video editing. *Screen, 42*(1), 21–48.

Vernallis, C. (2002). The Functions of Lyrics in Music Video. *Journal of Popular Music Studies, 14*(1), 11–31.

Vernallis, C. (2004). *Experiencing Music Video: Aesthetics and Cultural Context*. Columbia: Columbia University Press.

Vernallis, C. (2007). Strange People, Weird Objects: The Nature of Narrativity, Character, and Editing in Music Videos. In R. Beebe & J. Middleton (Eds.), *Medium Cool: Music Videos From Soundies to Cellphones* (pp. 303–328). Durham and London: Duke University Press.

Vernallis, C. (2008). Music Video, Songs, Sound: Experience, Technique and Emotion in *Eternal Sunshine of the Spotless Mind*. *Screen, 49*(3), 277–297.

Vernallis, C. (2013a). *Unruly Media: YouTube, Music Video and the New Digital Cinema*. Oxford: Oxford University Press.

Vernallis, C. (2013b). Music Video's Second Aesthetic? In J. Richardson, C. Gorbman, & C. Vernallis (Eds.), *The Oxford Handbook of New Audiovisual Aesthetics* (pp. 437–465). Oxford: Oxford University Press.

Vernallis, C., & Ueno, H. (2013). Interview with Video Director and Auteur Floria Sigismondi. *Music, Sound and the Moving Image, 7*(2), 167–194.

CHAPTER 10

Conclusions: Media Industry Studies—How and What Now?

Matthew Freeman

As I reach the end of this book, I will use this last chapter firstly to summarise what have emerged as the overarching points, ideas, and themes about a methodology of media industry studies, and secondly to reflect on potential future directions for this subfield. Let's be clear: Most fundamentally, media industry studies is about theorising the workings of the media industries—and that includes everything from macro social, economic, and political influences to micro production and distribution practices and professional ideologies, and also includes everything in between. The perceived value of actually doing media industry studies lies in collaboration, showing how dialogues between the worlds of academia and media industries can help develop and articulate new understandings of things like audience engagement and participation, market shares and sizes, institutional or industrial practices, processes, strategies of monetisation, and so on and so forth. So let's be clearer still: Tied up within this conception of studying the media industries is the implicit potential for knowledge exchange, and in that sense media industry studies is essentially applied research, but critical distance remains key.

M. Freeman (✉)
Bath Spa University, Bath, UK
e-mail: m.freeman@bathspa.ac.uk

© The Editor(s) (if applicable) and The Author(s) 2016   195
M. Freeman, *Industrial Approaches to Media*,
DOI 10.1057/978-1-137-55176-4_10

RESEARCH *ABOUT* MEDIA INDUSTRIES: TOWARD A COHERENT METHODOLOGY

Understanding and grappling with the methodological issues encountered when attempting to engage with and research the media industries as an object of study is central to media industry studies, yet this methodological challenge has this far tended to lurk in the background of such research. Rather than acknowledging the difficulties that manifest when trying to produce academic research that is somehow not only *about* the media industries but simultaneously beneficial *for* the media industries, as academics we are often trained to simply look past the limitations of our methodologies, or at least to disguise the potential shortcomings of our media industry research methodologies with clever signposting and contextualisation strategies.

However, in operating as one of the first books to focus explicitly on the practical, theoretical, and ethical principles of conducting media industry research, at least from a UK perspective—crossing the humanities and the social sciences, culture, and economics—it is my hope that the book can now act as a unique and invaluable guidebook to much ethical, theoretical, and practical information for students and emerging academics concerned with the complex methodologies involved in doing media industry studies. I hope to have provided a comprehensible yet theoretically focused analysis of how to produce research both about and for media industries.

In terms of proposing a coherent methodology for studying media industries, throughout this book I have reinforced the importance of borrowing approaches from other disciplines and adopting a multi-method approach in order to reflect the fact that media industries themselves cross disciplinary divides—operating socially, culturally, politically, economically, creatively, productively, and so on and so forth.

Hence given the opposing ontological ways in which the study of media industries can be conceptualised, it is crucial that media industry studies methodology affords a rich, diverse, and holistic body of study. And it is for this reason that I have emphasised the value of Anthony Giddens' classic *structuration theory* in its ability to conceptualise relationships between deep macro structure and micro agency as a two-way reciprocal process. Equally, the value of Giddens' structuration theory on the study of media industries has pointed to the value of cultural studies, a field of study that is profoundly multidisciplinary and contextualised in its attempts to make sense of highly complex and seemingly opposing cultural factors, forces, and influences.

This book's more sociological perspective is a key contribution to media industry studies methodology. Thinking of media industries as authors of society, if you will—and thus acknowledging, as Evans and McDonald did in Chap. 3, that the critical imperative of media industry studies 'involves looking beyond the showbiz gloss to make known how the media industries function as actors in, and arenas for, enacting economic, political, social and cultural power'—means researching the operations of media industries as social structures enacting economic, political, and cultural power, while those structures are manoeuvred by the acts of social agents.

Sociology, as a discipline, is innately cross-disciplinary, incorporating aspects of economics, technology, anthropology, and management studies, amongst others. It places contextualisation at its heart. And as Bauman and May (2001: 2) assert, 'what these neighboring bodies of knowledge have in common is that they are all concerned with the human-made world.' Of course, and despite what might be presumed to be an emphasis on more mechanical notions of production, technologies, and economics in some aspects of much media industry research, media industries are fundamentally made up of lots of people, who drive the working practices and operations of these industries, and upon whose ideas, creativity, and outputs media industries depend. Research methods that afford a rich understanding of people are therefore crucial.

Methodological considerations of industry in media studies have long singled out such industrial considerations as separate to other explorations of text or audience. However, while I am not proposing that researchers should necessarily merge studies of text, audience, and industry, I do assert that the methodological ethos of media industry studies means utilising more multiperspectival methods. In some ways, doing media industry studies means returning to the interdisciplinary research agendas and approaches made famous by the traditions of cultural studies. Echoing Henry Jenkins' call for more multiperspectival work in media industry studies, Douglas Kellner (1997: 102) calls cultural studies similarly 'multi-perspectival'. For our purposes then, this means using the perspectives of political economy, textual methods, and social analysis.

Paul du Gay and Michael Pryke (2002: 1) discuss elsewhere how debates around culture have re-emerged as 'critical to understanding what is happening to, as well as to practically intervening in, contemporary economics and organizational life.' Understanding the impact of market or even political forces on the operations of the media industries then is also 'a matter of culture, because it is through culture than people change the way they do things and see the world' (Mulgan 1997: 34).

'It is with trying to characterise a way of thinking that we call sociological' (Bauman and May 2001: 2), and through a sociological or sometimes cultural perspective I have proposed that media industry studies is most broadly about understanding one of three contexts of study—*the societal context, the corporate context,* or *the discursive context.* Each of these three contexts of study affords an understanding of media industries as very different things: first, as a 'structure' (where the media industries are understood as an outcome of the deep economic, social, and political forces in society); second, as an 'interaction' (where the media industries are understood as a medium where media practitioners define production cultures); and third as a 'modality' (which studies the very cultural transformations of how industry-as-outcome transforms into industry-as-medium, or even vice versa).

Specifically, and to address Paul McDonald's question from the start of this book about how different levels of analysis can be effectively integrated into studies of the media industries, it is worthwhile reiterating here that particular methodologies can be used to address specific interests and emphases of the workings of the media industries. As argued across Part II, political economy remains a key and valuable theoretical tool for tracing connections and impacts between deep social structures and media industry operation. Interviewing and ethnography, meanwhile, provide more specific insights into the practical workings of the corporate context of media industry studies, while trade paper and social media analysis—which can be extended to also include policy documentation, newspapers, etc.—perhaps best affords a rich understanding of the more cultural, discursive context of the media industry studies.

It is true that each of these individual methodologies emerged from many different disciplinary backgrounds—such as film and television studies, media and communication studies, business and management studies, and cultural studies, amongst others. Individually, they all have limitations. Taking one's eye off the media industries assumes that media texts are somehow autonomous objects produced only by human agents, while an analysis focussed too heavily at the macro level risks not satisfactorily accounting for how media texts come to be produced in the first place. But when these macro and micro approaches are harnessed *together,* they emerge as complementary methods for understanding 'an extraordinary range of texts, markets, economics, artistic traditions, business models, cultural policies, technologies, regulations, and creative expression' that is itself what it means 'to explore media industries in the twenty-first century' (Holt and Perren 2009: 1). In other words, I hope to have provided a greater sense of clarity and pointed exploration of the unified methodological study of media industry studies that Havens et al. (2009) characterised earlier as an overarching *Critical Media Industries Studies* approach.

RESEARCH *ABOUT* MEDIA INDUSTRIES: CHALLENGES AND OPPORTUNITIES

As has been explored, moreover, the theory and practice of doing media industries studies can often bring many methodological challenges and pitfalls to do with ethics and politics, which can bring further numerous difficulties that emerge from the interpretation of cultural data from interviews, archives, ethnography, and so on. Legally, too, issues may arise from questions over ownership and confidentiality, with the thorny issue of who implements final approval of all published findings—industry or academia—raising important methodological concerns about maintaining critical distance from the very media industry practitioners that you may wish to partner with.

Nevertheless, aside from such potential methodological concerns, we have seen throughout this book how the value of media industry studies can be to enrich and enhance perspectives and understandings—at its best, this subfield allows researchers to illuminate *intentionality* and *creative authorship* by considering many different perspectives. Indeed, my hope is that, in building on the ideas of Michele Hilmes (2014), I have shown how the concept of authorship can be centralised in media industry studies methodology as a focal and re-energised theoretical concept for attempting to conceptualise the through lines that may well materialise between expansive industrial modes of societal, corporate, and discursive contexts of study.

Media industry studies is indeed by its very nature expansive. For example, by having media practitioners sitting in a room together, they may well identify certain intertextual practices; they may well not actually call it 'intertextuality', of course, but the degree of insight and perspective gained from bringing scholars and practitioners together can work to expand scholarly understandings of that very concept. And yet for this kind of insight to materialise, the media industries themselves need to understand the value of academic research. Hence the need to develop shared goals and critical agendas across industry and academia—and why part of the need for this book is about understanding how to articulate shared aims and goals to the media industries.

Beyond these general and overarching conclusions, it is worth now reciting a few more specific pieces of methodological advice based on the themes of this book. A number of scholars, including Caldwell (2015) and Catherine Johnson (2014a, b), identify the turn towards more marginal or 'in-between' media industry studies, calling for the importance of looking at micro or cross-border workings of the media industries as well as the macro studies that have tended to dominate the subfield. By looking cross-industry, it becomes possible for academics to see what those working within a specific media industry sector perhaps cannot, and in turn to articulate the connections across multiple media industry sectors and even identify possible areas for future developments. While single sector media industry research allows for a degree of depth, with a clearly defined and bounded object of study, cross-sector media industry research is inherently expansive in scope and can afford a more fully contextualised piece of research that also enables for a degree of comparison. In any case, in today's world of convergence and digitisation, the media platform is perhaps no longer as important as it once was; it is arguably now more about the brand, the content, and its accessibility across platforms to various audiences. And this digital transformation has particular implications in terms of methodological approach—implications that I have attempted to address via an emphasis on multiple contexts.

In one sense, and following this logic, Caldwell (2015) argues that studying the multiplicities of media industry workings is important, for this can afford the potential to evolve the breadth of our critical thinking about media industries. And in another sense, studying the micro variation or cross-border workings of the media industries can be seen as an opportunity to overcome the perceived struggle of gaining access to the innards of the media industries, as Eva Novrup Redvall (2015) explains:

> It is my impression that it is easier to gain access in smaller production cultures where people are more likely to know each other in a variety of ways—also between the industry and academia. People are very dependent on each other in small nation production cultures, and at least in the Danish film and television industry I have experienced a very friendly and collaborative attitude, towards colleagues as well as towards scholars asking curious questions about how things are done.

Redvall, furthermore, also raises the importance of *timing* in much media industry studies, especially those that require strong collaborative involvement from industry partners. For instance, Redvall (2015) discusses how in her collaborative study of the Danish television channel DR1, she 'conducted the research at a time of perceived success for DR with huge national audience figures and international acclaim for series such as *The Killing* and *Borgen* meant a lot, as asking people to allow you to observe their work and tell them about their ideas of quality and best practice is a lot easier when they find that they are doing the right thing.' Moreover, Redvall (2015) concludes that besides the issue of timing in terms of gaining access, studying smaller media organisations—perhaps within small countries and contexts—might be fruitful in the sense that it can quite often allow research to occur in settings where 'the industry feels a *responsibility* to collaborate with scholars and allow for transparency, which is of course very helpful, even if it is always hard to get someone to speak more specifically about the exact financing figures and revenue streams.'

Additionally, and as Caldwell (2015) has argued, it is equally as important that media industry studies also includes failure studies, i.e., research that considers that what does *not* work, where tensions materialise, where failures occur, where money is lost, and where professional ideologies damage creative outputs. Studying the failures, as well as the successes, of the media industries might well be extremely productive in terms of generating new understandings about the media industries; scholarly insights about failures—and how to avoid such failures—could be highly valuable to the media industries as a source of knowledge exchange.

On the flip side, media industry studies can now look to the future: 'As researchers we should not only focus on what is actually out there, but also on what *could* be out there, how processes *could* be structured, and on how to possibly improve the media industries' (Redvall 2015). It seems crucial for media industry studies to ask critical questions about creative labour and the way in which media work is now organised, since many of those based in industry do not have the time to do so.

RESEARCH *FOR* MEDIA INDUSTRIES: THE MEANING OF COLLABORATION

So, the ultimate value of media industry studies to media industries lies in the knowledge of contextualisation, and to bridge understandings of societal contexts with those of corporate and discursive contexts in ways that can be communicated as a specific insights and objectives. And as John Mateer (2015) insists, that means that 'researchers need to have a rich understanding of a domain in order to ask pertinent questions that can uncover more nuanced elements of the subject.' For Mateer (2015), in fact, 'many researchers—but by no means all—looking at media industries do not have a sufficient understanding because their first-hand experience of industry is lacking and the research is flawed as a result.' Perhaps most conclusively, therefore, Mateer (2015) concludes that 'media industry studies academics need to adapt more to the workings of the commercial world to be able to support their own work.'

One notable example of how and where media industry studies academics can indeed become more accustomed to the workings of the commercial media world is via industry-engaging conferences and public events. For example, Jennifer Holt (2013a, b) refers to the *Law & Order* conference put on by the University of California Santa Barbara's Carsey-Wolf Center and the Film and Media Studies Department:

> This was an industry-funded event organized by scholars that brought journalists, executives, actors, producers, and academics together. In the four roundtables addressing the impact and significance of one of television's longest-running series, the participants shed new light on the issues of branding, global format circulation and production through their dialogue.

As Holt (2013a) goes on to explain, a conference event such as this one—bringing together journalists, executives, actors, and producers alongside academics—'offers one example of how these interactions can create broader perspective and perhaps benefit our research and pedagogy.' Studying via working with the media industries can contribute a lot in terms of creating a better understanding of the many influential media texts that we are all surrounded by every day. What is made—and what is not? Who is regarded as creative—and who is not? As Redvall (2015) further discusses this point: 'Media products influence our everyday life as well as our understanding of ourselves, others, and the world, and it is crucial to ask critical questions about the nature of the content that gets produced and distributed, but also about the structures—and constant power plays—behind the making of new products.'

Mateer (2015) agrees with this kind of assessment about the general value of collaboration between media studies and media industries: 'When trust is gained and there is mutual respect between the two camps, both sides can benefit greatly and significant advances can be made both academically and commercially.' However, specifically, what are these benefits? From the industry perspective, there is the opportunity for enhancing practice and procedure through the understanding and acceptance of formal evidence provided by academics. Fully engaging with the media industries in a meaningful, sustained, and respectful way—conceived in the form of a partnership rather than as 'subject-observers'—can successfully break down barriers and provide genuine insight into the domain that cannot easily be obtained otherwise.

Conversely, Derek Johnson (2014) claims, echoing the views of Caldwell and Redvall, that while there is still much value in making use of organisations that aim to put scholars and industry into dialogue, some scholars prefer to develop more organic one-on-one relationships with media industries and practitioners: 'I am hopeful that those kinds of relationships—driven less institutionally, and more by personal interest and investment—might encourage that kind of exchange and transfer of ideas in the future. That may be more of a long road. But it seems worth travelling.'

Nevertheless, while large- or small-scale collaborations between academia and the media industries may generate much value, it is also important to remember that such a collaborative approach to scholarship itself represents a fundamental change in research focus. For Mateer (2015), this change, based on shifts in funding bodies, means that funding bodies 'are now often looking for "benefit" ahead of knowledge'. Regardless, it does mean that 'researchers need to be aware of both academic and commercial needs when undertaking research into industry areas' (Mateer 2015).

Daniel Ashton (2015) sheds some specific light on how such 'benefits' might actually manifest in media industry studies, though his 'preference for the words "collaboration and exchange" over "impact" do suggest more of co-productive relationship in which impact is something established not "for the research" but "with" others involved in collaborating in the research.' Ashton (2015), for instance, points to a recent example of this kind of media industry collaboration in his work:

> For the industry partner, our relationship would raise different perspectives and questions, and the research process created opportunities for reflecting on their practices, understanding their sector through unconsidered questions, and then sharing this with their peers. On this final point, the means

of dissemination were vital. This research was published in an online, open access journal that provided a crossover between "the popular" and "the academic" as part of the aim to "move ideas outwards". For my industry co-author, the "impact" of our research was also a consideration and public accessibility through open access publishing, which was crucial for the ways they could establish "pathways to impact". Along the same lines, the creative commons license used by the journal ensured issues of copyright and intellectual property were clear and equitable.

Ashton, in other words, reiterates the shift towards more public-facing publishing, which was itself the focus of Chap. 9—here reiterating the relationship between open, public publishing methods and effective collaborative engagement with the media industries. Reflecting this theme of producing more 'open' research outputs—an idea that has been highlighted throughout this book—is Gianluca Sergi's insistence that approaching media industries with 'project-based pitches' tends to be far more effective in terms of engaging the media industries. Says Sergi (2014),

> [i]f you are going to try and get industry to do work with you, or even if you wish to do work for them, and invest their time, effort, expertise, and even money, you should avoid going in and saying, "I have an idea". It is much better if you go in and say, "I have a project: this is the aim, and this is how you can contribute to it."

The reason for Sergi's push towards 'projects' over 'ideas' is primarily because the former is how the media industries actually function. Thus making sure that you have a clear project—aims, rationale, methods, outputs, sustainability, etc.—that can be explained concisely is enormously important. In one sense, part of the political challenge of doing academic research that is not only *about* but also *for* the media industries is developing skills that make the scholar more publically engaged—further blurring traditional divides between notions of theory and practice—whilst simultaneously establishing a deeper understanding of the theoretical and practical workings of the media industries. Echoing this shift towards a level playing field between academia and industry, with consistent language and objectives identified on both sides, Sergi (2015) also highlights the importance of following up your progress with industry partners, even after the research is complete, in order to maintain professionalism: 'Who knows when you might wish to contact then again?'

Reiterating Emily Caston's ideas from earlier in the book, a useful tip is to pitch and situate your proposed media industry partners as 'co-researchers', rather than simply as subjects or objects of study, and to offer a clear purpose for your own involvement in their work. As Caston (2015) insists, '[m]edia practitioners do not need you to tell them how to do their job. But they often do not get the room or the time to reflect on their everyday working processes—thus working together provides this room and time to develop new strategies, methods, and outputs for doing their job.' Under this rubric, at least, our role as media industry studies scholars is perhaps to be brainstormers and analysts to help theoretically advance cutting-edge media industry workings, such as my own example of how the future of transmedia storytelling can be better theorised by examining its history, or Derek Johnson's example of how commercial applications of media licensing might be advanced via scholarly insight.

RESEARCH *FOR* MEDIA INDUSTRIES: WHERE NOW?

Once again, the ultimate question of *what media industry studies is actually for* raises its head: Is our role as academics to fundamentally reinforce the proverbial bubble—explaining how and why the media industries work the way that they do—or alternatively to fundamentally crack that bubble and in turn provide new knowledge so as to rebuild a whole new bubble as if from scratch? While I am in no position to answer that question, allow me to allude towards possible interpretations of the role of media industry studies by pointing towards the future work of others.

John Thornton Caldwell (2015), for one, points out that media production in the twenty-first century, at almost all levels, top to bottom, consists of large amounts of what he calls 'speculative work'. Caldwell (2015) argues that it is important to understand the value of this speculation as a methodological enquiry: What is its relationship to creativity, to funding models, to production settings, and to cultural moments? At what point does the media's speculative work stop being speculation and become some kind of algorithm for generating success? Are genres, for instance, algorithms for predicting success in the film and television industries? Could the future of media industry studies therefore seek to study and to theorise 'success algorithms' within and across different sectors? Could such work dovetail onto industry market research in ways that could both complement and enhance the findings of market research? In this vein, Caldwell (2015) further reinforces the view that the subfield of media industry studies could potentially aim to identify that which the subfield is *not* looking at, given the industrial sprawl of this particular subfield.

By way of example, Caldwell (2015) pinpoints the following as cornerstones of what media industry studies does—or might—focus on: 'Affiliation, contracting, deal-making, franchising, branding, consensus-building, networking, creativity-and-constraints, collective creativity, destabilising, dispersal, contention, and so on.' In addition, when asked the question 'What should media industry studies do now?', many people in this book's interview pool tended to reiterate the importance of forging *commercial* benefits—the type of projects demonstrated by Elizabeth Evans and Paul McDonald in Chap. 3. 'Economic impact' is a key criterion for many UK academic funding bodies. By way of example, Katherine Champion (2015) offers another insight into how such commercial benefit can be achieved. In her research, Champion worked with Gillian Doyle and Philip Schlesinger on the project *Multi-Platform Media and the Digital Challenge: Strategy, Distribution and Policy* (2012–2015). Here, one of the project's many objectives was to contextualise and to conceptually understand how stories can travel across platforms. Champion's research objective has clear economic impact potential, for it aims to identify which stories are likely to travel well across which platforms, which itself is the sort of commercial insight that media industries are interested in and can be verbalised to practitioners.

The critical possibilities of embarking on this kind collaboration with media industries have been seeded throughout this book and demonstrated in different ways, particularly in Evans and McDonald's discussion of the critical imperatives that might be behind collaboration with media industries, Jenkins' discussion of speaking back to industrial power, and Iosifidis' discussion of political economy's critique of class domination. Perhaps more than anything else, however, each of these three examples show the continued importance of distinguishing between speaking back to industrial power and working for it, demonstrating how academics can stake out a collaborative *but adversarial* position in between the worlds of academia and the media industries.

The future directions of media industry studies approaches are prosperous, then. Paul McDonald (2014) speculates that '[w]hile there is a sudden surge of interest in this subfield, I anticipate that in due course what we will find is that media industry studies will not be marked as a wave of interest; it will simply be something that has folded into the broader scope of media industries—in fact, we may already be in that position.' In fact, McDonald (2014) sees the destiny of media industry studies as being similar to what has happened with audience research. Much like audiences are now accepted as one of the critical domains of media studies, McDonald anticipates that the same emphasis will be placed on media industries. Says McDonald (2014), '[w]e cannot ignore and forget industry, for it is clearly part of the communication ecology.' Accordingly, and regardless of whether one self-identifies as working in the subfield of media industry studies or not, all future media scholars will likely have much investment in wanting to understand and to critically engage with matters of industry. However, beyond such speculative interpretations, who really knows how the subfield of media industry studies will develop next, or indeed if it will ever reach its end? For as John Ellis (2014) so eloquently concludes, 'the field of media industry studies does not always know where it is going, and that gives us somewhere to go…'

BIBLIOGRAPHY

Ashton, D. (2015). Author Interview: *Industrial Approaches to Media*. 17 June.
Bauman, Z., & May, M. (1990). *Thinking Sociologically*. Malden, MA: Blackwell Publishing.
Caldwell, J. T. (2008). *Production Culture: Industrial Reflexivity and Critical Practice in Film and Television*. Durham and London: Duke University Press.
Caldwell, J. T. (2009). "Both Sides of the Fence": Blurred Distinctions in Scholarship and Production (a Portfolio of Interviews). In V. Mayer, M. J. Banks, & J. T. Caldwell (Eds.), *Production Studies: Cultural Studies of Media Industries* (pp. 214–216). New York: Routledge.
Caldwell, J. T. (2013). Para-Industry: Researching Hollywood's Blackwaters. *Cinema Journal, 52*(3), 157–165.
Caldwell, J. T. (2014). Para-Industry, Shadow Academy. *Cultural Studies, 28*(4), 720–740.
Caldwell, J. T. (2015). Production Studies: Where Do We Go From Here?. Panel Presentation at the Conference of *New Directions in Film and Television Production Studies* (Bristol, April 14–15).
Caston, E. (2015). Author Interview: *Industrial Approaches to Media*. 20 June.
Champion, K. (2015). PhD Workshop on Researching Media at a Time of Transition, presentation at the University of Glasgow (Glasgow, June 10).
Du Gay, P., & Pryke, M. (2002). *Cultural Economy: Cultural Analysis and Commercial Life*. London: SAGE.
Ellis, J. (2015). The ADAPT Project. Panel Presentation at the Conference of *New Directions in Film and Television Production Studies* (Bristol, April 14–15).

Giddens, A. (1984). *The Constitution of Society: Outline of the Theory of Structuration*. Cambridge: Polity Press.

Havens, T., & Lotz, A. D. (2011). *Understanding Media Industries*. Oxford: Oxford University Press.

Havens, T., Lotz, A. D., & Tinic, S. (2009, June). Critical Media Industries Studies: A Research Approach. *Communication, Culture & Critique, 2*(2), 234–253.

Hilmes, M. (2014). An Interview with Professor Michele Hilmes. *Industrial Approaches to Media—The University of Nottingham*. Available at: http://www.nottingham.ac.uk/research/groups/isir/projects/industrial-approaches-to-media/index.aspx

Holt, J. (2011). *Empires of Entertainment: Media Industries and the Politics of Deregulation, 1980–1996*. New Brunswick: Rutgers University Press.

Holt, J. (2013a). The Future of Media Industry Studies—Academic-Industry Collaboration. *Media Commons* (May 30) Available at: http://mediacommons.futureofthebook.org/imr/2013/05/30/future-media-industry-studies-academic-industry-collaboration

Holt, J. (2013b). Two-Way Mirrors: Looking at the Future of Academic-Industry Engagement. *Cinema Journal, 52*(3), 183–188.

Holt, J., & Perren, A. (Eds.) (2009). *Media Industries: History, Theory, and Method*. Malden: Wiley-Blackwell.

Johnson, C. (2013). The Mutual Benefits of Engaging with Industry. *CST Online*. Accessed December 3, 2015, from http://cstonline.tv/mutual-benefits

Johnson, C. (2014a). Interviewing Media Professionals. *Industrial Approaches to Media—The University of Nottingham*. Available at: http://www.nottingham.ac.uk/research/groups/isir/projects/industrial-approaches-to-media/industrial-approaches-to-media-inaugural-event.aspx

Johnson, D. (2014b). Understanding Media Industries From All Perspectives. *Industrial Approaches to Media—The University of Nottingham*. Available at: http://www.nottingham.ac.uk/research/groups/isir/projects/industrial-approaches-to-media/derek-johnson.aspx

Kellner, D. (1997). Overcoming the Divide: Cultural Studies and Political Economy. In M. Ferguson & P. Golding (Eds.), *Cultural Studies in Question* (pp. 102–120). London: SAGE.

Mateer, J. (2015). Author Interview: *Industrial Approaches to Media*. 15 June.

McDonald, P. (2013). Introduction: In Focus – Media Industries Studies. *Cinema Journal, 52*(3), 145–149.

McDonald, P. (2014). An Interview with Professor Paul McDonald. *Industrial Approaches to Media—The University of Nottingham*. Available at: http://www.nottingham.ac.uk/research/groups/isir/projects/industrial-approaches-to-media/index.aspx

McDonald, P., & Wasko, J. (Eds.) (2008). *The Contemporary Hollywood Film Industry*. Malden: Wiley-Blackwell.

McDonald, M., Carman, E., Hoyt, E., & Drake, P. (Eds.) (2015). *Hollywood and the Law*. Basingstoke: Palgrave Macmillan.

Mulgan, G. (1997). *Life After Politics: New Ideas for the 21st Century*. London: Fontana Press.

Redvall, E. (2015). Author Interview: *Industrial Approaches to Media*. 1 June.

Sergi, G. (2014). The ABC of Working with Industry. *Industrial Approaches to Media—The University of Nottingham*. Available at: http://www.nottingham.ac.uk/research/groups/isir/projects/industrial-approaches-to-media/index.aspx

INDEX

A

academia
and film studies, 66
and media studies, 5, 33, 38, 202
and television industry, 24, 29, 31,
 34, 39, 41, 200
and television studies, 31, 33, 34,
 37, 184
academia-industry collaboration, 7,
 16, 43
Adorno, Theodor, 10, 74, 87
advertising, 32, 78, 79, 91, 102, 103,
 114, 120, 134, 137, 182, 184,
 187, 188
Advertising Age, 137
anthropology, 97, 197
The Apprentice, 29–38
Arts and Humanities Research
 Council, 121, 126n2, 154, 181
Ashton, Daniel, 3, 15, 38, 39, 42, 66,
 115, 116, 118, 119, 203, 204
audience, 7, 16, 18, 33, 34, 40, 48,
 50, 52, 53, 57–9, 66, 78, 93, 98,
 103, 110, 116, 123–5, 136, 137,
 139, 143, 145–7, 154, 162,

170–2, 175–80, 189, 190, 195,
 197, 201, 207
auteur, 36, 72, 74, 79
authorship, 12, 16, 17, 65–82, 111,
 120, 133, 199

B

Balio, Tino, 104
Batman, 178
Batman V Superman: Dawn of Justice,
 178
Baum, L. Frank, 2, 102
Benford, Steve, xi
BFI National Archive, 50, 160, 180
The Blair Witch Project, 168
Box Office Mojo, 162
Branding, 53, 67, 68, 78, 82, 103,
 168, 177
British Broadcasting Corporation
 (BBC), 30, 32, 34, 37, 68, 74,
 75, 78, 79, 94, 125, 183
British Library, 50, 160, 181–3, 186
Broadcasting & Cable, Billboard,
 137

© The Editor(s) (if applicable) and The Author(s) 2016   211
M. Freeman, *Industrial Approaches to Media*,
DOI 10.1057/978-1-137-55176-4

216 INDEX